The
Home Woodworker

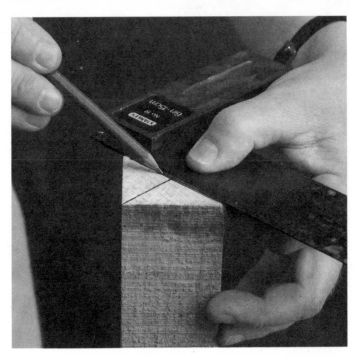

The
Home Woodworker

Edited by Julian Worthington

GUILD PUBLISHING
LONDON

Acknowledgments

All photographs are the property of Orbis Publishing Limited with the exception of those on pages 44, 45 and 46 which were supplied by Formica Ltd.

First published in Great Britain
by Orbis Publishing Limited, London 1982
© Orbis Publishing Limited 1982
This edition published 1985 by Book Club Associates,
by arrangement with Orbis Publishing Limited

Printed in Czechoslovakia
50159/3

Contents

Introduction

This book is intended as a useful guide for all types of woodworker. You may be an aspiring carpenter and want to learn every aspect of the craft, with the intention possibly of making your own furniture. You may already have the basic woodworking skills, but want to brush up on the various techniques, learn about woodturning and, maybe, get some ideas from the projects in the last section. At the other end of the scale, you may have done little or no work with wood – and even here this book will be an invaluable starting point.

The home handyman will already have discovered that there is no substitute for practice and this applies as much, if not more, with woodwork as with any other job in the house. You may feel that since wood is not the cheapest of materials to work with, you cannot afford to buy more than the project requires. But, if you do not have scrap pieces lying about to practise on, it is well worth the small extra cost to buy a bit more than you need to begin with. Mistakes can be even more costly in terms of material and time.

Obviously this will not be so necessary for basic woodworking projects, such as fixing up shelves, or if you use knock-down joints which are just screwed into place. But until you are well rehearsed in making the various carpentry joints, you should certainly learn the techniques on scrap pieces first. Cutting wood to size is another crucial part of the work – and here marking and scribing carefully will help save any expensive errors. Equally using the right saw – or the right chisel – in good condition will also increase your chances of success, as will holding the work securely and correctly.

There are many tools that can be used when working with wood, but you will find you do not need them all at once. Some are expensive, so do not invest large amounts on tools that you may hardly ever use. To supplement the basic range of hand tools – or, in some cases, to substitute them – study the range of power tool accessories. A power drill is a must, particularly where you are drilling into hard material such as walls. A saw attachment will save you much arm ache, although if you are doing a lot of cutting jobs it may well be worth your while buying a jig and/or circular saw. Measuring equipment may mean a sizeable initial outlay, but again there are certain items that must be considered essential, if you want to ensure good results every time. These include a metal straightedge, try square, spirit level and mortise gauge – and do not forget you must have a good quality cutting knife with lots of sharp blades.

Having the right equipment is one thing: using it correctly is quite another. There's no truer saying than 'a bad workman blames his tools'. If you have got good tools, however, and something goes wrong, it's the fault of the technique – not the tool. Be prepared to devote time to perfecting the different techniques of using each piece of equipment. It's a natural instinct for the beginner to rush at the job and, more often than not, spoil it.

Get used to the tools you have and how to use them so that by the time you come to work with them you will not have to think about them; they will feel almost like part of your hand.

One section is devoted entirely to joining wood. This skill is a must for the project maker, since the quality of the joints you make will affect not only the appearance of the finished work but also, and more importantly, its strength. Learn the basic joints, such as rebate, dowel, mitre, mortise and tenon and halving, first. These will be sufficient for most of the work you may need to do around the home. The other joints, particularly the dovetails, are for the expert carpenter – and something you may like to try your hand at when you have mastered the basic techniques. Often their effect is purely decorative.

Turning wood is another job you can try once you have learnt how to handle wood proficiently. This, of course, requires an additional outlay of a lathe or lathe attachment. But the fun you will get out of the extra range of projects you can make is certainly worth it. The principle of taking off bits of wood gradually, which applies to all levels of carpentry, is the key to success with turning. If you cut and shape wood gradually, you can to an extent control any small errors and finish up with a satisfying result. Remember – don't rush at it.

Finishing the work is almost as important as putting it together, since the results of your labour will be judged as much by how the job looks at the end as how well it has been constructed. Plan carefully the type of finish you want to put on the project and pay particular attention to the application. It is heart-breaking to spoil the job at this late stage.

However well you apply the skills involved in woodworking, your work will only be as good and effective as the material you are using. Buying timber is not as simple as it seems, even when you have worked out what type of wood – or board – you need and the quantities involved. That is why there is a guide to the faults you may encounter in timber and what effects they have. Some of these are more obvious to detect than others. So don't be rushed into taking the first pieces that come to hand – and don't be afraid to ask for better wood if you can't see any suitable material on display. The timber merchant is a good person to make friends with, since you will save yourself a lot of time and money by buying good quality material. Another important aspect of the material is how you handle and store it, particularly since you should allow the wood to acclimatise to the environment it will finally be in when made up.

Woodworking should be an enjoyable occupation for the home handyman – as well as a rewarding one. Once you have mastered the basic techniques involved, you will not have to rely on your local furniture showroom any more. And even if you do not want to concentrate on making furniture, just look around your home and see how much of it involves wood.

Timber and its uses

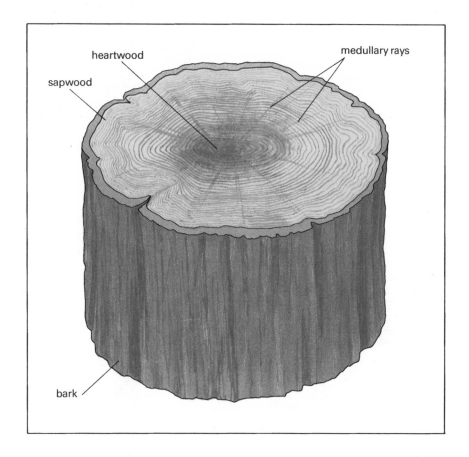

Choosing timber for projects around the home is
not easy unless you know what to buy and how to
avoid expensive mistakes. Because timber is no
longer a cheap item, you don't want to waste money
on inferior quality or on the wrong type of wood
for the job. Check on the different kinds of
softwood, hardwood and man-made boards that are
available and make sure you know what they are
most suitable for. You should also be able to
recognize any flaws in the material before you buy.
It is also important to store the timber correctly
before use and to work it when it is in the right
condition. You may have a reliable timber merchant
who will help you in your choice, but it is best to go
forearmed with the information given in this
section.

Man-made boards

Above Three faces of ply: (from the top) simulated wood grain, wood veneer and decorative plastic laminate
Right Types of man-made board
1, 2 & 3 Standard plywood – three, five and seven-ply
4 & 5 Laminboard
6 & 7 Blockboard
8 Chipboard

Man-made boards are cheaper than traditional timber and therefore ideal for the home handyman. They come in a wide range of finishes for use as floors, walls, ceilings, shelves, fittings and furniture. Some boards are also suitable for exterior use.

Plywood

These boards are made by bonding together three or more veneers of softwood or hardwood or a combination of both. There is always an odd number of veneers and the direction of the grain runs alternately to make the panels stable. If an even number of veneers were used the panel would warp; the more veneers used, the stronger the plywood.

Exterior grade plywood is used for outdoor constructions such as dog kennels and sheds and is sometimes used as a cladding material, particularly for insert panels such as those often found under windows. Inside, plywood is used for such things as wall-panelling, flooring and furniture making. It has an advantage over other man-made boards in that thin flexible sheets can be curved.

The sizes most commonly stocked are 1220 × 1220mm (4 × 4ft), 2440 × 1220mm (8 × 4ft), 1525 × 1525mm (5 × 5ft) and 3050 × 1525mm (10 × 5ft), all available in 3–24mm ($\frac{1}{8}$–1in) thicknesses.

Finishes

For interior use there are a number of decorative veneers for plywood, some of which are cut from

top class hardwoods. There are also less expensive simulated finishes which are printed on paper and glued to the plywood's surface. All these decorative boards are used extensively for panelling to provide a warm, rich feel to a room.

Boards are also available ready-painted or pre-primed for painting and you can buy plastic laminated boards suitable for shelves, worktops and fittings. Exterior quality plywood is specially bonded with a strong, water-resistant adhesive and is available in such finishes as glass fibre and petroleum-based film overlay.

Working with plywood

Store plywood in dry conditions, stacked flat. If the sheets are to be used in a centrally heated room, store them in similar conditions before use to allow the moisture content of the sheets to adjust to the atmosphere; this will prevent later shrinkage.

Fixing Plywood may be fixed in place with adhesive and screws or nails, or by rivets or bolts. Instructions for the best method of fixing particular panels can be obtained from the manufacturer or supplier. But for general purposes, where ordinary nailing is acceptable, plywood panels can be secured with battens fixed to the wall. The battens must support all edges of each plywood sheet. In addition battens should support the sheets at intervals of 400mm (or 16in) for 6mm ($\frac{1}{4}$in) thick board, 600mm (or 24in) for 9mm ($\frac{3}{8}$in) and 900mm (or 36in) for 12mm ($\frac{1}{2}$in).

When gluing plywood, roughen the surface with coarse glasspaper so the adhesive grips. If you are joining two sheets of ply make sure the joining faces have the grain running in the same direction, but we recommend you avoid joining even numbers of sheets. If joining an odd number of sheets make sure the grains on the inside faces of the sheets you are joining run in opposite directions.

Sharp blows to the edge of ply can cause damage, so protect exposed edges with lipping if they are likely to get knocked.

Sawing Cut thicknesses of up to 3mm ($\frac{1}{8}$in) with a sharp knife. For ply up to 12mm ($\frac{1}{2}$in) thick, use a fine tooth panel saw and for thicker sheets use a coarse tooth panel saw. To prevent splitting, score through the outer veneer on both sides of the sheet, then saw out the waste.

Chipboard

Wood chipboard is made by bonding together wood particles with a synthetic resin adhesive under heat and pressure to form a rigid board with a smooth surface. Most boards have three or more layers with fine particles on the faces and coarse particles in the middle. Single-layer boards usually have a coarser surface since larger chips are used. Other types of particles are also used, the most common being flax shivers which form flaxboard. But wood chipboard is the most common of this family of boards, known collectively as particle boards.

Although there is an exterior grade chipboard used outdoors by the building trade, those at present available to the home handyman are for interior use only. The main grades are standard, flooring, and moisture-resistant for high humidity conditions. There are also flame-retardant boards and pre-felted roofing boards.

Uses and finishes Chipboard is widely used for built-in furniture, fittings, work surfaces, wall linings and partitions. Semi-finished boards have a

Top row Chipboard is available in a variety of finishes, a few of which we illustrate here; (from the left) melamine, hessian and wood veneer
Bottom row Three types of hardboard; (from the left) standard, reeded (embossed) and tiled effect

surface prepared for painting. Fully finished boards are available ready-painted, with decorative wood veneers, and with hard-wearing washable surfaces of melamine and vinyl which are suitable for kitchen use. Boards faced with textiles such as hessian or felt are also available.

The most common sheet sizes are 2440 × 1220 and 610mm (8 × 4 and 2ft) in 12, 15 and 18mm ($\frac{1}{2}$, $\frac{5}{8}$ and $\frac{3}{4}$in) thicknesses, but there are other sizes, including very large sheets. Chipboard is also available in metric sizes only of 2400 × 1200 and 600mm.

Many of the fully finished boards come in sizes for specific uses, such as shelving, and these are useful for DIY work. Those faced with melamine are especially suitable for interior fittings, shelves, cupboards and fitted units.

Flooring grade chipboard is marked 'flooring' and no other type of chipboard should be used for this purpose. It is available in 2440 × 1200 and 610mm (8 × 4 and 2ft) sheets and in 18 and 22mm ($\frac{3}{4}$ and $\frac{7}{8}$in) thicknesses with tongued and grooved edges for easy laying and fixing. If you are replacing an old boarded floor with chipboard, check with the manufacturer or supplier that the joist spacing of your floor is suitable for a chipboard floor.

Working with chipboard
Store chipboard flat in dry conditions and handle carefully since the edges and corners are vulnerable.
Fixing Nails, pins and screws may be used on chipboard, but they should always be fixed through the chipboard and into the support. If you pin, nail or screw into chipboard, the fixings will pull out easily. (Drill small pilot holes, especially when nailing, to make fixing easier.) The screw-holding power of chipboard depends on the type and density of the board and the type of screw used, so check with the manufacturer or supplier. The screw-holding power is improved if double-threaded or chipboard screws are used. Follow the manufacturer's instructions for fixing special purpose boards. Any woodworking adhesive may be used but preferably a synthetic resin type.

To cut chipboard, use a panel, circular or jig saw, smoothing edges with a plane and/or glasspaper.

Blockboard and laminboard

Bonded under high pressure, blockboard is composed of a core of softwood strips up to 25mm (1in) wide placed edge to edge and sandwiched between veneers of birch or a similar hardwood, the grain of which runs at right-angles to the grain of the core. Laminboard is constructed in the same way, but has a core of narrower strips of wood and is heavier than blockboard.

Both blockboard and laminboard are bonded with an interior grade adhesive, so they cannot be used outdoors. They have good resistance to warping, which makes them useful for large, flat surfaces. As the core runs the length of the sheet, it is stronger in length than width. So, when using blockboard or laminboard for such items as a door or long table, make sure the core runs lengthwise to give maximum strength. Blockboard is used for shelves, doors, panelling and partitions. Laminboard, which is more expensive, is normally used in high quality work and furniture making.

The surfaces of standard boards can be painted, while finished boards are available with a variety of applied surfaces such as decorative wood veneers and plastic laminate facings.

Sizes commonly stocked are 2440, 3050 or 3660 × 1220mm (8, 10 or 12 × 4ft) and 2440, 3050 or 3660 × 1525mm (8, 10 or 12 × 5ft).

Working with blockboard and laminboard
Store the sheets as for plywood. When applying a finish to blockboard or laminboard, whether it is paint, veneer or paper, you must treat both surfaces of the board. If only one side is finished, surface tensions are created which pull the sheet into a curve. The edges of these sheets do not clean up well and are not attractive, so cover exposed edges with lipping or fill and paint them.

Hardboard

This is made by breaking down wood fibres and reconstituting them under heat and pressure to form sheets. The three main types are standard, medium and oil-tempered and there are also a

Above Some of the range of perforated hardboards: the fretted ones make interesting room dividers, while the peg board type is ideal for hanging tools and kitchen utensils

number of specially finished boards for specific purposes.

Standard With a smooth surface on one side and a mesh texture on the other, this is used for wall and ceiling panelling, floors, door panels, built-in cupboards and fitments, toys and pelmets. It comes in 610 and 1220mm (2 and 4ft) widths and 1220–5490mm (4–18ft) lengths. Thicknesses are 2–12mm ($\frac{1}{16}-\frac{1}{2}$in), the most commonly used being 3, 5 and 6mm ($\frac{1}{8}$, $\frac{3}{16}$ and $\frac{1}{4}$in).

Tempered Treated, usually with oil, to give extra strength and water resistance, tempered hardboard is particularly suitable for exterior use, as wall claddings, fascias, extensions and sheds. It is obtainable painted, duo-faced (both sides smooth), and perforated and in the same sheet sizes as standard hardboard.

Medium Although less dense than standard hardboard, medium board is thicker and therefore more rigid. There are two types: LM (low density) which will take drawing pins and can be used for pin boards and notice boards, and HM (high density) which is suitable for wall and ceiling lining, partitions, toys and relief carving. Sheet sizes go from 1830 to 3660mm × 1220mm (6 to 12ft × 4ft) and 6–22mm ($\frac{1}{4}-\frac{7}{8}$in) thick.

Decorated Lacquered or enamelled hardboard has a hygienic, easily washable surface which is suitable for wall and ceiling linings in kitchens and bathrooms, splashbacks and kitchen cabinets. Special panels are available for baths.

Moulded hardboard is embossed with patterns giving a variety of effects such as leather grain or tiled, reeded or fluted. It is used for panelling, decorative fittings and pelmets.

Hardboard faced on one side with rigid PVC, flexible PVC or melamine is available in plain colours, patterns and wood grains. These boards are suitable for all vertical panelling and the melamine-faced boards can be used for kitchen work surfaces and splashbacks.

Standard, tempered and plastic-faced boards are available with perforated surfaces suitable for hanging kitchen utensils, tools and small shelves on peg board hooks and supports, and for ventilation panels and room dividers.

Working with hardboard
Store sheets flat and protect the corners and edges from damage. When handling hardboard, take care not to damage the smooth surface.

Conditioning To prevent sheets buckling due to a change in moisture content, manufacturers recommend they should be conditioned before use. There are two ways to do this.

For standard and LM (low density) type medium and tempered boards, scrub the backs with water, using 1 litre (2 pints) to every 2440 × 1220mm (8 × 4ft) sheet. Then stack the sheets flat, back to back, for 24–48 hours (48–72 hours for tempered boards).

For HM (high density) type medium boards and all boards to be used in centrally heated surroundings, stack the sheets on edge in the room where they are to be used, separating them with wood offcuts to allow the air to circulate. Leave HM medium boards for 48 hours and other boards for 72 hours.

Cutting Use a fine tooth saw and cut into the face of the board, supporting it on both sides of the cutting line. Pre-decorated and plastic-covered boards should first be scored along the cutting line using a sharp knife and straight-edge to prevent the edges chipping.

Fixing Hardboard may be fixed by screws, hardboard pins, nails or adhesives; follow the manufacturer's recommendations relating to the particular type of board and its use. Nails should be rust-resistant and preferably the round head type.

You can use any petroleum-based impact adhesive (for instant fixing) and woodworking PVA or synthetic resin-based ones (which require pinning or cramping while setting).

Decorating Boards which are not already primed should be treated with special hardboard primer/sealer before being painted or papered. Diluted emulsion paint (one part of water to four of paint) may be used as a primer unless the boards are to be papered. Wood primers should not be used.

Softwood

Softwoods come from coniferous trees, usually of an evergreen type with needle-like leaves. They are relatively inexpensive, light and easy to work with, making them popular for DIY jobs.

Types and uses

There are many types of softwood, including fir, cedar, cypress, pitch pine, larch, sequoia, juniper and hemlock. Most are produced commercially but they are not always readily obtainable outside the country of origin. There are four softwoods available in Britain.

European redwood Usually known as deal or pine, this is the softwood mostly used in houses. It comes from Northern and Eastern Europe and is light yellow with a heart wood of a darker red. A relatively strong timber, it is used for construction, joinery and sometimes furniture and has an attractive appearance when finished with stain or clear lacquer.

Spruce Often called whitewood, this is the second most popular type and is grown in Northern and Eastern Europe, North America and Northern Asia. A chief source of pulp for newsprint, it is also used in houses for joists, rafters, studding, internal joinery and furniture. It is light and easy to work and takes a good finish.

Parana pine Harder than European redwood, it is distinguishable by its characteristic red streaks and whitish-yellow grain. This pine comes from South America and its fine even texture and minimum of knots make it ideal for indoor joinery such as staircases. It is easy to work and because of this and its knot-free quality is particularly popular for DIY work. Since parana pine is inclined to twist, it is rather unsuitable for open shelving; so confine its use to work that is braced and rigid.

Yew This tree grows in Central Europe, Britain and other parts of Western Europe and its timber has been traditionally used to make simple 'cottage style' furniture such as Windsor chairs. It turns well on a lathe, is resilient and resistant to splitting, and has a reddish brown colour.

1

Buying softwood

Softwood is often sold graded: by degrees of clearness (how few knots there are), by description (as either best or second class timber) or, as in the case of European redwood, by its colouring – or by some combination of these terms.

Normally when buying softwood from your timber merchant or stockist you will have a choice between deal (pine) and one or two other types. Deal is the cheapest softwood available and suitable for a wide range of uses, though obviously if the job specifically requires another type of timber you should buy that type.

For most general construction purposes you can buy deal or occasionally spruce. In cases where the appearance of the wood is not going to be important, buy sawn unplaned timber. If you are intending to build internal structures such as fitted cupboards, staircases, storage units, doors and window frames, you will need the best available planed softwood you can find.

You should watch out for defects such as warp-

1 Chairs such as this one, with woven rush seat, are often made out of deal (**above**). Available in large quantities, deal is strong for its weight and good for joinery and making furniture
2 This sturdy kitchen stool is made from spruce (**above**), a light but strong wood which finishes well

ing, splits, bowing, dead knots and excessive moisture in the timber. But sometimes where the structure will not be required to bear very heavy loads and where appearance is not important, knotty, warped or slightly split timber (which can be cut down) will be suitable for the job. Some suppliers may give a discount on this 'second class' timber. Make sure you are dealing with a reputable supplier, since the official classifications of inferior and superior grade timber are not always adhered to. If in doubt, try another source.

You can visit demolition sites to see if any old timber is available. Sometimes contractors will sell this at very low prices if they are anxious to clear the site quickly. As long as it is sound and free from infestation the timber can be used to good effect for rough construction work.

Finished timber Softwood is sold in two forms, sawn or planed. The reduction in size which results from planing or finishing can be as much as 6mm (¼in) all round, though timber merchants generally keep to the margin of 3mm (⅛in), except with some

of the larger timbers. Timber is most frequently supplied in nominal thicknesses of 12mm (½in), 25mm (1in), 32mm (1¼in), 38mm (1½in) and 50mm (2in); these will, when finished, reduce to approximately 9, 22, 29, 35 and 44mm respectively. Widths are generally available from 25 to 229mm (1–9in); other sizes have to be specially ordered.

Working with softwood

Since softwood marks and dents fairly easily, make sure you work in a clear, uncluttered area to avoid the risk of objects falling or being pushed onto unfinished work. To avoid splitting the wood when nailing, use oval nails with the grain; if screwing into the wood, drill pilot holes for the screws. If you are using softwoods for constructions outside such as sheds and fences, remember they are less durable than oak or similar hardwoods traditionally used for these purposes and should be liberally coated with wood preservative. You ought also to use galvanized or sherardized screws and nails to avoid unsightly rust marks.

3 Lay an attractive floor with wood blocks made from parana pine (**above**). Valued for its fine, knot-free quality, parana pine is best used where the beauty of the grain can be displayed
4 A simple candlestick made from a branch of yew (**above**), one of the heaviest softwoods noted for its strength.

Hardwood

Most hardwoods come from broad-leaved deciduous trees. Generally more difficult to work than softwoods, they are also heavier and more expensive, but they do last longer.

Types of hardwood

There are over one hundred varieties of hardwood but many are not manufactured as timber. Of those which are commercially available, the most popular in Britain are mentioned here.

Mahogany This is the premier hardwood, prized for its stability and the way it lends itself to a really fine finish. It is rich reddish brown in colour, durable but lightweight and reasonably easy to work. The most sought-after variety comes from Cuba and America. It is used for high-class furniture, fine joinery, panelling and doors.

Teak With its great durability, this is mainly used in shipbuilding, although it is also used for joinery, furniture, panelling and, like many other hardwoods, veneering. A difficult wood to work, it has a greasy feel and must be finished with a special oil. It comes mainly from Burma and South-East Asia and is golden or deep brown.

Walnut A top-class wood, walnut works easily and is noted for its excellent finish. It is used for furniture, decorative panelling and veneering, fine joinery and bowls and other turned items. A light-to-medium weight wood, it varies from grey brown to purple brown in colour and different types are grown in North, Central and South America, Europe and South-West Asia.

Oak The traditional ship and housebuilding timber of Britain, this is now mainly used for furniture, joinery, panelling, floors and stout exterior doors; outdoors it is used as fencing material. It is heavy and quite difficult to work, but very strong. Grown all over Europe as well as in Japan and America, it varies in colour from a pale whitish yellow to a reddish yellow.

Beech This medium weight wood is used extensively in making furniture, particularly chairs, since it steam-bends easily and takes a good finish. It is also used for domestic floors and for making mallets, shooting boards and other items for the carpenter's workshop. A pale brown wood, it is grown in Europe, East and North America and the northern regions of the Near East.

Birch A strong, fairly heavy straight-grained wood, this is used for furniture and in pulp form for paper. It is more familiar as plywood than as solid timber and in this form is used for building and flooring. It grows mainly in Canada and North East Europe and is almost white in colour.

Ash This is a medium weight, very pale wood and its resilient toughness makes it suitable for hammer, axe and pick handles and ladder rungs; it is also used for sports equipment. The most sought-after variety is English ash, although it also grows in Europe, Japan and North America.

Ramin A white wood with a straight grain, this is obtained almost entirely from Indonesia, Malaysia and Sarawak. It has a particularly smooth feel and appearance when planed and is used extensively for mouldings and dowelling. It tends to split more easily than other hardwoods and is not suitable for use outdoors.

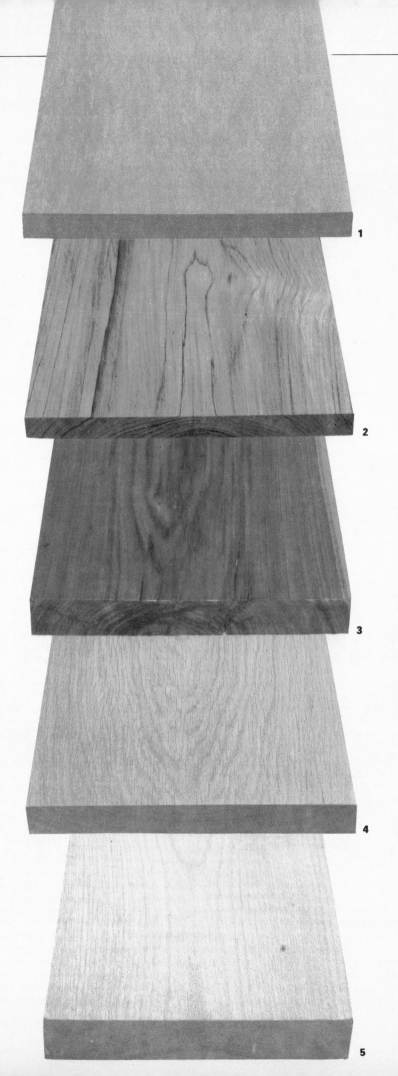

1
2
3
4
5

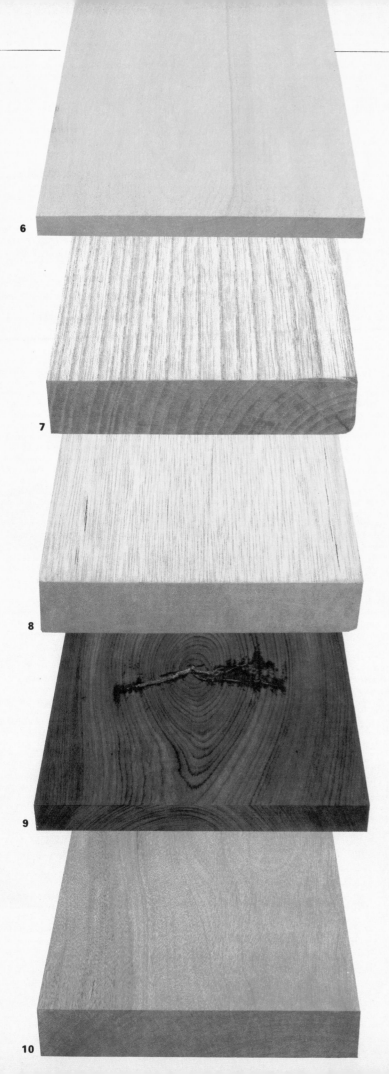

Rosewood This is a premier furniture timber with a pleasant fragrance and fine, elegant grain which can be given a high polish; but is difficult to work. It comes from South America, the West Indies and central and southern India and is dark in colour. The most sought-after variety is Rio rosewood which has a marble-like surface; other types, often grouped under the name of Mexican rosewood or tigerwood, tend to be a yellowish-brown in colour, are coarser on the surface and crack easily.

Gabun Coming from the African tropical forests of Gabun, Cameroun and Guinea, this is almost pink in colour, glossy and virtually knot-free. It looks like mahogany and is sometimes sold as African mahogany but is less expensive. It is used for furniture, veneering, joinery and for making up sheets of plywood.

Buying hardwoods

The trees from which hardwood timber is produced grow relatively slowly and generally require a more favourable growing environment than those which produce softwoods. This means that although there are a greater number of hardwood types and a wider range marketed, they are not so readily available in large quantities than softwoods and therefore much more costly. Unless you specifically require hardwood for the job you have in mind, it is worth choosing a suitable softwood instead.

Normally when buying hardwood from a general purpose shop you will be faced with a limited and expensive choice of timber. If you go to a specialist hardwood supplier, you will have much more choice, but again there is little chance of any bargain prices. The exception to the general rule is ramin, which is readily available at at least half the cost of most other hardwoods. This type of wood is worth using for all indoor purposes where another hardwood is not an essential requirement. When you want to use hardwood for outdoor work such as fence posts or gates it is best to buy oak – or mahogany for door sills. Your supplier will give advice on which timber you should buy and in what quantity to save unnecessary waste.

Working with hardwood

First familiarize yourself with the characteristics of the wood you are going to work with. If it has a close, even-grained appearance, it will probably be easy to turn on a lathe; if it is very knotty or has a very uneven grain, it will not. Check the wood's resistance to splitting by hammering various types of nails into an offcut. If it splits easily, you will have to use screws or joints rather than nails. You can learn something of how easy the wood will be to work by sawing, planing and chiselling the offcut. If the surface of the wood has a slightly greasy touch, you will have to use oil and not lacquer to finish it, so experiment with your proposed finish on a piece of scrap wood before applying it to any completed job. For outdoor work, remember to use galvanized or sherardized nails and screws and treat the wood for extra protection from the elements.

The most popular hardwoods
1 Mahogany. **2** Teak. **3** Walnut. **4** Oak.
5 Beech. **6** Birch. **7** Ash. **8** Ramin.
9 Rosewood. **10** Gabun

Special use of hardwood

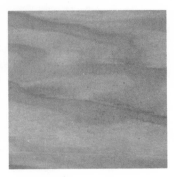

Zebra

Zebra wood or Zebrano, which grows in tropical forests in Brazil and Africa, is straw-coloured or pale brown with very dark stripes. Although strong, it is liable to distort and should be worked in small lengths; commonly used as a sliced veneer for decorative inlaying

Olive

From the olive tree grown in Mediterranean countries and parts of Africa, this wood is pale to medium brown with dark grey or black markings. Hard to saw, it can however be worked with shaping tools and is usually used for small carved or turned decorative items

Rosewood

The finest rosewood is very dark and is used for top quality furniture; the richness of colour tends to disappear when the wood is exposed to light and air. Rosewood is seen at its best when used for making valuable objects such as wood flutes

Briar

This wood comes from a type of Erica, a shrub grown in the Canary Islands, the Mediterranean and tropical Africa. The hard, almost red, wood of the roots is especially suitable for carving and turning and is often used for making smokers' pipes

Ebony

Ebony comes in several colours, including jet-black, dark brown with black stripes and mottled grey or brown. Grown in parts of the Far East and tropical Africa, it is available in small sizes and is used for a wide range of musical instruments

Pockwood

Otherwise known as lignum vitae, this very strong and exceptionally hard wood comes from the West Indies and Central and South America. Normally greenish-black in colour, it was used to make ships' propeller shafts; it can be turned to make ashtrays and bowls

Lippings and mouldings

Many jobs tackled by the DIY man need lipping or moulding to finish off joints and edges and it is important to choose the right type and to apply it correctly. Lipping is used to protect edges of man-made boards and softwood, while moulding covers joints and gaps and gives a decorative finish. Moulding comes in a wide variety of shapes, so you need to decide carefully which one to use for a particular job.

Lippings

Lipping is a strip of wood applied to the edges of man-made boards and softwood to protect them from wear and tear and to give a neat finish. Hardwood or softwood can be used, but hardwood provides greater resistance to wear. You can buy lipping in various widths and thicknesses or you can make it yourself from offcuts of seasoned hardwood: unwanted furniture can often provide suitable hardwood for lipping and many timber suppliers sell offcuts and odd lengths at reasonable prices. Most lipping is square or rectangular in section, although it is also available shaped or flanged for decoration as well as protection.

Lipping is essential for edging a ply or hard-board flush-faced door, whether it is to be left in the natural finish or painted. Blockboard doors should also be lipped to seal exposed sawn edges. A lipped finish to a tiled sill allows square-edged field tiles to be taken flush to the top edge of the lipping, giving a neat finish to the sill and eliminating the possibility of damage to overhanging tiles.

Hardwood lipping gives better protection to a laminate surface than a strip of laminate. If the laminate edging is slightly damaged, it has to be removed and replaced; damaged hardwood lipping, on the other hand, can be planed or scraped back using a cabinet scraper to a give a new surface. Shaped lipping can provide a door pull for a cupboard or a finger grip for a drawer.

Applying lipping

Lipping is usually glued, or glued and pinned; it can also be glued and screwed, but this is advisable only if the screws are decorative. Gluing is preferable if appearance is important, since pins may be difficult to disguise completely. If you are gluing

1 Applying lipping to a tiled sill; this gives a neat finish and protects the edges of the tiles against chipping
2a Shaped lipping used as a door pull on a cupboard
2b Shaped lipping used for drawer finger grips
3 Before applying lipping, check it is straight and square with the help of a try square
4 Position lipping so the edges are slightly proud of the board surfaces; trim away the overhang later
5 If you want to mitre the corners on external edges of the lipping, shape the ends before fixing
6 Butt-joining the lipping at the corners is much easier than mitring; make sure the ends are square-cut to provide a flush finish

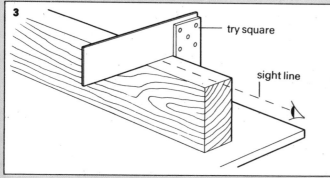

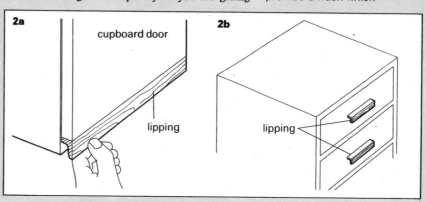

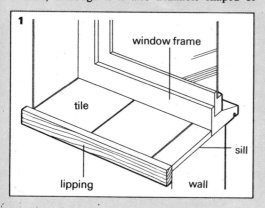

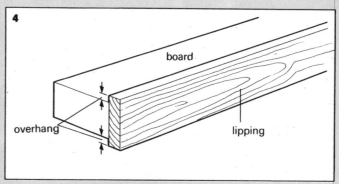

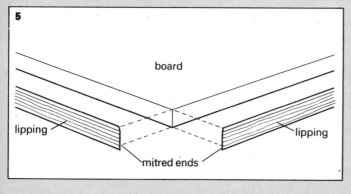

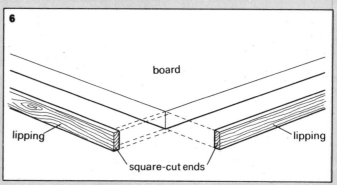

only, you will need to apply pressure while the adhesive is drying.

Preparing the surfaces The edge of the board to be lipped must be square-cut, straight and smoothly finished. Check the squareness of the edge with a try square; for straightness, hold the edge against a level surface such as a flush door or table top, or sight along the length at eye level.

Follow the same procedure to check the back edge of the lipping material is true and try the edge against the board. The back edge of the lipping should close tight and square when brought up to the board edge. Any signs of daylight indicate high spots along one or both of the butting edges; remove these with a sharp, finely set block plane or a medium-cut file. It is worth spending a little time to get the surfaces right at this stage.

Choose a lipping which is slightly wider than the thickness of the boards. The outer faces of the lipping can be trimmed when the adhesive is dry, so keep the top and bottom edges of the lipping just proud of the board surfaces when fixing.

Dealing with corners If you use mitre-cut corners on external edges, form them before fixing the lipping and work to exact dimensions to ensure a perfect fit. You will, however, find it easier to butt the corners. Fix the short sides in place first and trim them flush with the front edges of the board. Then fix the long sides, butting them against the ends of the short sides and trim back the ends of the long sides flush with the side lipping. It is important to file or plane away from the corner, since the grain will break away unless the front edge of the lipping is clamped against a supporting timber or shooting board.

Choosing adhesive Impact adhesive provides the quickest method of fixing, but PVA adhesive gives a stronger bond on wood and the excess is more easily removed. If using impact adhesive, first prime the edge of the board with adhesive and let it dry; this is particularly important in the case of chipboard, which is very porous. If the surface being lipped is likely to get wet in use, glue it with water-resistant adhesive.

Gluing and pinning Apply the adhesive and fit the lipping in place. Using veneer or panel pins, punch the pins below the surface of the lipping and fill with matching filler. Wipe away excess adhesive.

Applying pressure If you are not using pins, you will need to apply pressure to keep the lipping in place while the adhesive is drying. If possible, use a sash cramp or edging clamp; if not, tie round string or rope to hold the lipping in place. Place a wad of paper between the string or rope and the lipping, where the pressure is, to avoid marking the wood. Wipe away excess adhesive.

Trimming When the adhesive has dried, trim the outer edges of the lipping with a finely set, razor sharp block plane. When trimming back to a laminated surface, take care not to scuff it with the plane: use your fingers to sense how close the trimming is to the decorative surface and finish with a fine file until both surfaces are flush. A cabinet scraper can be used when a perfect flush finish is required between two wood surfaces.

Mouldings

Used to cover joints, gaps and edges, moulding is usually decorative as well as functional; some mouldings are used for decoration only. There are various shapes for different purposes and each

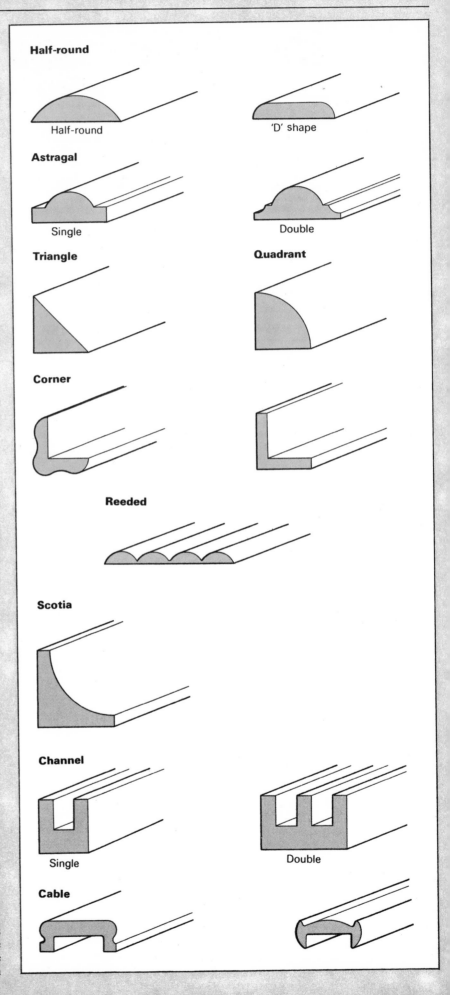

Half-round

Half-round

'D' shape

Astragal

Single

Double

Triangle

Quadrant

Corner

Reeded

Scotia

Channel

Single

Double

Cable

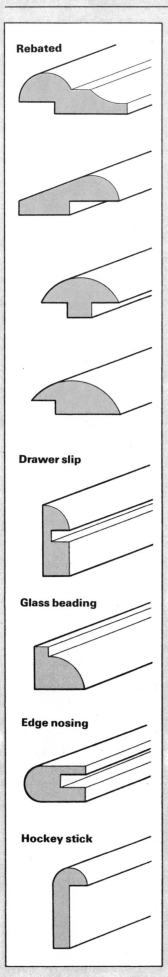

Rebated

Drawer slip

Glass beading

Edge nosing

Hockey stick

comes in a range of sizes. The most commonly used shapes are described below; there are also specialist mouldings used in cabinet making, picture frames, trays, toys and handles, and even sash mouldings for windows.

Half-round For hiding joints of butted panels. There is also a flat-topped or 'D' shape half-round.

Astragal Used as for half-round, an astragal has a 'shoulder' each side of the round part; a double astragal has two 'shoulders' each side.

Quadrant Probably the most widely used moulding; typical applications include covering an internal joint and hiding a gap between the skirting and floorboards.

Triangle Used for covering internal corners.

Corner For covering external corners and as an alternative to mitring where this would be difficult on thin panels; it is also used just for decoration.

Reeded This covers joints or can be used just for decoration.

Scotia For decorative use and for covering the joint between the skirting and floorboards.

Channel Used for glass or timber sliding doors. A deeper grooved moulding is positioned at the top of the door opening to enable the doors to be lifted into the channels when fitting. Single and double tracks are available.

Rebated These are popular as a cover strip for standard panel edges.

Drawer slip Useful for securing a drawer bottom to sides which are too thin to be rebated. The base slides into the groove.

Glass beading For fixing glass into a frame. If the frame does not have a rebate, the moulding can be used inside with putty outside. If the frame has a rebate, the glass can be bedded on putty in the rebate and covered outside with moulding. This moulding is also used inside for dry-glazing cabinet doors.

Edge nosing For covering edges of standard hardboard and plywood.

Cable For covering exposed wires and cables.

Base and architrave Used to cover joints between walls and window frames, door frames and fitted cupboards.

Hockey stick For lipping or edging panels and doors. It is sometimes fitted with the curve facing outwards to act as a closing seal for double doors.

Weatherboard (door drip) Fixed to the bottom of an exterior door to deflect rainwater and prevent it seeping into the gap below the door.

Door stop Fitted to the door frame to stop the door in the closed position.

Cornice Used at the join of the ceiling and wall.

Dado rail Fitted to the wall 1070mm (or 3ft 6in) from the floor.

Skirting Covers the join between the wall and the floor.

Applying moulding

The procedure for applying moulding is basically the same as for lipping. If the moulding is to be painted or applied where the use of pins will be unnoticeable, you can glue and pin it. If, however, it is a decorative moulding, glue it without pinning. Where access is difficult, making it impossible to cramp the moulding while the adhesive dries, use impact adhesive.

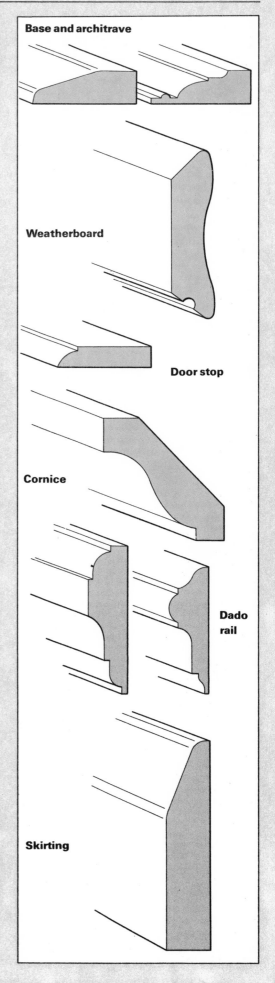

Base and architrave

Weatherboard

Door stop

Cornice

Dado rail

Skirting

Converting and seasoning timber

Before buying timber, try to discover from your supplier what processes the wood has undergone and the conditions in which it has been stored. Armed with this information you should be able to determine the quality of the timber and its moisture content and assess its suitability for the project you have in mind.

Tree growth A tree grows by continually forming a new outer layer of wood beneath the bark; this new wood is called the sapwood since it is in these layers that the sap is carried. The change in growing conditions due to seasonal climatic changes causes the new sapwood to be laid down faster at certain times than others. This causes a change of colour in the sapwood and is the reason for the annual rings; each ring represents one season's growth. In trees grown in temperate climates the light rings are the spring growth and the dark rings the slower summer growth.

As the tree gets bigger, the older wood towards the centre carries less and less sap and gradually dies. This wood formed from dead cells is called heartwood and is the best timber for joinery purposes since it is a better colour, stronger and less liable to insect attack than sapwood. Small groups of cells run out radially from the centre of the tree and form the medullary rays; these do not show at all in many woods, but are a decorative feature in oak and beech.

Felling This is best carried out in winter when the sap content of the tree is at its minimum. The tree is then trimmed and transported to the timber conversion mill as quickly as possible.

Timber conversion

Conversion is the process whereby a tree is sawn into planks; there are several ways in which this may be carried out, depending on the type and condition of the tree and the use to which the timber is to be put.

The most common method – and the one by which nearly all softwood is converted – is where the tree is cut into a series of slices; this is called the slash or through-and-through method. The planks cut from the centre of the tree are the best, since those on the top and bottom have a wide, waney edge and are also liable to cup.

For more expensive woods where a better figure or grain pattern is obtained by cutting with the medullary rays, a method known as quarter-sawing is used; this is a more wasteful method of conversion than the slash method, but results in more decorative and much more stable planks. It is normally used only with hardwoods.

With slash-sawing, some radial and some tangential planks will be obtained; with quarter-sawn timber, all the planks are radially cut.

Moisture in timber

The moisture content of timber is the percentage of water by weight in the wood; the water is contained in the cell cavities and in the cell walls.

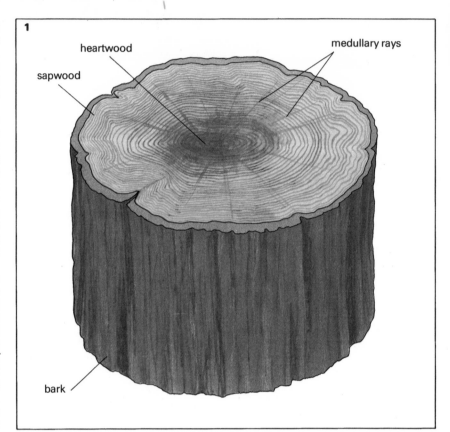

1

sapwood

heartwood

medullary rays

bark

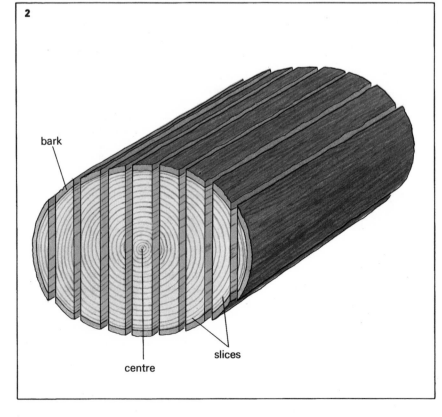

2

bark

centre

slices

In a growing tree the moisture content can be as high as 200 percent.

Once the tree is felled it starts to lose moisture. This process is accelerated by conversion; the timber will continue to lose moisture as long as the air surrounding it is dry enough to absorb the water and until a state of equilibrium is reached, when the moisture content of the timber is the same as that of the surrounding air.

The water in the cell cavities is the first to be given up; this continues until the moisture content has dropped to 27–30 percent. The loss of this water causes no dimensional change in the wood. As the moisture in the cell walls is given up, however, a dimensional change does take place. This is called shrinkage and continues until the equilibrium point is reached and no more water is lost. For timber stored in outside yards, this equilibrium occurs at about 18 percent moisture content. Bear in mind, however, the wood will continually adjust its moisture content to that of the surrounding air; if it is brought indoors to a centrally heated room, its moisture content will slowly drop to about ten percent, causing more shrinkage to occur.

Shrinkage It is not possible to give any hard and fast rules about how much and in which direction wood will shrink; however there are some general points which you should bear in mind.

● Shrinkage along the grain is so small it may be ignored.

● Shrinkage takes place mainly along the annual rings and tends to straighten them out; this means a tangentially cut plank will usually cup to some degree.

● Shrinkage is most noticeable across the grain of a plank, causing it to become narrower.

● Different woods shrink in different manners. Cedar, for example, shrinks about half as much as European redwood (the most popular softwood); beech shrinks more than this. A radially sawn beech plank 250mm (or 10in) wide will shrink about 8mm

(or $\frac{5}{16}$ in) in width if moved from an outside store to a hot, centrally heated room.

● While certain paints and varnishes have a slight delaying effect, they will not stop wood finding its equilibrium level and therefore shrinking or expanding.

● A further complication of shrinkage occurs if the grain on a plank is twisted; this is called distortion and causes the plank to twist and warp.

Seasoning timber
Seasoning is the controlled drying-out of timber. The oldest process (which is still much used today) is the natural or outdoor method; the planks are stacked in open sheds with small pieces of wood (called stickers) between them to assist the free circulation of air. This method takes a long time, especially with hardwoods – about one year for timber 25mm (or 1in) thick. The average value of the moisture content for a fully seasoned plank by this method is 18 percent; lower figures are not possible because of the humidity of outside conditions. Some timbers, such as oak, tend to become waterproof when dry; this means the centre of a thick plank may be still moist and unseasoned after many years of natural seasoning.

A quicker and more controlled method involves the use of a kiln; here the timber is stacked in a closed kiln and, by controlling the temperature and humidity in the kiln, the moisture content of the wood is lowered. This process takes weeks instead of years.

A kiln may be used to dry out wood to any required moisture content, but only large quantities of timber will be considered economical. Kiln-drying should be used only where carefully controlled storage conditions exist for the wood after seasoning. There is little point in seasoning timber down to say eight percent and then storing it in an outside shed; the moisture content would soon be raised to 18 percent.

As a general rule, most softwood is naturally seasoned and most hardwood is kiln-dried; however, the best guide to the moisture content of timber about to be purchased is where it is stored. If it is kept outside under cover, it is safe to assume the moisture content is 18 percent. If it is stored indoors in a heated environment, the moisture content will be lower; how much lower depends on how long the timber has been there and the temperature at which it has been kept. The term kiln-seasoned has little significance unless you know when it was seasoned and what has happened to it since.

Home seasoning If a timber construction is to remain stable and not shrink, the moisture content must remain constant; it follows the same moisture content should be present when the object is made. The following table gives approximate moisture content requirements for certain applications.

Application	Moisture content (%)
Garden tools and equipment	18
External doors	15
Indoor furniture – bedrooms	13
Indoor furniture – centrally heated rooms	12
Parquet tiles over underfloor heating	8

(With the exception of garden tools, all items have a lower moisture content than that of naturally seasoned timber.)

1 Section through a tree trunk indicating the sapwood and heartwood; medullary rays do not show in all woods, but are a decorative feature in oak and beech
2 The slash or through method of converting timber; the planks cut from the tree centre are the best
3 The quarter sawing method of converting timber; the planks are more stable and decorative than those produced by the slash method

3

bark

slices

medullary rays

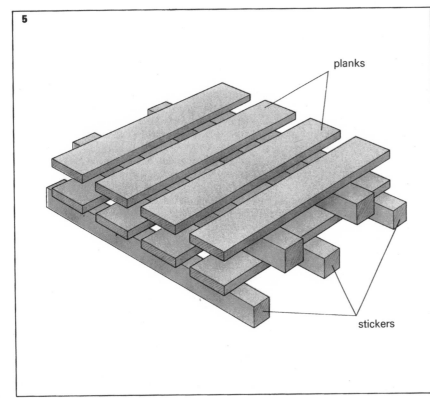

radial cut

tangential cut

planks

stickers

4a With radial cutting, the cuts are made from the centre of the timber along the medullary rays. **4b** With tangential cutting, the cuts are made across the medullary rays. **5** Stacking timber to allow air to circulate

When buying timber, therefore, have a good look at the timber merchant's store; this will allow you to make an approximate assessment of the moisture content of the timber you are about to buy.

Storing When the timber has been cut roughly to size (allowing plenty for wastage), it should be stored where the finished article is to be situated. Stack the planks vertically or horizontally with small pieces of waste wood between them to allow air to circulate. It will take at least two weeks for the timber to reach its equilibrium point. If these simple precautions are not taken, a project which may have taken many hours of work will shrink and distort, causing doors to stick, drawers to jam, joints to open – and many other faults.

Warning Beware the term 'seasoned' timber; it means very little. Even antique furniture will shrink and warp if brought from a cool bedroom to a hot, centrally heated sitting room. Timber never loses its ability to absorb or dissipate moisture to reach equilibrium with the surrounding air.

Buying timber

Where timber is to be used for furniture or any other function where strength and appearance are important, it is essential the best available material is purchased. A reputable timber merchant will allow you to select wood from stock to suit your own requirements and you should always take advantage of this; never buy timber without inspecting it first – which means you should never order timber by telephone.

Man-made boards
When buying man-made boards such as plywood, blockboard, chipboard, laminboard and hardboard, check both surfaces are free from scratches and dents; pay particular attention to the corners of the board, back and front. With veneered or melamine-coated chipboard, the edges should be checked carefully since these can be easily damaged in transit. Boards which are twisted or warped should be avoided; the one exception to this is 6mm ($\frac{1}{4}$in) hardboard which can be flattened by soaking it with water and laying it on a flat surface. The boards should be stored on edge or completely flat; they require no special treatment before use and may be used immediately after purchase. Again the exception to this is hardboard, which should be conditioned before use to prevent buckling; conditioning hardboard has been covered earlier in the book.

Natural timber
When purchasing softwood and hardwood, much more care is necessary. Before use, the wood must be home-seasoned to enable the moisture content to adjust to that of the surrounding air; this was covered earlier in the book. Always buy the boards

Above Always inspect timber before you buy; if the timber merchant will not allow you to do this, it is advisable to shop elsewhere

with a generous allowance for wastage on length; this is to allow the required pieces to be cut using the wood to its best advantage.

There are many flaws which can exist in natural timber. Some are completely unacceptable and affected boards should be avoided; others may be cut out, but remember to make allowances for this when calculating the amount of timber you need.

Decay This is caused by fungal attack and may be detected by soft patches and discolouration, usually due to the board being stored in damp conditions. The only treatment for decay is to cut out the affected portion and burn it.

Checks This term usually refers to end checks which are splits or cracks in the end of boards; they are caused by the moisture in the end of the board drying out more quickly than that in the centre. End checks may be on the surface or pass through the board; the only treatment is to cut off the faulty end.

Shakes These are separations or splits between the annual rings of the board; the opening may vary from a hairline to 2mm ($\frac{1}{12}$in) and may be on the surface or right through the board. There is no effective cure for a shake and you should avoid buying any boards affected in this way.

Splits Splits are large separations of the fibres and are the signs of physical damage to the board. Affected boards should be avoided at all costs.

Knots A knot is where a branch left the tree and new wood has grown over. If the branch was alive when it was grown over, the result is a 'live' knot which will remain in the board; if the branch was dead, a 'dead' knot results and this will drop out in time. Knots can provide an attractive feature and are perfectly acceptable as long as the board is used for decorative purposes and not for strength. For example, timber with knots can be used successfully as wall cladding, but should not be used for such things as table legs.

The main problem with knots occurs when planing or otherwise working them because they tend to leave a rough or pitted surface. Loose or dead knots with black rings around them should be avoided since they will almost certainly drop out when the timber is fully seasoned. Discard any boards which have half a knot showing on an edge.

Thunder shakes These are small shakes across the grain of the board and are caused by wind or storm damage tearing the fibres. Thunder shakes always weaken the board considerably and should be avoided.

Holes Various pests attack living trees and tunnel through the wood, causing holes of 1–10mm ($\frac{1}{24}$–$\frac{13}{32}$in) in diameter. The holes appear mainly in hardwoods such as African walnut. The pests have long since left the boards by the time they reach the timber yard and the presence of such holes does not mean the board is infested with woodworm. There is, however, no cure for this condition; the affected area of the board must be cut out and discarded.

Resin streaks This is a condition which affects mainly softwoods; dark brown streaks run down the annual rings and may ooze sticky resin. The resin will eventually dry up, but the brown streaks will remain. Proper home seasoning will allow any exposed streaks to discharge their resin, but will not stop discharge occurring from new streaks which may appear as the wood is worked. Excess resin clogs glasspaper instantly, rendering it useless, and will stick to the sole of a plane; allow the resin to

run away before continuing work.

Bark pockets This is a fairly rare condition caused by the tree being damaged during its growth; new wood eventually grows over the wound, but the damaged bark remains inside the tree. The faulty piece of wood must be discarded.

Waney edge When a board has one edge with bark on it or the brown edge beneath the bark, it is called waney-edged. In a few cases this edge may be used as a decorative feature, but normally the faulty edge has to be sawn off.

Cupping As a slash-sawn board seasons or dries out, the annual rings tend to straighten up; this gives a concave shape to a wide board. It is part of a natural process which is difficult to stop and is the main reason why narrow boards are used in preference to wide ones for making such things as table tops, since the cupping can be placed in opposite directions to cancel itself out. The fault may be cured by ripping the wide board into a series of narrow boards and planing the edges square before gluing them together again. To avoid the defect altogether, quarter sawn boards should be bought, but these are normally available only in hardwood.

Twisting This is when a board twists in a corkscrew fashion along its length. It is sometimes possible to correct this fault by clamping the board in a position to reverse the twist; but such measures are not usually successful, so avoid affected boards.

Some of the flaws which can be found in timber:
1 Decay
2 Checks
3 Shakes
4 Splits
5 Dead knots
6 Live knots
7 Thunder shakes
8 Holes
9 Resin streaks
10 Waney edge
11 Cupping
12 Ripples
13 Incomplete planing
14 Out of square
15 Twisting
16 Bowing

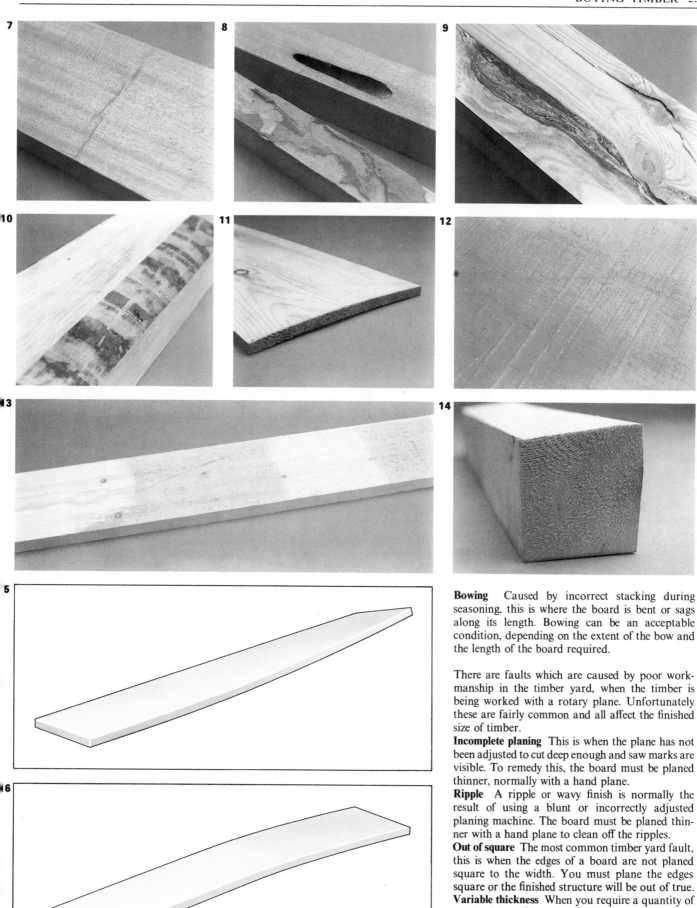

Bowing Caused by incorrect stacking during seasoning, this is where the board is bent or sags along its length. Bowing can be an acceptable condition, depending on the extent of the bow and the length of the board required.

There are faults which are caused by poor workmanship in the timber yard, when the timber is being worked with a rotary plane. Unfortunately these are fairly common and all affect the finished size of timber.

Incomplete planing This is when the plane has not been adjusted to cut deep enough and saw marks are visible. To remedy this, the board must be planed thinner, normally with a hand plane.

Ripple A ripple or wavy finish is normally the result of using a blunt or incorrectly adjusted planing machine. The board must be planed thinner with a hand plane to clean off the ripples.

Out of square The most common timber yard fault, this is when the edges of a board are not planed square to the width. You must plane the edges square or the finished structure will be out of true.

Variable thickness When you require a quantity of wood of the same section, always check all boards are finished to exactly the same width and thickness: PAR (planed all round) timber is planed only to nominal dimensions and all timber for one job should be obtainable from the same batch.

Basic techniques

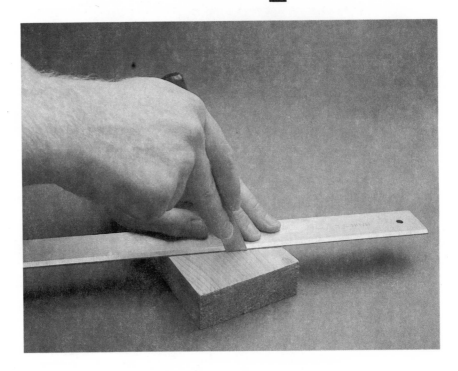

There are some general aspects of woodworking that you must be able to cope with efficiently to get the best out of the work. Follow the simple techniques on the easy way to cut man-made boards and learn how to make your own saw horses. A shooting board is another valuable item you can make yourself. Check on the best way to mark and scribe wood to eliminate any errors in cutting. This section also deals with different ways of finishing the work, such as filling in the grain and staining, laying veneer and putting on laminate, and shows you how to fit a recessed hinge neatly and effectively.

Making a shooting board

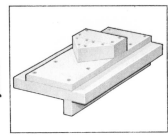

This board is used for shooting (planing the end of) a sawn piece of timber either at the mitre angle of 45 degrees or at right-angles. The board must be made from beech or a similar close-grain hardwood. Our design makes shooting at either angle a simple job.

stage 1

Measure and mark out all the pieces of timber according to the dimensions shown (**see 1**). Accuracy is essential so cut with a panel saw on the waste side of the lines, except for the holdfast E and the base A, which can be cut from the same piece of 22mm timber (457 × 301mm). Here you must saw along the line. Also cut along the line to saw out the triangular mitre wood-stops D, using a tenon saw; make sure the grain runs along the longest side of the triangle (**see 2**). Plane down the timber to the cut-line where you have cut on the waste side. Smooth with medium glasspaper the timber you have cut on the line; don't use a plane here or you will alter the size. To plane down to the line hold the timber horizontally in a vice. If the vice has metal jaws place pieces of scrap wood between the timber and the jaws for protection. Apply steady pressure on the plane and make long, even strokes to remove the same amount of wood right across the edge. Make sure the blade is not cutting too deep or to one side — your plane will have at least two adjustment devices. Check you are planing square by holding the timber up to the light with the planed side uppermost. Place your try square at regular intervals along the surface; if any light shines through, you have taken off more wood from that area than the rest.

1 Assembly diagram (dimensions in millimetres)

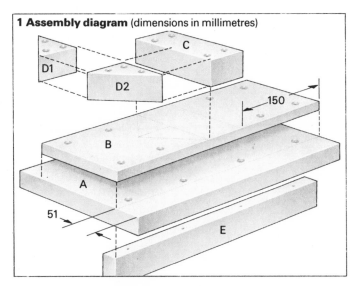

2 Cutting and drilling plan

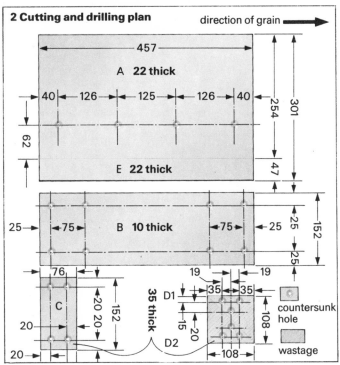

direction of grain ➡

stage 2

Drill 5mm clearance holes through all pieces, except the holdfast E, at the positions shown (**see 1**), using a piece of scrap wood underneath the drilling point to avoid damaging your worktop. Countersink all the holes to take No 8 screws. Place the holdfast E squarely against the base A at the position shown (**see 1**) and mark with a bradawl through the holes in A where the pilot holes will go in the top edge of E. Drill 3mm holes at these points and glue and screw the base A firmly to the holdfast E. Apply a layer of woodworking adhesive to the top edge of E and screw the two pieces of timber

together with No 8 countersunk screws while the adhesive is still wet. Wipe off any excess adhesive immediately with a clean dampened cloth.

Mark the pilot holes to be drilled in the base A through the holes already drilled in the shooting guide B. Glue and screw B to A as before, applying adhesive to the bottom face of B.

To fix the two mitre wood-stops D to the wood-stop C apply adhesive to one of the long edges of C and both 76mm edges of each part D. Fit the three pieces of timber together (**see 1**) and hold them together tightly with a web-clamp while the adhesive dries (**see 3a**). Alternatively tie a length of strong rope loosely round the edges of the three pieces (padded with newspaper) and twist with a screwdriver or strong piece of wood until tight (**see 3b**). When your clamp is tight wipe off excess adhesive as before. When the adhesive has properly dried remove the clamp and place onto the shooting guide B in the position shown (**see 1**). Mark onto B where the pilot holes will go as before, but this time drill them right through B into A. Glue the bottom of C and D and screw firmly to the shooting guide B with No 8 countersunk screws 63mm long.

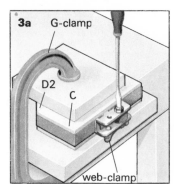

3a G-clamp

web-clamp

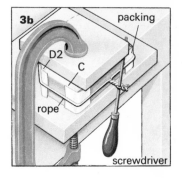

3b packing

rope

screwdriver

Fitting a recessed hinge

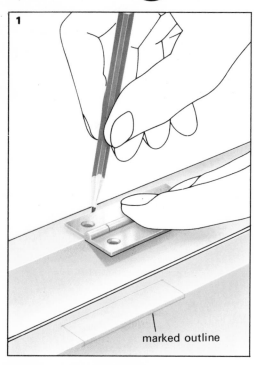

marked outline

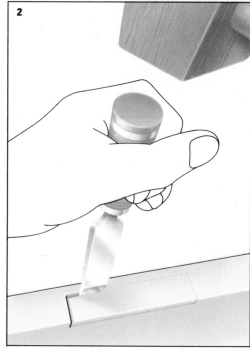

1 Using the hinge leaf as a guide trace the outline of the recess with a sharp pencil. The knuckle must lie just clear of the edge of the piece of wood. Mark the thickness of the hinge on the face of the wood down from the fixing edge

2 Score the outline of the hinge with a sharp knife. Hold the chisel vertically on the line with the bevel facing the waste side and tap the handle lightly with a mallet (or hammer if the chisel has a plastic handle) until the blade almost reaches the required depth

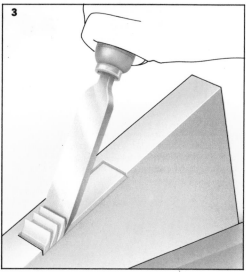

pilot hole

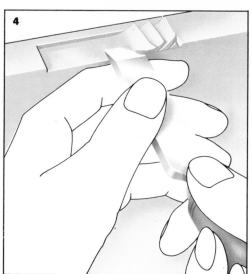

3 With the chisel bevel face downwards, clean out the recess making shallow-angled cuts to remove the waste wood to the required depth of the recess

4 Cut out any remaining slivers of wood from the recess by tapping lightly on the chisel (bevel face upwards) across the grain of the recess and along the base line

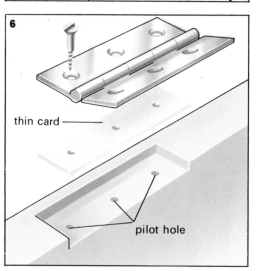

thin card

pilot hole

5 Place the hinge leaf in the recess to see if it has been cut to the right size and depth

6 If the recess is cut too deep, pack it with a small piece of card to bring the leaf flush with the wood surface. If it is not deep enough chisel out more wood

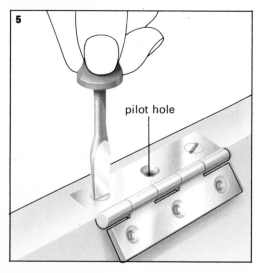

Working with man-made boards

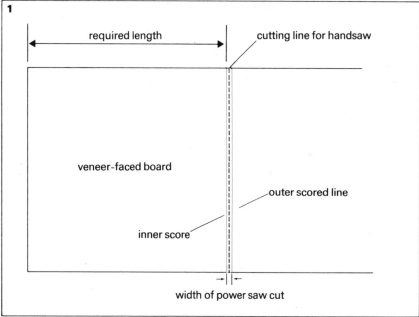

Man made boards have numerous advantages for use in the home; but because of their size they can be rather difficult to handle. The first job is to reduce them to a more manageable size; for this you will need two saw horses – three or possibly four for very large boards. We describe how to make a saw horse on page 31.

Cutting boards
If you decide to cut the board into halves or quarters to make it easier to handle, alter your cutting plan so the offcuts you are left with are large enough to be used in another project; the best possible use should be gained from each board.
Scoring Boards which have a veneered surface must first be scored with a sharp knife; this prevents the saw tearing the surface. If you are using a power saw with a thick blade, score two lines to allow for the width of the blade; remember to include this in your initial measurements. Score the outer line (with the blade width added) and an inner line without the blade width (**see 1**).
Sawing Use a panel saw for fibreboard or hardboard; power saws should be used for thicker boards such as chipboard, plywood and laminboard. When using a hand saw, score the cutting line on both sides of the board unless the project requires only one clean side; with power saws, just score the top side because these cut on the upward stroke only. When dealing with a non-veneered board, mark the cutting line in pencil.
Shaping Mark out with a pencil or scriber and use a jig or coping saw to cut the required shape. If the shaped piece is to fit into a certain area of the project and is not symmetrical, ensure the best side of the material faces you as you mark out and saw. Following a cutting plan, you may find two cuts are required to remove the shape completely; use weights and clamps to support it as you cut it from the board (**see 2**).
Cutting planks It is economical to saw your own planks, for shelving for example, from a board. To cut a board down its length, use saw horses (or tables or benches) each side of the cutting line (**see 3**). To cut across its width, support it each side of the cutting line and at both ends; this prevents play as you make the cut (**see 4**). Use old timber planks placed underneath thin sheets of board.

1 Scoring veneer-faced board. **2** Using weights and clamps as supports when cutting shape from board. **3** Positioning saw horse for cutting board along length

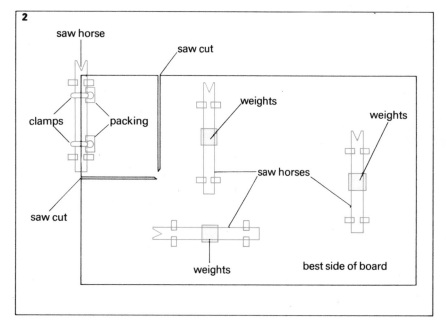

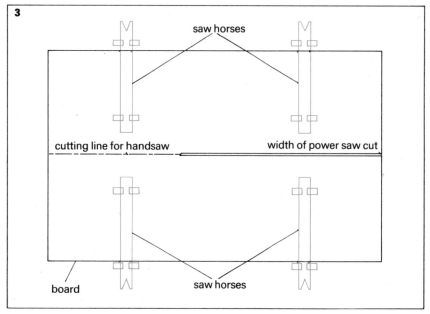

such as plywood and hardboard; clamp them firmly to the board to prevent play. Cutting boards into planks will require a saw which cuts on the downward stroke to reduce play around the cut. Support the planks on saw horses and also support the ends of the board as before. If you rest the thin board on two tables, you can make the cut as you would for sheets of normal thickness (**see 5**).

Warning Select your boards carefully, looking for broken corners or damaged veneers; choosing timber has been covered earlier in the book. It is cheaper to buy whole sheets, but timber yards may cut them for you; this may involve a charge, as could delivery. Try to avoid storing large boards at home for a long period since they are easily damaged; but remember to buy them in advance if they will need seasoning.

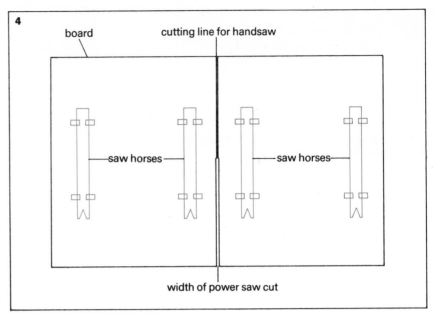

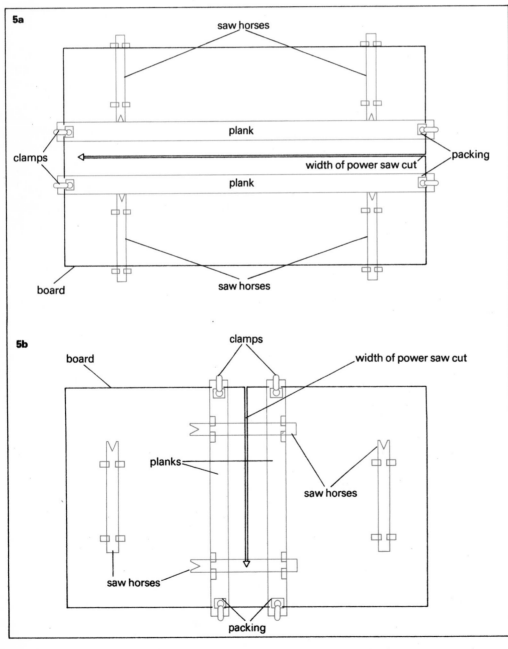

4 Positioning saw horses for cutting board across width
5a Supporting board with old timber planks each side of cutting line; clamp planks firmly to both ends of board
5b When cutting, depth of power saw cut should be not more than thickness of supporting planks — and preferably less — to ensure blade clears saw horses

Making a saw horse

Tools and materials

timber (see cutting list)
measuring tape and pencil
try square and sliding bevel
fine-tooth panel saw
tenon saw, block plane
medium fine glasspaper
25mm chisel, protractor
galvanized round head nails
   50mm long
water-resistant woodworking
adhesive

Saw horses are essential
when cutting up large
man-made boards and long
timber planks. You can make
them easily yourself — and
save a lot of money since you
may need as many as four
horses when working with
large sheets. Our design
enables the horses to be
stacked neatly on top of each
other so storage is no great
problem.
Saw horses are also useful to
support a board to serve, for
example, as a makeshift
wallpapering table or to take
vices and clamps for a
temporary worktop.
Use knot-free timber for
strength and galvanized nails
and exterior-grade plywood
so the horse can be used
outside without being
damaged by the rain.
The 'V' shape on the horse
supports the cutting area
when sawing angles in a
board or piece of timber. The
legs are recessed into the top
at an angle for strength and
stability.

stage 1

Measure and cut all the
pieces of timber with a
fine-tooth panel saw to the
dimensions shown (see
cutting list); smooth all
surfaces of all cut pieces
with medium fine glasspaper.
Cut the 'V' shape at one end
of the top A with a tenon
saw according to the
dimensions shown (see
assembly diagram) and
smooth the inside edges as
before.
Mark out the recesses in the
top A according to the
dimensions shown (see
assembly diagram) and

form each one by making
two cuts with a tenon saw to
the depth lines; keep slightly
to the waste side of the
cutting lines. Chop out the
waste from between the cut
lines with a 25mm chisel.
Check with a sliding bevel
the angle in each recess is
70 degrees.
Using a sliding bevel, mark
out the 70 degree angle
rebate at one end of all four
legs B according to the
dimensions shown (see
assembly diagram) and cut
out the waste from each one
with a tenon saw. Check the
legs fit snugly inside the
recesses in the top A and
trim the insides of the
recesses, if necessary, with a
chisel.

stage 2

Apply adhesive to the insides
of the recesses in the top A
and to the rebates in the
legs B and fix each leg firmly
in position with two 50mm
long round head nails. Wipe
off excess adhesive with a
clean dampened cloth.
Glue and nail the plywood
braces C to the legs (see
assembly diagram) so the
side edges overhang by an
equal amount. When the
adhesive has set hard, trim off
the protruding top edges of
the legs with a block plane;
remove the protruding side
edges of the braces with a
fine-tooth panel saw then
medium fine glasspaper.
Place the assembled saw
horse on a level surface and
position a piece of scrap
wood (about 22mm thick)
against the bottom end of
each leg in turn; draw a line
on the leg using the top edge
of the scrap wood as a
marker. Cut off the bottom of
each leg, sawing along the
marked line, and smooth the
saw cuts with medium fine
glasspaper.

Cutting list for softwood & exterior grade plywood

Description	Key	Quantity	Dimensions
Top	A	1	1000 × 98 × 44mm
Legs	B	4	600 × 44 × 44mm
Braces (plywood)	C	2	250 × 150 × 12mm

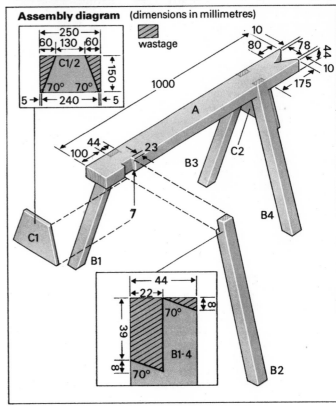

Assembly diagram (dimensions in millimetres)

Marking and scribing

In any woodworking job it goes without saying that accurate marking out and scribing of timber is vital if you want to obtain the best results. As a general rule you can get by with the minimum of equipment, which includes a pencil, straight-edge, steel rule, or tape, and marking knife. More accurate tools are available, such as gauges, compasses and dividers, which are a worthwhile investment if you are doing a lot of joinery work.

If you fail to mark out timber correctly, you will end up with poor joints and probably an unstable construction; and if you have to start again, a lot of time and money will have been wasted. So marking and scribing are jobs you must take time and care over.

Of the two basic items, in principle a marking knife is used where precision is all important, such as in cabinet making; a pencil is used for more general carpentry work where such a high degree of accuracy may not be required. A pencil is also used to mark waste areas of timber which have to be removed and also to identify the face side and edge of timber.

Marking knife
This tool consists of an angled steel blade, which is ground and sharpened on one side only. When marking, the knife is held with the flat side of the blade against a metal straight-edge, which can be the blade of a try square or a steel rule. The cut the knife makes in the timber being worked will help prevent a saw or chisel splintering the work when cutting through.

The knife is suitable for marking the cutting lines on veneered surfaces. By sawing along scored lines you will be far less likely to tear the veneered surface; but because the scored lines are quite difficult to see, it is a good idea to go over them with a pencil so they show up quite clearly.

Multi-blade knife
Multi-blade knives for marking are also available; these are particularly useful since you can fit the relevant blade for the work involved. You can buy these knives with either fixed or retractable blade fittings. A range of blades is available for different types of work.
Normal duty A general purpose blade for marking out wood, trimming leather and suede and cutting paper, card and polystyrene tiles.
Heavy duty Used for scraping off paint or vanish and cutting plastic (not laminate), flooring tiles and roofing felt.
Hooked Ideal for cutting vinyl and textiles.
Angled Used for scoring long lines on timber and plastic and for cutting card. It can also be used for routing and cutting carpet, roofing felt and vinyl.
Concave Will cut carpet, roofing felt and vinyl. Also used for routing.
Convex Especially useful for cutting wallpaper; will also score most materials and cut carpet.
Laminate Designed especially to score laminate.
Warning Inaccurately scored lines cannot be removed. Until you are confident you can get it right first time, it is wise to set out the cutting lines on the timber to be worked with a pencil first.

These can always be removed with a rubber or fine glasspaper. When you have checked for accuracy, you can score over the pencil marks.

Pencil
When marking timber, don't be tempted to pick up and use the first pencil stub which comes to hand. The pencil should be of a reasonable length so you can hold it comfortably for precise marking. It should be sharpened to a chisel point so you get clean, fine lines. For most work an HB grade pencil is suitable; this is hard enough to retain its point for some time, while soft enough not to damage the surface of the work.

Use an even softer grade pencil, such as a 2B, if

1 Using a marking knife held flat against a metal straight-edge to make an initial cutting line on a piece of timber
2 When marking the cutting lines on laminate, go over them with a pencil so they will show up more clearly as a guide for the saw
3 A cutting gauge, which has a blade instead of the point fixed to the normal marking gauge
4 A single point gauge

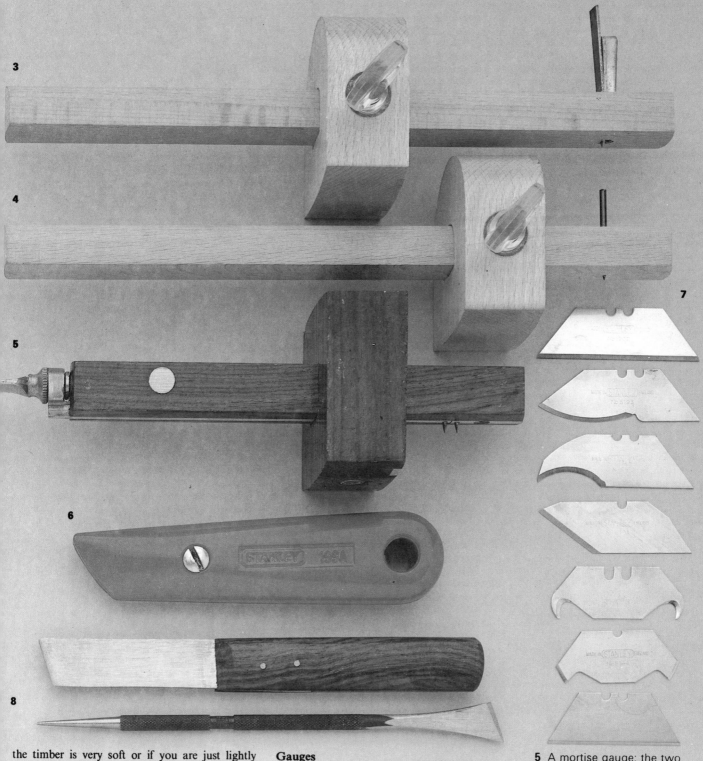

3

4

5

6

7

8

the timber is very soft or if you are just lightly marking the work for accuracy prior to using a marking knife. Use a harder grade pencil, such as an H or 2H, for fine marking where a marking knife is not available and where hard-surfaced timber is being worked.

For general marking of waste areas and with heavy work, it is best to use a carpenter's pencil, which has a wide rectangular lead available in soft, medium and hard grades. The medium grade is suitable for most work. The lead should be sharpened with a sharp knife and the end scraped to a chisel edge. If it wears down while working, you can rub it against medium glasspaper held on a flat work surface to renew the edge.

Gauges
Woodworkers' gauges are the most accurate tools to use when scribing or cutting lines in timber; their one limitation is that they can only be used to scribe or cut lines parallel to the edge or end of timber. To mark out curves and circles you will need a pair of compasses or – for larger areas – a timber lath, trammel heads or large blackboard-type compasses.

Single point The most widely used type is the single point marking gauge, the stem of which has a hardened steel point that protrudes about 3mm (⅛in) from it at one end. A stock slides along the stem and is held in place with a thumbscrew. To set the gauge, position the stock at the approximate

5 A mortise gauge: the two points – one of which is fixed and the other adjustable – mark out parallel lines
6 A multi-blade knife which holds a range of blades
7 Types of blade used with the multi-blade knife: (**from top**) heavy duty, convex, concave, angled, hooked, laminate and standard
8 Two types of marking knife which are fitted with a fixed, angled blade

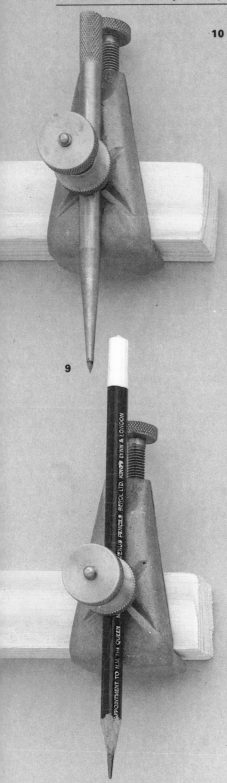

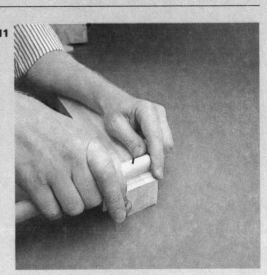

dimension required, then partially tighten the thumbscrew and tap the end of the stem gently on the bench until the point is the required distance from the stock, which can be checked with a rule. To mark the timber, grip the gauge with your thumb and first finger round the stock and your other fingers on the stem and run the gauge down the timber: keep the point at an angle to the work and the stock firmly against the edge of the work. Score lightly several times, allowing the point to mark a little deeper each time until the line can be seen clearly. If the gauge is not held firmly to the work, it can wander and follow the grain of the timber and you will not get an accurate parallel line. Always mark out with the stock on the face side of the work.

Keep the point sharp by using a small oilstone whenever necessary; when the gauge is not in use, slide the stock up to the point to protect it.

Cutting This gauge is similar to the marking gauge, except that it has a blade instead of a point – and this is held in place by a wedge. Use it like the marking gauge when cutting through thin materials such as veneers, light plywood, card and thin plastic. Use the gauge on each side of the material until the cuts meet. A cutting gauge can also be used to mark out timber across the grain, since it cuts into the work and will therefore not tear the grain.

Mortise This has two points (one is fixed and the other slides) and a sliding stock. The gauge is used to set out the parallel lines when making mortise and tenon joints. The method of using this gauge will be covered later in the book.

When a gauge is not available, a pencil and rule used carefully in conjunction with a try square can help you draw reasonably parallel lines. Hold the rule firmly in one hand with your thumb on the required measurement and your fingers steadying the rule underneath and touching the edge of the work. The end of the rule acts as a guide for your pencil. Check with a try square to make sure the line is parallel.

Compasses

Ordinary pencil compasses can be used to mark small radius curves and circles on timber. The legs are first set to the required distance apart and the point of the compasses is then placed at the centre of the circle; the leg holding the pencil is swung carefully round several times to mark out the curve or circle.

9 Trammel heads mounted on a timber beam are used for marking large accurate curves and circles
10 If your carpenter's pencil wears down when in use, sharpen it by rubbing on medium glasspaper
11 Using a single point gauge to mark timber
12 Wing dividers, which have points on both legs, are used for scribing equal distances on work

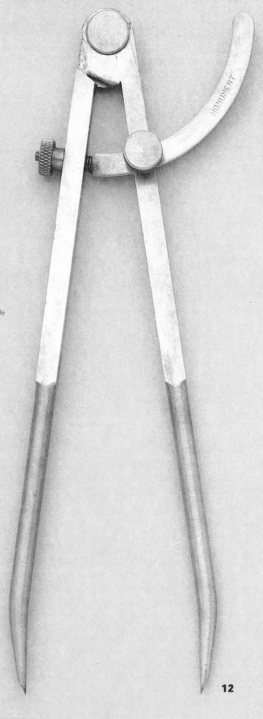

12

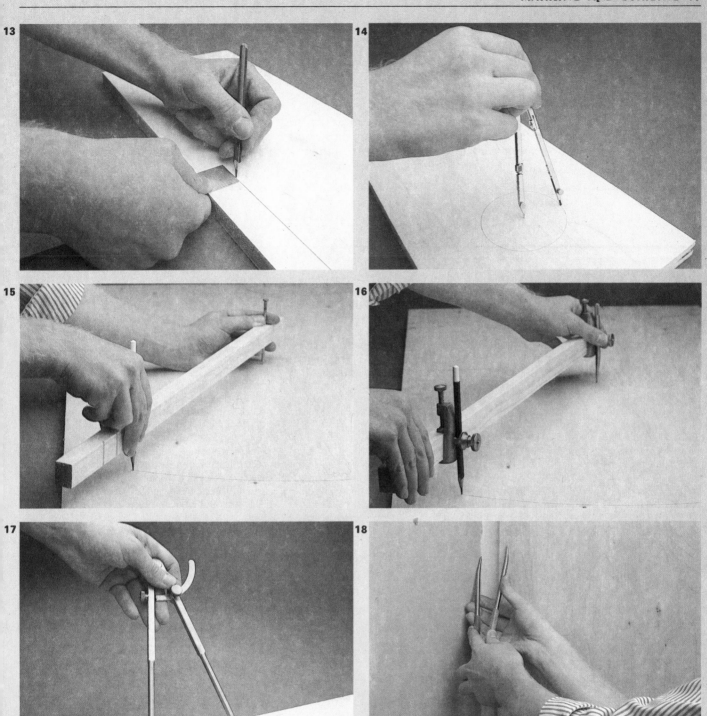

Wing compasses These are suitable for more accurate marking. One leg has a point and the other is flattened and sharpened so it scores the surface of the timber as it is moved. This helps to ensure a clean edge when cutting with a saw or chisel.

Timber lath This is useful for marking out larger circles. A nail or pin is driven in near one end of the lath to act as a pivot and a pencil is held in a notch or hole near the opposite end at the required distance from the nail for the radius to be marked on the work.

Trammel heads For really accurate marking of large curves or circles, trammel heads mounted on a timber beam should be used. Both heads are pointed for scribing and one usually has a socket so a pencil can be fitted. This apparatus is used in a similar way to compasses; place one point at the centre of the circle and move the other point (or pencil) to mark the required radius.

Wing dividers With points on both legs, these are used for stepping out equal distances along a length of timber. They can also be used to scribe a line along a length of timber when it is necessary to fit this to an irregular surface; the outline is transferred from the irregular surface onto the timber to be fitted.

13 Marking a parallel line with a rule and pencil; check with a try square
14 Using compasses to mark small curves
15 Using a timber lath to mark large curves
16 Using trammel heads on a beam to mark large curves
17 Using wing dividers to step out equal distances on a piece of timber
18 Using wing dividers to scribe irregular outlines onto work to be fitted

Staining wood

You may have pieces of furniture in the home made of reasonable quality wood. But are you making the most of their natural effect? Dyes, stains, oils and lacquers can each help to produce an even better finish.

Nature has given wood its own inherent beauty, so what are you going to do after you have built that new sideboard or bedroom unit? Are you going to hide the wood's natural grain with paint – or bring it to life with a dye, oil or stain? You may have an old piece of furniture that has become an eyesore thanks to innumerable coats of dark varnish or paint over the years. That, too, can be brought back to life with the proper treatment.

With better woods being so expensive, you may well decide to opt for cheaper varieties or man-made products such as plywood, chipboard and blockboard, which you can enhance with modern finishes that have superseded the traditional French polishing, button polishing and shellac varnishes.

Preparing the surface
The first essential, whether the item is old or new, is to make sure the surface is clean and smooth. All nails must be hidden, screws countersunk and any gaps filled with a cellulose wood filler; or you can work in a mixture of sawdust and wood adhesive,

which is much cheaper than using a proprietary filler. If a natural finish is required, use a matching wood filler.

If the wood has previously been waxed, varnished or painted, this must all be removed. Take off wax or an oily film with fine wire wool soaked in white spirit and dry off with an absorbent cloth. Repeat this process for each coat until you reach the bare wood, then smooth it lightly with fine glasspaper. Remove varnish or hardened wax in the same way, but use coarse wire wool.

To remove paint you can use a chemical stripper and paint scraper, an electric sander (either the type attached to an electric drill or a purpose-made orbital sander), a modern gas cartridge blowtorch or the old-fashioned meths burner in conjunction with a paint scraper. If you use an orbital or circular sander and wish to apply a clear finish, make sure you rub along the grain of the wood with fine glasspaper to remove any marks made by the sander. Don't use an electric sander on veneered wood since it might rip off the veneer. Only use a burner if you intend to repaint the wood or use a dark stain since any burn marks will show through light finishes.

Warning When using a chemical stripper always wear gloves to protect your hands and treat veneered wood very gently at the edges because the chemical could seep under the veneer and break down the adhesive that keeps it in place. Before you

Some of the colourful results of applying water-based dyes to hardwood
1 Rosewood
2 Teak
3 Red mahogany
4 Medium oak
5 Red cedar
6 Black forest
7 Swedish dawn
8 Sauna blue
9 Yellowstone
10 Carmesine

start work on an old piece of furniture look inside a drawer or at any unpainted surface you can find to check the wood grain and natural colouring: you can always test the dye or stain you want to use on these hidden areas – or paint a small area to check the effect.

When you have reached the original surface, wipe it over with fine wire wool soaked in white spirit. Glasspaper down again, fill any cracks with cellulose wood filler, or sawdust and wood adhesive, and glasspaper smooth.

Finishing the wood

If you decide on a paint finish, you must put on a coat of shellac knotting (if there are visible knots) and allow to dry before applying primer, undercoat and topcoat, leaving each coat to dry before applying the next. If, however, you want the natural look, you have several choices.

Wood dye Perhaps the easiest colouring to use and therefore ideal for the beginner, it is available in a range of wood or bright furnishing colours. The dye is in a powder form which you mix with cold water, or ready-mixed. And you can mix more than one dye to get the exact colour you want.

Apply the dye along the grain with a brush, cloth or sponge. As this penetrates the wood to give an even, permanent colour it means any subsequent chips or scratches will not expose bare wood. Several coats will give a deeper colour without masking the grain. Use a half-strength solution on end grain for a uniform finish since this is naturally darker. Dyes should be used sparingly at the edges of veneered woods to prevent the solution seeping under the veneer and lifting it.

These dyes are claimed to be non-toxic and the vivid clear colours make them ideal for nursery furniture and toys. When the colouring is dry, rub down lightly with fine glasspaper and protect the dye against heat and stains by applying a coat of transparent matt or gloss polyurethane lacquer for a hard-wearing finish.

Soluble oil stain Available in a choice of shades, soluble oil stain usually comes in liquid form. Apply along the grain with a cloth, making sure you do not go over the same area twice or the finish will be patchy. Use a half-strength solution on end grain. The great advantage of this type of stain is that it does not cause the grain to rise so there is no need to rub down the surface with glasspaper or wire wool before applying the final finish.

Linseed oil This darkens the wood and is suitable for most dark woods. Paler shades can be obtained by diluting the oil with an equal amount of turpentine. Apply sparingly along the grain with a soft cloth, rubbing it well in. Repeat once every day for two or three weeks until the wood will accept no more. Rub over with a soft cloth, finishing with a wax polish to bring up the shine.

Teak oil This can be used for any natural wood. It is an alternative to linseed oil, although it dries more quickly and has a more pleasant odour.

Vegetable oil Usually olive or corn oil, it is used to finish wood bowls and food containers. Apply with a soft cloth, but never finish with wax polish.

Polyurethane Available in clear gloss or matt and bright colours, apply it with a soft brush. Since the colour does not penetrate the wood, the original wood colour will appear if the surface is scratched or damaged. To safeguard against this, apply at least three coats, although with some colours you may cloud the grain pattern.

The effects of soluble oil stains on hardwood
11 Walnut
12 Mahogany
13 Dark oak
14 Golden oak
15 Teak
Oils and lacquers can bring out the best in good grain hardwood.
16 Clear matt polyurethane
17 Coloured polyurethane
18 Linseed oil
19 Clear gloss polyurethane
20 Teak oil

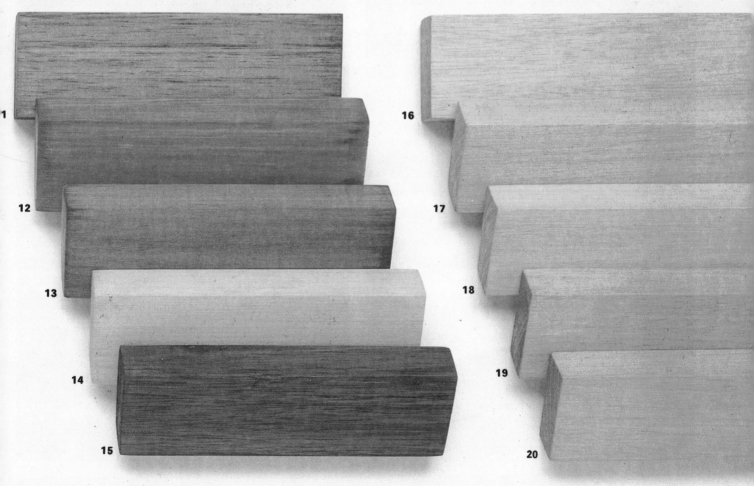

Wood finishing

There is a wide variety of ways in which to finish wood – some more difficult than others; the most commonly used methods are covered here. The standard procedure of finishing is to sand, fill, stain (if required), fill the grain, restore the colour (these last two stages apply only to wood with open pores) and seal.

Preparing work

Before attempting any staining, varnishing or polishing, you must ensure the surface of the work is smooth and dust free. If necessary, fill cracks and holes with the appropriate type of filler before carefully rubbing down with flour glasspaper to give you a sound finishing surface. When you are satisfied the work has been adequately prepared, move it to a clean, dry, dust-free environment; be careful to remove or cover all furniture and floor coverings since you may splash and mark them.

Staining

Stains come ready-mixed or as a pigment which you mix with oil, water or spirits. Some pigments are natural products, others are chemical; available in crystal or powder form, most are fairly easy to mix and work with. Once you have decided on a stain,

check a compatible finish is available. The simplest way to ensure this to is buy ready-mixed stains and polishes produced by the same manufacturer; otherwise you will have to match up the stains and finishes yourself.

Water stains These are usually supplied in powder form. Recommended mixing proportions are given in the manufacturer's instructions and, if these are adhered to, you will obtain a consistent mixture and shade. It is advisable to keep to set quantities when mixing up any stain, especially if it is to be used over a large area; when small amounts are required, the golden rule is to prepare more than you need so you will not have to mix up a second batch which could vary in shade or tone. Before applying the stain, dampen and raise the grain, then sand it down; this will prevent the grain rising later and spoiling the final finish. Water stains are easy to apply and penetrate the timber to a greater depth than other stains; this makes them suitable for furniture or toys which are roughly treated. Also water stains will not cause a chemical reaction with the finish.

Oil stains The base of these stains is naptha oil, a coal/petroleum by-product. They must not be used if a polyurethane finish is to follow, since a reaction will set in between the stain and the finish. Oil stains come ready-mixed as well as in pigment form.

1a & b Start applying stain about 25mm in from one end and work towards the other; at the other end, start 25mm in from the edge as before, overlapping the stain as you work back over the unstained area

2a & b Continue applying stain in this way until the whole surface is covered; use long even strokes and always work with the grain

1a

1b

2a

2b

3

4

3 Before starting any finishing work, stop all cracks and holes with filler
4 When applying stain to awkward areas such as moulding, you will find it easier to use a fitch brush
5 If you are working with a wood which has an open grain, you must fill the grain; work the filler over the surface and wipe off any excess with a rag

5

Spirit stains These stains are less popular than the others because their volatile nature and quick-drying properties make them difficult to work with. They are mostly based on methylated spirit and, like oil stains, contain aniline dyes as the colouring agent; this means they should not be used in conjunction with a polyurethane finish. Speed of application is essential; it is inadvisable to cover large areas with this type of stain since some parts will dry before others, leading to patchiness.

Using stains

The basic tool for applying stain is a brush and, as a general guide, the larger the surface to be treated, the larger the brush; awkward areas such as mouldings should be worked with a fitch brush. On large areas, such as table tops, use a dry sponge or lint-free rag so an even covering can be applied quickly.

Before staining, remove all fittings from the work and, if possible, place the surface to be stained in a horizontal position. Start applying the stain about 25mm (1in) in from one end and work towards the other; recommence 25mm (1in) in from that end, overlapping the stained edge to cover the unstained area. Use long, even strokes and always work with the grain.

You can rub the stain into the wood with a clean cloth to guard against splashing; this is most important when one area of the work is to be stained a different colour from the rest. To minimize absorption, lightly wipe the surface with a clean cloth, maintaining even pressure. If you want a darker colour, apply a second coat. Always treat the end grain with a half-strength mixture – you will

have to thin ready-mix stains – so it will end up the same colour as the rest.

Never leave part of the job unfinished, since it will be difficult to obtain the exact shade again. Check no area has been missed and set the work aside for several hours to dry.

Filling the grain

Grain fillers are not required with softwoods, most man-made boards and ramin, but they are essential for a good finish with open grain woods like oak and mahogany. There is a large variety of fillers, but the two most commonly used are plaster of Paris and paste. Colouring pigments and water, spirits or oil (depending on the type of stain used) are added to produce a creamy slurry which is worked over the wood with a brush or rag. The excess is wiped off with a rag and the surface lightly rubbed down with flour glasspaper.

Plaster of Paris Since this sets very rapidly, large areas should not be attempted at one time and any excess must be removed as quickly as possible with a coarse rag; an offcut of tapered dowel can be used to remove filler from recesses. After the plaster has set hard and been rubbed down, the full colour of the stain can be restored by rubbing in raw linseed oil which removes any remaining plaster. If you are going to apply French polish to the work, you must fix the stain with two or three coats of French polish before applying the plaster of Paris filler. Don't use plaster of Paris with polyurethane since it will cause a chemical reaction.

Paste This is available ready-mixed in a variety of wood shades. Follow the manufacturer's instructions – they do not differ markedly from those for plaster of Paris – and leave for 24 hours to harden.

Finishing

When deciding on a finishing method for wood, always consider the use to which it will be put, since some finishes are more suitable for a particular purpose than others. Also, if you have had little experience, it would be best to choose one of the simpler finishes to achieve good results, rather than attempt something complex and spoil the work.

Using French polish

For many years French polish was the prime method of furniture finishing; if applied properly, it can give superb results. It does, however, take much patient and painstaking practice to acquire the

6 To apply French polish, use a rubber made up of rags and wadding

7 Use light, even strokes in a series of up and down, circular and figure of eight motions

8 With teak oil, rub well into the grain using a soft rag

necessary skills and techniques. French polish is difficult to apply to carved or moulded surfaces because for a perfect finish the surface must be as smooth and as flat as possible. The finish is not resistant to heat, water or scratches.

French polish is obtainable ready-mixed in a large variety of colours and shades. Alternatively you can buy shellac – the basic ingredient – and dissolve it in methylated spirit; use about one kilogram of shellac to four and a half litres of methylated spirit (or 2½lb shellac to 1gal methylated spirit). Apply the liquid polish with a pear-shaped rubber made of rags and wadding; use light, even strokes in a series of up and down, circular and figure of eight motions. Alternate these strokes until a high, almost mirror-like gloss is achieved. As more polish is applied, the methylated spirit evaporates and it becomes progressively difficult to keep the rubber moving across the tacky surface. You can overcome this by dropping the smallest amount of linseed oil onto the rubber; but be careful to use only the barest minimum otherwise the oil will smear and mark the surface.

Using polyurethane

Polyurethane is the most popular and durable of finishes and has several advantages over French polish. It is tough and resistant to heat, water and scratching; it can be applied quickly and easily with a brush and it sets to a good finish in gloss, matt or eggshell. Polyurethane must not be used with any stain or filler which has been mixed with linseed oil, but it can be used over many finishes provided they have hardened. You must remove all traces of wax and oil with turpentine before

application. If applying more than one coat, leave each to dry thoroughly before applying the next; buff alternate coats with the finest grade of steel wool, ensuring the penultimate coat is buffed (but not the final one).

Using rubbing varnish

This varnish dries exceptionally hard and is easy to apply. Several finishes can be achieved, but the natural appearance is gloss; you can obtain a matt or eggshell effect by rubbing down with the finest steel wool combined with wax polish. In a warm room, apply the varnish carefully with a brush; leave it to harden for at least 24 hours before rubbing down with silicon carbide paper and soapy water and applying a second coat. After two days, rub down the final coat with rottenstone – a powdered abrasive which you work over the surface with a damp pad. Wipe the surface clean and polish it with liquid car polish; don't use an ordinary wax.

Using oil

Oil polishing is a simple procedure, but it does require a lot of energy. Oil is rubbed into the grain with a soft rag over varying lengths of time, depending on the oil used.

Linseed oil This should be applied at regular intervals over a five to six week period so a water-resistant finish is built up.

Teak oil Although primarily intended for teak, this can be used on other oily woods and is particularly suitable for furniture which is to be used outside. Teak oil contains drying agents which speed up application and also improve its resistance to heat in comparison with linseed oil. It will never polish up to a very high gloss finish, so is unsuitable for good quality furniture. Destroy the cloths after use since they will be highly inflammable.

Danish oil This can be used on all types of wood, is easy to apply and is suitable for both interior and exterior use, although periodic re-oiling will be necessary if used outside.

Olive oil This should be used as a finish on work which will come into contact with food.

Using wax

Originally the basic ingredient of wax polish was beeswax, but some modern polishes contain silicone since this is more resistant to marking. Wax polish can be applied effectively to most wood and, with age, can result in a fine stain gloss. It can also be used successfully over other finishes to give added lustre. Rub it into the grain with a lint-free rag.

Laying veneer

Veneers are thin slices of timber cut from round or squared-off logs. There are two basic types: constructional veneers are often thick and used in the manufacture of plywood and laminates, while face veneers are usually thin and decorative. You can lay face veneer to give a premier finish to less decorative timber surfaces.

There is a large number of face veneers available for cabinet making; most hardwoods make excellent veneers and some, such as mahogany, walnut, rosewood and ebony, are prized for their grain effect and colouring. Particular cuts from certain tree sections also give spectacular effects, especially when bookleaved or quartered to give symmetrical patterns.

Besides face veneers, there is a wide range of easily cut pliable sheet veneers and edging strips. Different types are applied in different ways; the most common is pre-glued and you apply it using a warm domestic iron. When using these veneers always follow the manufacturers instructions carefully to ensure good results.

Warning Remember a veneered surface must be balanced; always lay a sheet of cheaper veneer of the same thickness on the reverse side of the work. This will prevent the veneer shrinking and pulling the groundwork into a concave shape.

Choosing veneer
Face veneers should be used for any work which requires a premier finish. Veneer is expensive so examine it carefully before you buy. Check the veneer is squarely cut; if not, or if it is supplied with a waney edge, ensure you will be able to cut a piece from it to suit the project you have in mind. Also check the veneer is flat, has not split or flaked off and knots have not shrunk out of it. You may be able to rectify cracks during laying by gluing the edges together with a little adhesive; this is possible only with small cracks, however, and you should never buy veneer which has wide cracks.

Handling veneer
Never fold or roll up your sheets of veneer; if not kept flat, veneer could crack and break up. Avoid putting it in contact with varnish, dirt, grease or any other substance which could stain or mark it; you cannot clean up veneer easily using cleansing agents or abrasives.

Preparing groundwork
The surface upon which you lay the veneer, known as the groundwork, must be well prepared and of a good quality. It would be unwise to use ordinary softwood as groundwork since its tendency to distort will affect the veneer. The best groundwork to use is mahogany-faced plywood; gabun or Malay-faced plywood is a good substitute and laminboard, blockboard or even chipboard faced with the same timbers is satisfactory. Birch-faced varieties of these boards and plain chipboard are also suitable for veneers, but the tightly packed resinous surface will not readily accept the adhesive, unless it is well keyed. Plain chipboard is, however, an ideal groundwork for iron-on veneers since it will not need to be keyed.

Hardwoods, of course, make excellent groundwork for veneers, although they are expensive and you will probably be obscuring a perfectly good natural timber finish if you veneer over them.

Warning Veneer should never be used to disguise damaged timber or bad joints.

Cutting Once you have chosen suitable groundwork, it can be cut to the required size and shape; this is straightforward if your work is to be rectangular. If you require curved or shaped groundwork, you should cut slits in the reverse face of the timber at regular intervals; make the slits equal to two thirds of the thickness of the timber you are using. If your groundwork is thin, you can simply soak it in water and bend it to the shape you require; this is one advantage of using thin plywood as a groundwork.

Never attempt to bend groundwork which is more than 6mm ($\frac{1}{4}$in) thick; you will have to cut slits above this thickness. Also try to avoid cutting very tight curves since this will cause difficulties when making the shape of your veneers match each other. Cut the groundwork to size using a jigsaw, pad saw or coping saw; remember to score surface veneers on the groundwork to ensure the edges remain intact during cutting.

Filling Any cracks in the groundwork should be filled and any dents should be swelled out using a domestic iron and water. Drill out any dead knots with a bit of a larger diameter than the knot and plug the hole with dowel smeared with adhesive. Smooth the plug flush with the surface and lightly clean up the groundwork with abrasive paper.

1 The effect of bookleaving – when two identical veneers are put together to form a symmetrical pattern
2 The effect of quartering – when four identical veneers are put together to form a symmetrical pattern
3 Some of the wide range of veneers available: (from left) industrial, sycamore, sapele, mahogany, gabun and red meranti

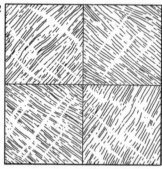

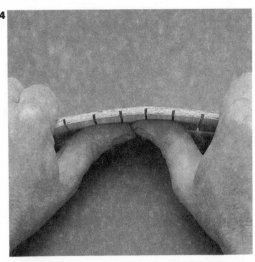

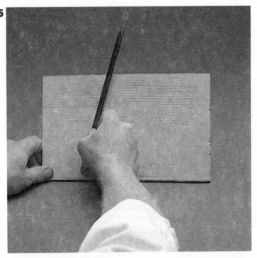

4 For curved groundwork, cut slits in the reverse face of the timber and bend it to the required shape
5 If necessary, provide a key for the adhesive by scoring the surface of the groundwork with a hacksaw blade
6 You can join cracks in veneer with wet gummed paper
7 Apply the veneer and smooth it down with a veneer hammer, then remove the gummed paper

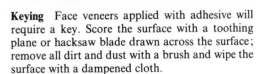

Keying Face veneers applied with adhesive will require a key. Score the surface with a toothing plane or hacksaw blade drawn across the surface; remove all dirt and dust with a brush and wipe the surface with a dampened cloth.

Preparing veneer

Before the veneer can be cut to shape and size, you will have to rectify any warping or distortion. Warm two flat boards with a domestic iron, sprinkle clean water on each side of the veneer and stack it between the boards. Weight the boards with bricks; after several hours the veneer will become pliable enough to lay.

Cutting Once the veneer is flat, use a sharp cutting knife against a metal straight-edge to cut squares or rectangles. A very sharp knife and stiff template will be required to cut shapes and curves; place the veneer face down on a clean flat surface and cut round the template as evenly as possible. Leave final trimming until the veneer is in place. When cutting across the grain of the veneer, make several runs at the cut using only light pressure. To build up a symmetrical pattern you will have to use the same template for each veneer you cut; so take care not to damage the template when cutting round it.

Choosing adhesives

The iron-on veneers sold in DIY shops use thermo adhesives which bond with heat from a domestic iron. True veneers can be applied with pearl adhesive, resinous adhesives and PVA adhesives.

Pearl The traditional veneer adhesive, this is mixed with water and heated in a glue pot. Once it has been stirred and heated you will have to use it quickly, since you will have little time to move the veneer once it is applied to the work.

PVA As with pearl, this adhesive must be applied evenly to the groundwork using an old brush. Don't apply PVA to plain chipboard since the surface will not absorb the adhesive; this will cause it to penetrate the veneer, resulting in shrinkage and cracking as it dries. PVA adhesive is slow in setting and you will have to use two pieces of plywood (known as cauls) clamped together until it has dried.

Resinous This type of adhesive, including urea formaldehyde and cascanite, is similar to PVA adhesive in most respects, but is more suitable for use on plain chipboard. The resin in the adhesive is compatible with that in the chipboard and this bonds them together.

Applying veneer

Apply iron-on veneer following the manufacturer's instructions carefully. Joints may be overlapped by about 19mm ($\frac{3}{4}$in) and cut through using a marking or cutting knife and a metal straight-edge; you can also butt join iron-on veneer.

Using veneer hammer True veneer can be applied using a veneer hammer; this method is ideal for flat surfaces and small veneered areas since you can easily position the veneer and flatten it by hand. Brush pearl adhesive evenly over the groundwork, dampen the veneer, coat it with adhesive and place it carefully in position; press the hammer onto the veneer and run it over the surface in a zig-zag fashion to remove all air bubbles. All areas of veneer should be covered using an even, steady pressure up and down the entire surface. You can use a domestic iron, set at a medium heat, instead of a veneer hammer, but first spray water onto the veneer to avoid burning, cracking or shrinking. You cannot use the hammer method if you use PVA or resinous adhesives; the veneer will lift as soon as the hammer is removed.

Using cauls Cauls are flat sheets of plywood used each side of the work to press the veneer flat. You will also need battens slightly curved on one side and some clamps. The battens are placed each side of the cauls with their curved sides facing the cauls; place a G-clamp at both ends of each pair of battens and tighten them to force the cauls together. This will squeeze the veneer flat and force excess adhesive out through the edges. Use some paper to protect the clamps and cauls from adhesive that is squeezed out. You will have to make specially shaped cauls when working with curved areas and unusual designs.

Making joints To join pieces of veneer, you should revert to the hammer method since the natural tendency of the cauls is to press the sheets outwards; this could make the veneers drift apart. Veneers can be butt-jointed or you can overlap them by about 19mm ($\frac{3}{4}$in) and cut through both sheets with a sharp knife; remove the waste to give a neat join.

Finishing Once your veneer has set firmly in place, use abrasive paper to clean it up. If the veneer has cracked, you will have to veneer it over again; run the new veneer in the opposite direction. As a general rule in cabinet making, it is best to counter-veneer (veneer over twice). The normal range of finishes, such as varnish, polyurethane lacquer and French polish, can be applied to all veneered work; the application of these finishes has been covered earlier in the book.

Repairing veneer

Although you must take extra care, it is quite a straightforward task to patch a damaged piece of veneer. However, refinishing large areas of older veneered work should be left to a professional restorer.

Patching It is most important to use a patch which matches the original veneer in colour, texture and grain pattern. Place the matching piece over the damaged area and line up the two grains. Make a boat-shaped cut, larger than the area of damage, through both veneers. Use a chisel to cut the scored portion from the old veneer and to remove the adhesive and dirt from the groundwork. Apply impact adhesive to the hole and to the new patch; press the patch into place with a veneer hammer and clamp or weight the piece down until it is firmly set. Wax and polish the new veneer to match the existing finish.

You may be able to avoid replacing a section of veneer which has blistered. Cut the blister open and squeeze some adhesive into the cut using a glue injector; clamp the veneer down until the adhesive has set hard. Once the adhesive has set, you can use a chisel to scrape off the excess; lightly sand the repaired area and apply a matching finish.

8

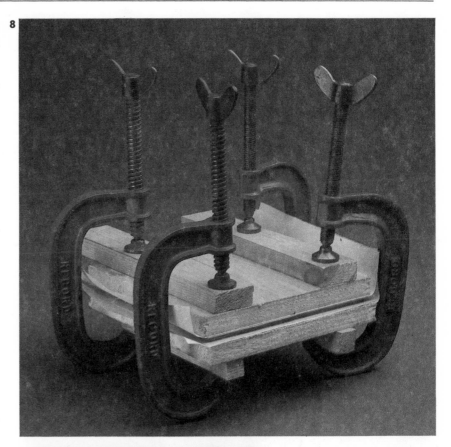

9

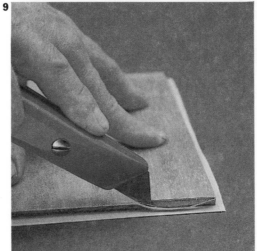

10

8 You can press the veneer flat onto the groundwork by sandwiching it between two flat, thick plywood cauls, placing very slightly curved battens on top and underneath and clamping the whole lot together; use pieces of paper between the veneer and the cauls for protection

9 Trim off excess veneer by running the blade of a sharp trimming knife along the edge of the groundwork

10 You can repair damaged veneer, but make sure you use a patch which is of the same colour, texture and grain pattern as the original

Working with laminate

Walk into most new or modernized homes and you are sure to find some decorative laminate – shiny or matt, patterned or plain – complementing the existing colour scheme. Hard-wearing and easy to clean, laminate will cover any type of surface.

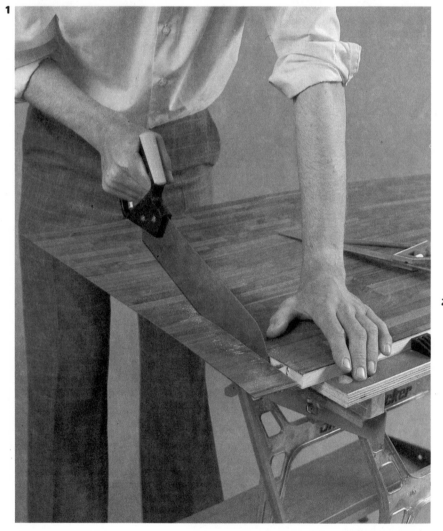

1 Saw at shallow angle to cut laminate
2 On large sheets score through laminate with trimming knife or score halfway through and snap sheet cleanly along scored line

Plastic laminate is made from layers of resin-impregnated paper, bonded under high pressure and temperature into a rigid sheet. Sold under various brand names, such as Formica, this decorative laminate is available from DIY shops in several sheet sizes which you can cut to the required shape at home or have cut for you at extra cost.

For economical edgings use laminate offcuts or buy a roll of edging strip to match the main decorative face. This type of edging is just a thinner gauge of laminate and will not have the wearing quality of standard sheet.

Warning The edging strip will lift away from the surface if the core board has an excessively porous edge – a fault with some cheaper quality chipboards. To overcome this, prime the porous edge with a thin application of impact (contact) adhesive before fixing the edging.

Laminate is normally glued to the work surface with impact (contact) adhesive. This sticks as soon as the two surfaces are brought together and forms a permanent bond, so the positioning of the laminate must be spot-on. Certain thixotropic brands do allow a little time for adjustment. Being less runny, these types are ideal when using laminate on overhead surfaces, such as the undersides of fixed shelves. Try to avoid sticking laminate to natural wood, as not even well-seasoned timber will make a suitable base. Man-made boards such as plywood, chipboard and blockboard make the perfect work surface.

When laminate is applied to free-hanging surfaces, such as doors, a certain amount of pull is exerted on the core material, causing it to bend and bow. To avoid this, you should always apply a compensating laminate to the back of the work surface. If you want a really attractive finish, use the same laminate on both sides, but an unfaced balancing veneer is cheaper and will do the job. Rigidly fixed boards will not warp so need only be covered on the visible face.

Cutting laminate sheet

Mark your intended cut line in pencil on the decorative face of the sheet, allowing an excess of 3mm ($\frac{1}{8}$in) all round for final trimming. Place the sheet so it is supported firmly along its entire length and near to the cutting line. Use a fine tooth veneer saw at a shallow angle to cut through the sheet. Hold the waste piece during cutting to prevent it tearing away from the main sheet.

When cutting large pieces of laminate, place the sheet on a flat surface with an offcut of hardboard

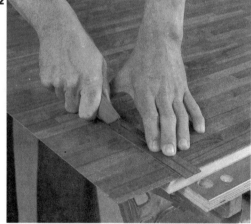

under the cutting line. Using a straight-edge (or a piece of timber, metal or even a strip of laminate) as a guide, mark a pencil line, then score through the surface of the laminate, using either a special laminate-cutter or a laminate-cutting blade held in a trimming type knife. Now score right through the laminate, gradually increasing the pressure as the score line deepens.

Another way of cutting is to score about halfway through the board and, holding down the straight-edge, raise the waste piece upwards until the laminate snaps cleanly along the scored line.

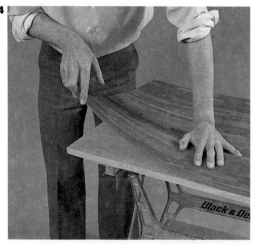

3 Spread adhesive. **4** Position laminate; align edges. **5** Use battens to stop bonding before alignment

6 Align laminate with drawing pins if using edging strip or wood lipping
7 Clamp for synthetic resin bonding

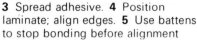

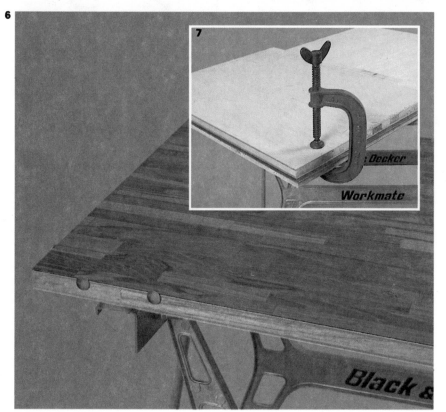

Bonding

Spread the adhesive to give an even covering to both the work surface and the laminate, making sure all edges are evenly coated. Leave until tacky or according to manufacturer's instructions.

One way to ensure the laminate is correctly positioned is to lay a number of thin timber battens across the work surface (they will not stick since they have not been coated with adhesive). Place the laminate on the battens, aligning it with the work surface, and remember to allow a 3mm ($\frac{1}{8}$in) overlap all round. Carefully remove each batten in turn, working from one end and pressing down the laminate to expel any air. Finally, using a hammer and block of wood (to protect the decorative face), work over the entire surface, banging firmly to ensure a good impact bond.

If your laminate surface is liable to constant water splashes you must use a synthetic resin adhesive which gives a high resistance to water. This type of adhesive is spread on one surface only, but the laminate must be held under pressure for 4–5 hours while it sets. To protect the face and ensure a firm bond, place timber offcuts between laminate and clamps (one at each corner).

When edging with proprietary strips or hardwood lipping **(see Edging)**, align the laminate using drawing pins as stop guides. Press the pins into two or more edges, with their heads protruding above the work surface, 3mm ($\frac{1}{8}$in) proud of the edge to allow for the overlap.

Warning Many adhesives are highly inflammable, especially the petroleum-based impact types, so never use these near a naked flame.

Trimming

To take off the overlap, use an adjustable block plane. It must be really sharp as the resin in laminate will quickly blunt the blade. Always plane from the edge towards the centre to prevent the laminate chipping at the corners.

A special trimming tool is available for trimming larger overhangs and curved profiles up to 12mm ($\frac{1}{2}$in). You can use a fine flat file instead. Work squarely along the top face edge – not at an angle – and put pressure only on the forward movement towards the laminate face to prevent your surface from splintering.

For a perfect finish, complete the job with a steel scraper. This is especially useful when trimming back the top surface where an edging has already been fixed.

Edging

Where possible, you should always fix edging strips before covering the main surface. If using laminate offcuts, fix them as you would the main sheet. If using a synthetic resin adhesive, hold the edge pieces in place with adhesive tape until they are set.

Proprietary edging strips bought in rolls have the adhesive already on the backing. Make sure that the work surface is square, clean and smooth and place the strip along the edge, allowing an equal margin at each side for trimming. Cover the strip with brown paper and with a warm domestic iron press slowly and firmly along the length. Follow up by running a small block of wood over the paper to obtain a good bond. After about an hour you can trim off the overlap.

An attractive alternative to laminate edging is a hardwood lipping glued into place and trimmed to form a flush finish.

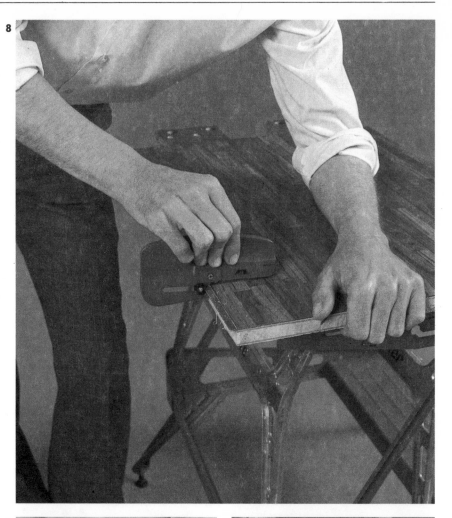

8

8 Cut large overhangs with trimming tool
9 Plane off overlap from edge to centre
10 Finish off with steel scraper
11 Position edging strip on surface
12 Iron down using brown paper

9

10

11

12

For cutting
fine tooth veneer saw or laminate-cutter or trimming knife with laminate-cutting blade

For trimming
adjustable block plane or fine flat file

For aligning while fixing
thin battens, hammer and block of wood drawing pins (if using edging)

For bonding
impact (contact) adhesive

For water-resistant fixing
12mm ($\frac{1}{2}$in) timber offcuts, four clamps synthetic resin adhesive
adhesive tape

For fixing self-adhesive edging strip
brown paper, domestic iron

For fixing hardwood lipping
woodworking adhesive

equipment

Joining wood

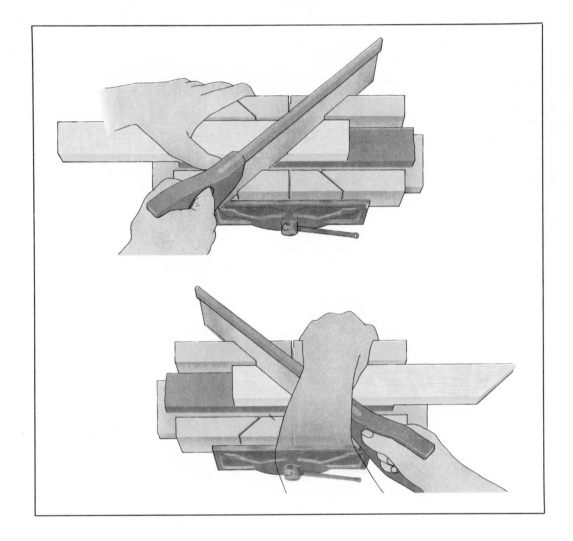

Most jobs involve joining wood and there is quite a range of woodworking joints that can be used, depending on the project. Some are easier than others, so it is best to use these where you can. Some are particularly intricate and often their main value is an aesthetic one, if you want to produce the highest quality woodwork. This section also shows you how to repair loose or damaged joints. It is important to know the relative strengths and benefits of individual joints so that you use the right one. Practice will help you perfect the techniques – and it is a good habit to try the joint out first on a piece of scrap wood.

Rebate joints

One of the quickest and easiest ways of joining two pieces of timber to form a right-angle, rebate joints are often used when making drawers, boxes and other similar containers that will not be subjected to great stress.

This joint is made by cutting a rebate in one or both pieces of timber to be joined together so all surfaces are flush when the joint is complete. The joint is then secured with adhesive and often with nails or screws as well for additional strength. There are two basic principles to remember. First, never cut the rebate more than three-quarters, or less than half, the timber thickness. Secondly, always cut slightly to the waste side of the saw line to obtain a tight join, rubbing down with medium glasspaper afterwards to provide a suitable surface for the adhesive.

Single rebate joint

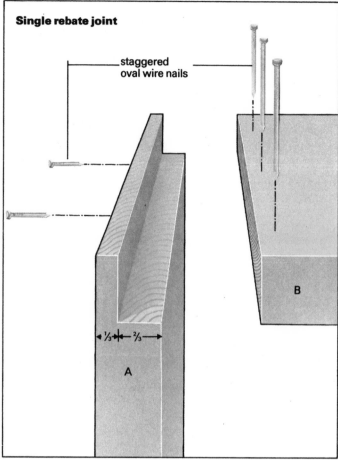

staggered oval wire nails

Double rebate joint

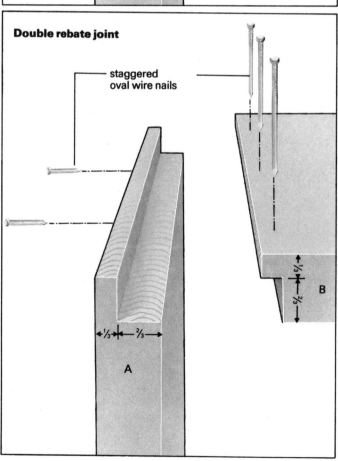

staggered oval wire nails

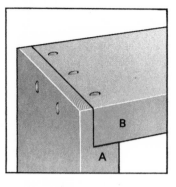

Single rebate
Using a measuring tape and try square, mark out the shape of the rebate in rail A. Cut the rebate squarely with a tenon saw to the same depth as the thickness of rail B. Smooth the saw cuts with medium glasspaper.
There is no cutting to be done on rail B so apply woodworking adhesive to the inside edges of the rebate in A. Place the end of B inside the rebate and glue and screw (or pin) through whatever will be the unexposed face when the work is complete. Wipe off excess adhesive with a clean dampened cloth.

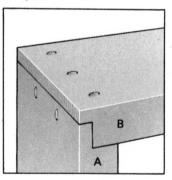

Double rebate
Mark out and cut the rebate squarely in rail A with a tenon saw to a depth of not more than three-quarters of the thickness of rail B. Trace the shape of this rebate onto rail B with a sharp pencil and then cut the rebate in B. Smooth all saw cuts with medium glasspaper, apply woodworking adhesive to one of the rebates and bring the two rails together screwing (or pinning) through the unexposed face. Wipe off excess adhesive.

Dowel joints

A dowel is a circular-section pin used to hold two pieces of timber together. You can buy ready-made dowels but it is far cheaper to cut your own from lengths of hardwood dowelling rod, chamfering them at one end. A dowel should be about four times as long as its diameter, so an 18mm (¾in) diameter dowel would be about 75mm (3in) long.

You must check with a try square before starting work that the two pieces of timber you are joining are cut square and sit flush together.

To make a dowel joint, drill corresponding holes in the two pieces of wood being joined. Then glue the dowels in the holes and join the pieces of wood together over them. The job is straight-forward but it will only be successful if you take great care when marking and drilling the holes. Make sure you drill the holes square to the surface; a dowelling jig will help you to do this **(see 2)**. The holes must be at exactly the right spot in each piece of wood and to the right depth. If they are not deep enough the wood will not join up over the dowels; if one hole is deeper than the other the joint will be weak. The diameter of the hole is critical, too, since the dowel must fit snugly into it.

Edge-to-edge
Make sure all surfaces are planed square. With hard pencil, mark guide-lines across both pieces of timber where dowels are to be sited. Intersect these with central line along each piece of wood to form crosses where holes to take dowels are to be drilled.
1 For drilling, mark centre of each cross with bradawl
2 Using correct size bit for dowelling, drill holes (with diameter about a third thickness of wood) to depth of not less than half dowel length (inset)
3 Cut dowels to length; with medium fine glasspaper slightly chamfer one end and saw shallow groove along each dowel to let excess adhesive escape (inset). Glue and insert dowels in one piece of wood, apply adhesive to protruding dowels and timber faces to be joined and fit other piece of timber over dowels. Finally clamp two together and remove excess adhesive while wet with clean dampened cloth

Edge-to-panel
4 When joining upright to panel or to bearer, mark dowel locations by clamping upright and bearer together at 90 degree angle or in 'L' shape, using scrap pieces of wood for protection. Check surfaces are flush with one another to ensure accurate marking. Make pencil crosses for drilling dowel holes as before
5 As pencil marks on upright are markers for inside of frame, turn upright round and continue guide-lines across top of faces to be joined
6 Mark each join A, B etc. to ensure right pieces stay together. Stagger holes if at right-angles to each other to allow sufficient clearance when making up frame
7 Drill holes to depth of not more than half thickness of upright (top hole) and with diameter about one third thickness of edge (lower hole). Glue and fit dowels as before

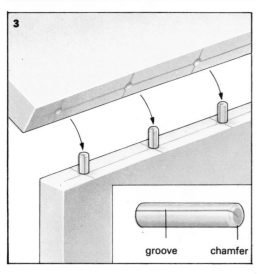

1 — bradawl

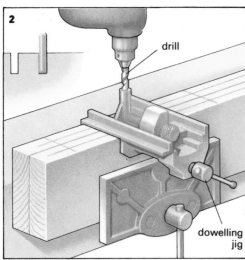

2 — drill — dowelling jig

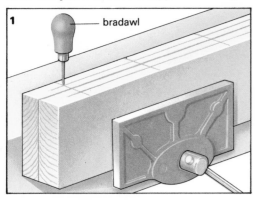

3 — groove — chamfer

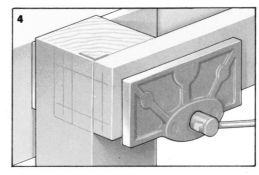

4

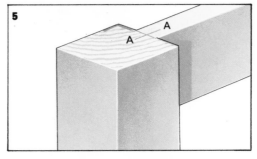

5 — A A A

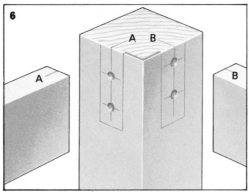

6 — A B / A / A — B

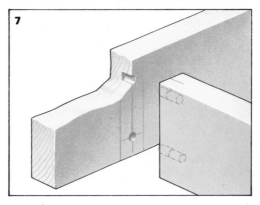

7

Mitre joints

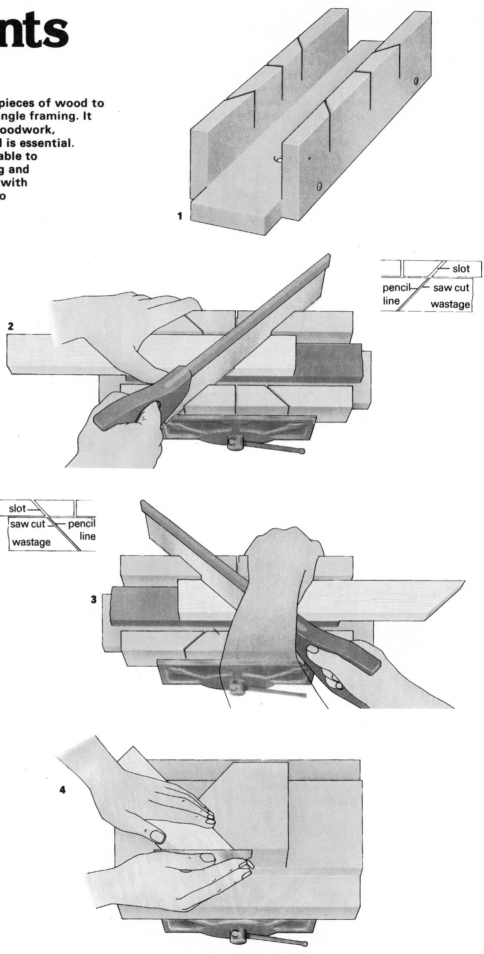

Mitring is a neat way of joining pieces of wood to form a rectangle and any right-angle framing. It is not difficult but, as with all woodwork, accuracy when cutting the wood is essential. Various jigs and guides are available to help you ensure precision cutting and we describe some of them here, with full details of how to use them to obtain perfect corner joints.

Mitre box

1 First secure the mitre box either by screwing it to your bench or by gripping the bottom 12mm ($\frac{1}{2}$in) in a vice. Mark the cut in pencil on the face of the wood to be mitred, allowing about 1mm ($\frac{1}{32}$in) for trimming

2 Place the wood in the box against the far side and on top of a piece of scrap wood to raise it above the bottom of the slots. The pencil mark should be just within the slot so you cut on the waste side of the mark (**inset**). Holding the wood firmly against the box, tenon saw carefully down the slot and through the wood, starting with the saw at a slight angle (tip downwards) and levelling it out as you near the bottom. Don't hurry the job as you may cut into the sides of the slot and make the wrong angle

3 To cut the opposite angle on the same piece of wood move the wood along the box and, with your left hand holding the wood firmly against the far side of the box, saw under your left arm, starting with the saw at an angle and levelling it out as before

4 For trimming, use your plane and a mitre shooting board to prevent splitting the wood

Mitre guide

5 A useful gadget for cutting mitres on wide planks of wood. It comprises an upright with a spring clip to hold a panel or backless tenon saw; the upright swivels

on a fixed base plate which you screw to the workpiece. You can set the upright at any angle for cutting mitres to fit out-of-true corners.
First measure and mark in pencil the wood to the maximum length required, allowing about 1mm ($\frac{1}{32}$in) for trimming. Select your angle, tighten the swivel nut and screw the base plate to the wood. Position your saw in the spring clip and lower it onto the wood, aligning with the pencil mark
Draw the saw back to make the initial cut at the edge nearest you and saw with the blade at a slight angle, handle downwards, levelling out as the base of the cut is reached. If mitring both ends of the wood, make sure you cut the angles in opposite directions. Trim smooth with a plane, using a mitre shooting board

5

Sawing jig
6 The jig shown here is a Jointmaster. It comprises a metal base with strategically placed holes on the surface to take nylon rods which hold the wood in position and indicate angles of varying degrees. On the base are two slotted pillars to hold the saw in place while cutting. When using this type of jig you alter the position of the wood but saw in the same direction
7 First insert a nylon rod in the appropriate 45 degree hole and lay the wood against the rod and the far saw pillar. Ensure precise positioning of the cut by lining up the wood under the saw, which is held in position by the nylon springs in the pillars. You will find the wedge (supplied with this jig) useful for holding the wood firmly in place. Insert a rod in the nearest convenient hole in the jig so it presses the wedge tightly against the wood. Move the saw backwards and forwards within the guides, making light cuts on only forward strokes
8 An alternative method of cutting mitres with this jig is to place a nylon rod in each of the two holes immediately in front of the far saw pillar, with another rod placed in the appropriate near corner hole. First cut one end of the wood square and then insert this end between the two adjacent rods and against the inside of the near corner one. No allowance need be made for wastage with this method of cutting the

mitre angle. If the wood you are cutting is very thin and liable to slip between the two rods, place another strip of wood against the one to be cut to make the whole piece thicker

Joint fixing
9 There are several methods of fixing, but the simplest and most common is gluing and pinning. You will only be able to join one corner at a time so glue both surfaces and clamp them, between padding, in a vice. This ensures that when you pin through the joint at right-angles to each outer edge you do not knock it out of alignment. With your nail punch, sink the pin heads below the surface and fill as required. If the wood is too wide to take pins, glue and dowel instead.

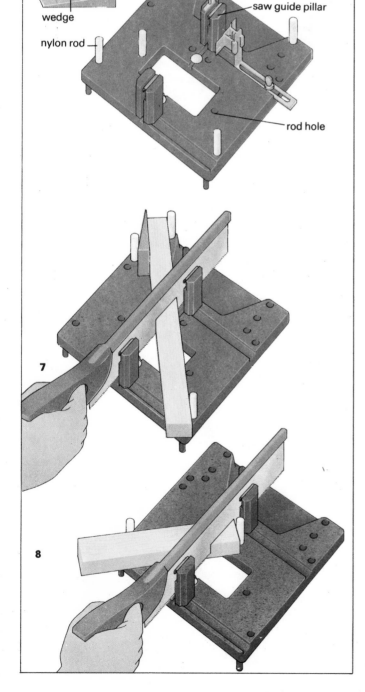

6

wedge

nylon rod

saw guide pillar

rod hole

7

8

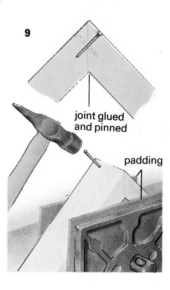

9

joint glued and pinned

padding

Repairing loose joints

If you find any loose joints, take them apart and rub off the old adhesive with medium glasspaper. Glue them back together with woodworking adhesive and clamp them tightly while the adhesive sets.Wipe off any excess with a clean dampened cloth. A G-clamp is ideal for most joints (see 1a), but a web clamp is especially useful when fixing tables and chairs (see 1b).

If you do not have a web clamp you can improvise with a length of strong rope (see 1c). Tie the rope loosely round the structure and twist it with a screwdriver or strong piece of wood until tight. Always pad between the rope and timber with plenty of newspaper to avoid damaging the surfaces. Dovetail joints are usually found in rows of at least three, so if one or two have broken the structure should still be sound. If a dovetail has broken fill the hole with cellulose filler or plastic wood.

If a mortise and tenon joint is broken or badly worn, trim the untrue edges of the tenon with a tenon saw (see 2a) and glue and pin a piece of hardwood (cut to size) to it so the tenon will be a tight fit inside the mortise (see 2b). With L-joints you might have to renew the triangular or square blocks by cutting out new ones from a piece of hardwood.

If a dowel joint has broken, drill out the old dowel with a drill bit of the correct diameter and insert a new dowel

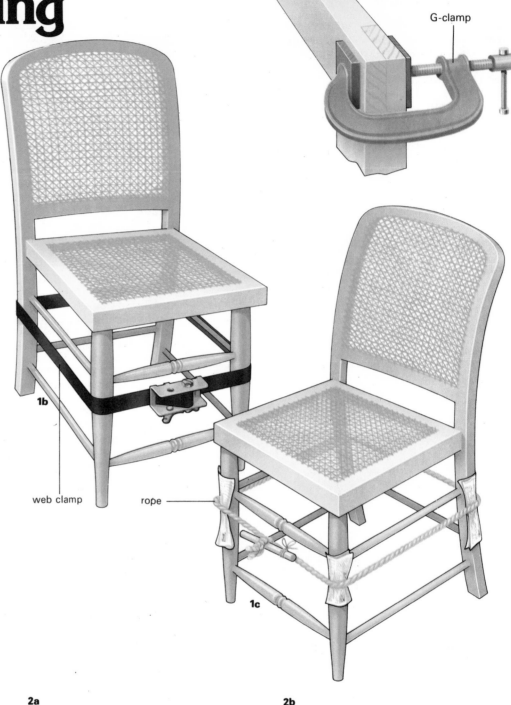

1a

G-clamp

1b

web clamp

rope

1c

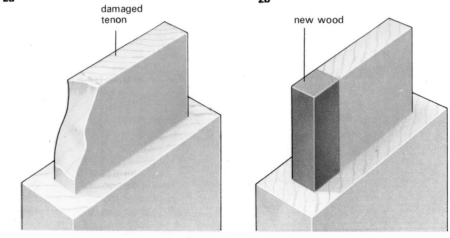

2a

damaged tenon

2b

new wood

Mortise and tenon joints

The strength of the mortise and tenon joint makes it ideal for use in heavy framing and general furniture work. To ensure a really strong T-joint the tenon must fit tightly into the mortise, so take great care when marking the timber and always cut on the waste side. The joint is made by shaping one end of a piece of timber into a tenon to fit into a slot (mortise) made in the other piece. The thickness of the tenon must never be more than one third the thickness of the timber in which it is cut.

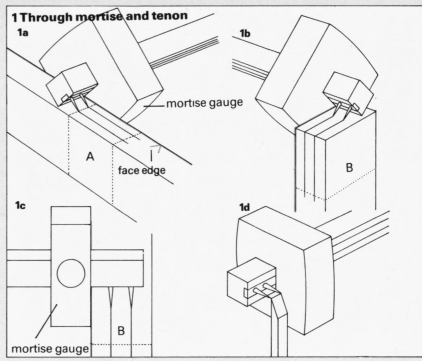

1 Through mortise and tenon
1a
mortise gauge
A
face edge
1b
B
1c
1d
mortise gauge
B

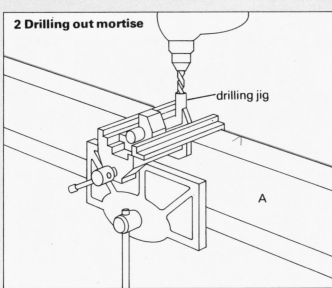

2 Drilling out mortise
drilling jig
A

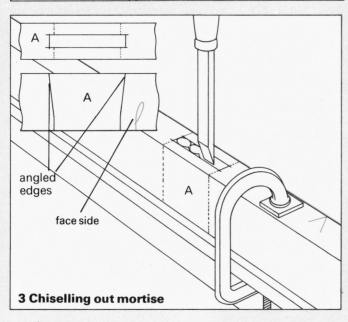

A
A
angled edges
A
face side
3 Chiselling out mortise

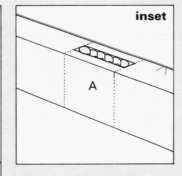

inset
A

There are several kinds of mortise and tenon joints. They all serve much the same purpose; some are stronger, while in others the joint construction is hidden.

Through mortise and tenon
Mark all face edges and face sides (**see diagrams for code**). On the face edge of timber A, mark the length of the mortise, which will be the same as the width of the piece of timber – B – from which the tenon is to be cut. With a pencil and try square mark lines where the joint is to be made, around all four edges of timber A (see 1a). The tenon for this joint must be of the same depth as the mortise. Mark this depth round the four edges of timber B (see 1b). Measure the thickness of tenon timber B, divide this by three and set your mortise gauge to that measurement (see 1c). Release the thumbscrews

holding the pointer and stock, adjusting these so the distances between each and the fixed pointer are one third the width of timber B. If using only a mortise chisel to cut out the mortise, check its blade is the same width as the distance between the pointers on the gauge (**see 1d**). This distance must be one third of the thickness of timber B.
Keeping the stock of the gauge up against the face side of the timber, mark out the mortise (see 1a) and the tenon (see 1b).
To drill out the mortise, clamp timber A in a vice and, with the aid of a jig, make a series of holes in the area marked (**see 2 and inset**). Use a drill bit slightly narrower than the final width of the mortise required and rest your work on a piece of scrap wood to prevent tearing the timber as you drill through. With a pair of G-clamps secure timber A to a workbench, making sure you put a piece of scrap wood underneath and padding between the clamps and the work (see 3). Chisel out the mortise with the correct width blade – if you have not already drilled holes. Angle it slightly to cut away from the mortise to allow space for wedges (to be inserted from opposite edge to face edge).

4 Cutting tenon
4a Sawing at an angle

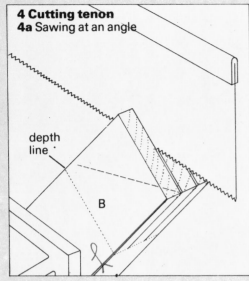

depth
line

B

4b Sawing parallel to depth line

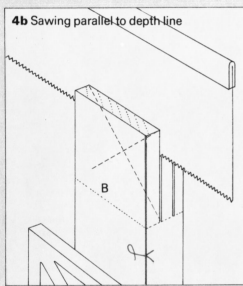

B

4c Removing waste

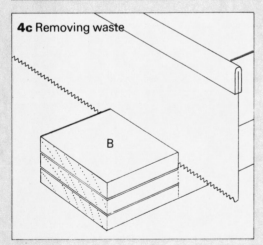

B

To cut out the tenon in timber B, place the timber at an angle in a vice and cut with a tenon saw at an angle down both sides of the tenon to the depth line already marked (see 4a). Turn the wood round and repeat the procedure. Secure timber B vertically in the vice and saw to the depth line on both sides (see 4b). Place timber B horizontally in the vice and remove the waste by cutting along the depth lines (see 4c).

5 Inserting wedges

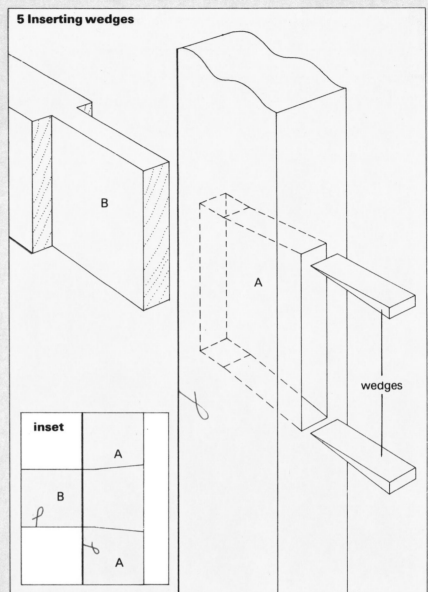

B

A

wedges

inset

A

B

A

6 Alternative wedging

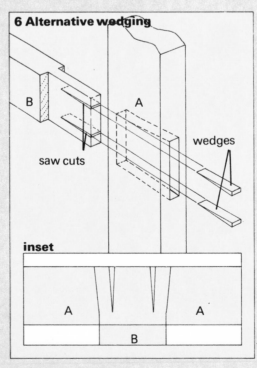

B

A

wedges

saw cuts

inset

A

A

B

Apply woodworking adhesive to the tenon and the inside of the mortise and fit them together. From matching wood cut two thin tapered wedges the same width as the mortise. Apply adhesive to the wedges and insert them in the gaps already cut, using a mallet or hammer and block of wood. Hammer the wedges alternately to keep the tenon straight in the mortise (see 5). Clamp the joint between padding until dry. Saw off the ends of the wedges and smooth the joint with fine glasspaper or a block plane (see inset). Another method of wedging (see 6) is to saw slots about two-thirds down depth of tenon, 4mm ($\frac{3}{16}$ in) in from edges. Tap wedges in slots to lock tenon in position (see inset).

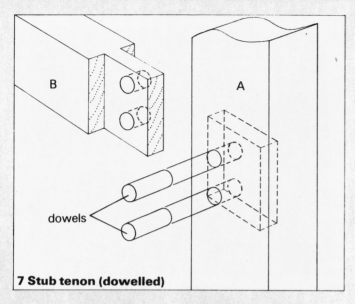

7 Stub tenon (dowelled)

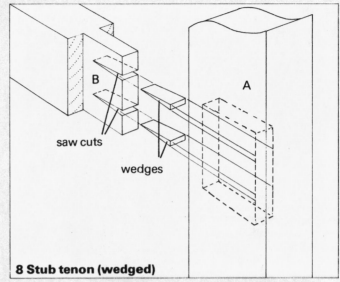

8 Stub tenon (wedged)

Stub tenon
A neater version of the mortise and tenon, since the tenon stops short and does not appear on the outside. The joint is strengthened by securing with dowels (**see 7**). Wedges can be used instead of dowels. Here you must partially insert the wedges first (**see 8**).

Haunched tenon
This is similar to the through tenon, but has a haunch (shoulder) on the top of the tenon – and a matching recess in the upper end of the mortise – for extra strength. The haunch piece protrudes no more than one quarter along the tenon and should be cut down the same distance to form a square (**see 9**).

Double or multiple tenon
For use on really wide joints where a single tenon would give a weak joint. Any number of tenons may be cut as long as their widths and the gaps between are the same (**see 10**).

Twin tenon
Often used for the centre or lock rail of door frames. The tenons are linked by a haunch for greater strength and the mortise is 'stopped' to correspond (**see 11**).

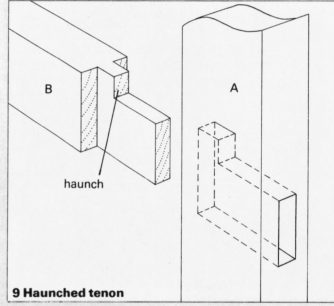

9 Haunched tenon

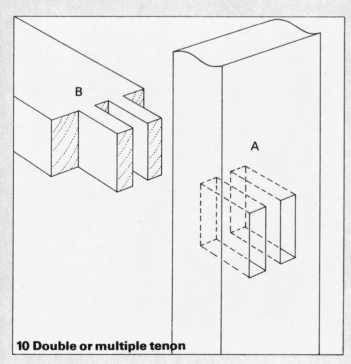

10 Double or multiple tenon

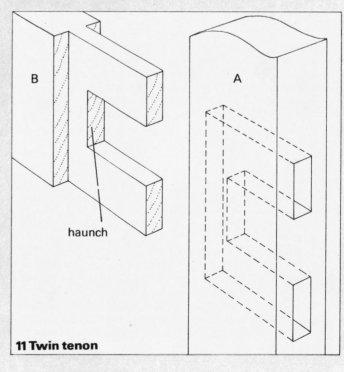

11 Twin tenon

Halving joints

One of the quickest and easiest ways to join two pieces of timber, halving joints are mainly used in constructing light frames where the joint will not be subjected to too much stress. The joint is made by cutting a recess in both pieces of timber so all surfaces are flush when the recesses are brought together and secured with woodworking adhesive. For extra strength the joint can be fixed with nails or screws as well.

'L' joint of timbers the same thickness

Top 'T' joint
Above Cross joint

'L' joint of timbers of different thicknesses

Mitred 'L' joint

1 'L' joint

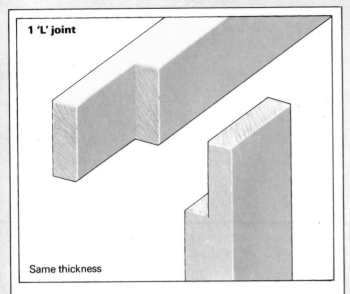

Same thickness

1 When both pieces of timber are the same thickness, cut each recess to half that thickness. Use your measuring tape, pencil and try square to mark out the dimensions accurately and cut out squarely with a tenon saw the recess in both rails.

Smooth all cuts with medium glasspaper. Apply woodworking adhesive to both recesses and secure the joint by screwing (or pinning) from the face that will be hidden when the structure is finished. Wipe off any excess adhesive.

4 Cross joint

3 'T' joint

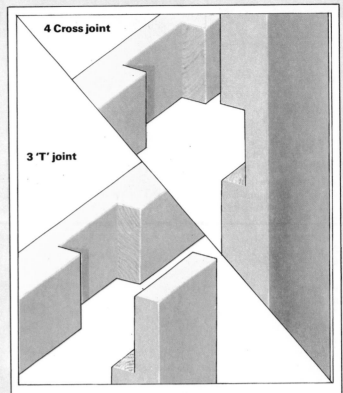

3 To make a 'T' joint, mark out the recess in one rail and cut squarely to the depth line with a tenon saw. Chisel out the wood from between the cut lines. Cut the same depth recess in the other rail. Smooth all cuts with

medium glasspaper, apply woodworking adhesive to both recesses and secure. **4** To make a cross joint, mark out, cut and chisel out recesses in both rails, apply woodworking adhesive to both recesses and secure the joint.

2 'L' joint

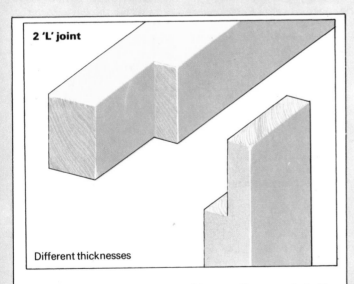

Different thicknesses

2 When the pieces of timber are not the same thickness, mark out and cut the recess in the

thinner rail to exactly half its thickness. Then mark and cut same depth recess in thicker rail.

5 Mitred joint

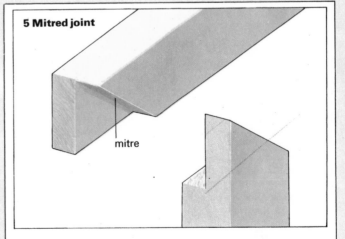

mitre

5 To make a mitred 'L' joint, place one rail in a mitre box (or guide) and cut the mitre angle to half the rail thickness. Place the rail vertically in a vice and tenon saw the mitre angle to remove the waste. Place the other rail in the mitre box (or guide) and cut through the mitre angle. Mark the base

of the mitre squarely across the rail and cut along the base line to half the rail thickness. Place the rail vertically in a vice and remove the waste, keeping the saw parallel to the base line. Smooth all cuts with medium glasspaper, apply woodworking adhesive to edges and secure joint.

Left The basic frame shown here is constructed entirely by using halving joints. A simple 'L' joint is used in each corner, but you could use a mitred 'L' joint for a neater finish. A cross joint is used in the middle of the frame and the remainder are all 'T' joints.

Bridle joints

There are two main types of bridle joint—the mitred and the 'T'. One real advantage with these joints is they can withstand pressure from above and from the side. Mitred bridle joints are used to join pieces of timber of the same width and thickness—in making such things as mirror frames. 'T' bridle joints are used in general furniture making.

When making a bridle joint, the same basic principles apply as those for tenon joints; the thickness of the tenon should not be more than one third the thickness of the timber from which it is cut. If there are two tenons, the combined thickness should not be more than two thirds the thickness. If one tenon is more than a third the thickness, the other tenon should be correspondingly thinner. No tenon, however, should be less than a quarter the thickness of the timber from which it is cut.

You can further strengthen these joints once they are glued in place by pinning or screwing them together. Before marking and cutting out any joints, mark on both pieces of timber all face edges and face sides (see diagrams for symbols).

Mitred bridle joint
1 With a measuring tape, pencil and try square, measure and mark accurately on all four edges at one end of timber B the depth of the slot to be cut out, which will be the same measurement as the width of timber A from which the tenon will be cut. Also mark the depth of the tenon on A (the width of timber B). The depth of the slot in B will taper at an angle when the end has been mitred. Mark the mitre line across both sides from the top corner on the face edge to the depth line on the inside edge. Check the mitre angle is accurate with a

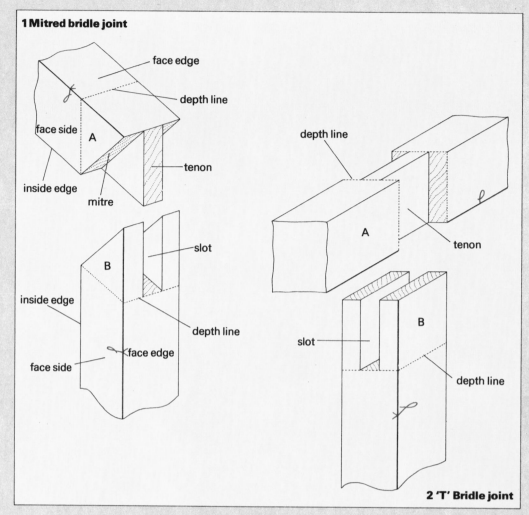

1 Mitred bridle joint

face edge
depth line
face side
A
inside edge
mitre
tenon

B
slot
inside edge
depth line
face side
face edge

depth line
A
tenon
slot
B
depth line

2 'T' Bridle joint

mitre square. Place timber B horizontally in a vice and saw through the mitre line.
With a mortise gauge set to the required width of the tenon, which in this case will be one third the thickness of timber A, mark out on the mitred face and the face edge of B the position of the slot down to the depth line. Remember to keep the stock of the gauge against the face side of the timber. Place the timber vertically in the vice and tenon saw down the slot lines to the required depth. Carefully remove the waste from the slot with a mortise chisel, working from both sides towards the centre. With the mortise gauge set as before, mark across the end and along the inside face edge of timber A the position of the tenon as far as the depth line. Mark out the mitre line to be cut as for timber B on both sides of A. Place the timber horizontally in the vice and cut down the the mitre line on each side of A as far as the lines marked

by the gauge. Place the timber upwards at an angle in the vice and saw down the lines marked by the gauge at the same angle as the mitre to remove the waste from either side of the tenon. Smooth all cut edges with medium fine glasspaper and fit the joint together, making sure it sits firmly. Glue the joint and secure it in a G-clamp until it has stuck. Alternatively glue and then pin or screw the joint.

'T' bridle joint
The 'T' joint can be used to join two pieces of timber that have at least one side the same measurement. One of the most common applications of this joint is where an upright timber joins a load-bearing horizontal timber.
2 To join two pieces of timber with dimensionally matching sides, face the larger sides of each piece (if they exist) to the front. Mark out accurately the position of the tenon on the horizontal timber A and the slot in the

vertical timber B in the same way as for the mitred joint. Remember the depth of the slot will be the same as the width of timber A and the width of the tenon must be about a third the thickness of A.
Place timber A horizontally in the vice with the face side upwards and cut down either end of the tenon as far as the line marked with the gauge. Turn the timber over and cut down from the other face in the same way. Remove the two waste pieces with a mortise chisel, working from both sides towards the centre. Place timber B vertically in the vice and cut down the lines marked by the gauge, which will correspond to the width of the tenon in A, to the depth line. Carefully chisel out the slot waste, working from both sides towards the centre.

Box joints

Box joints are mostly used in the construction of furniture and cabinet work. Both pieces of wood being joined must be the same width and, ideally, the same thickness as well.

'L' joint

Using a measuring tape, pencil and try square, mark out an uneven number of tenons and recesses across the width of both pieces of timber. Make sure each tenon is at least 10mm wide; if less, the joint will be considerably weakened. In one rail there should be more tenons than recesses and less in the other rail, so when the rails are joined together the tenons in one fit neatly inside the recesses in the other rail. Place each rail vertically in a vice and cut down to the depth line with a tenon saw where you have marked the tenons and recesses. Chop out the waste from between the cut lines with a chisel. Apply woodworking adhesive to the fixing edges of the tenons and recesses on both rails and join the two, clamping them (and pinning for extra strength if needed) until the adhesive has set. Wipe off excess adhesive with a clean dampened cloth.

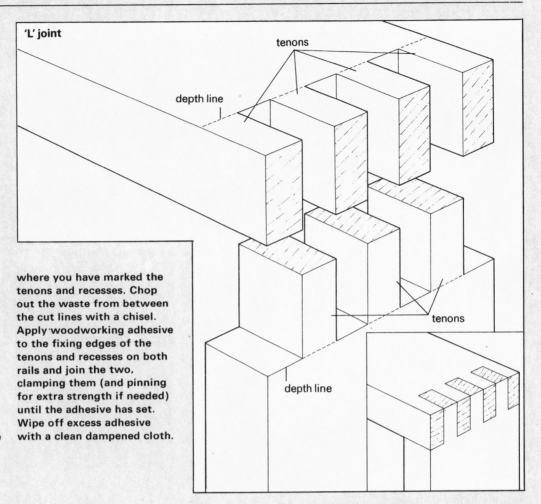

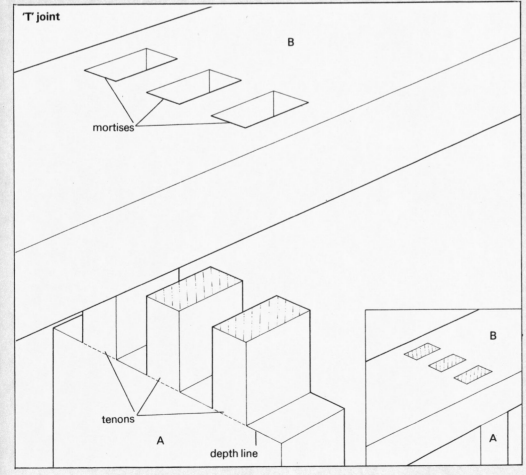

'T' joint

Mark and cut out the tenons and recesses in rail A in the same way as for the 'L' joint. Mark out the mortises in rail B to the same dimensions as the tenons in rail A; remove the waste from inside these lines by drilling a hole through the rail and chopping out the rest with a chisel. Apply woodworking adhesive to all the fixing edges on the tenons and recesses on rail A and to the inside surfaces of the mortises in rail B. Bring the two rails together, clamping them (and pinning for extra strength if necessary) until the adhesive has set. Wipe off excess adhesive with a clean dampened cloth.

For cabinet work where a hidden joint is required, a stopped 'T' joint is used. To make this, measure and cut the tenons and recesses in rail A half the thickness of rail B; the mortises in rail B must be the same depth as these.

Housing joints

The housing joint is used in cabinet work, furniture making and shelving systems, but should not be used when there is a risk of the timber bowing since this causes the joints to work loose. The uprights must be rigid and vertical (as in the confines of an alcove) and you may need to build in an extra upright or make the crosspieces shorter to avoid bowing. The joint is mostly used with timber of equal width and thickness, but the thickness and width of the upright should never be more than twice that of the crosspiece.

Simple housing

Using a try square, mark a line at the required height across the upright where the top edge of the crosspiece will enter the housing. Mark another line underneath this so the width of the housing is exactly the same as the thickness of the crosspiece to ensure a tight fit. Continue these lines onto both edges of the upright and mark on the depth line. If you are making a series of joints (such as for a shelving system), the depth lines must all be the same depth (about half the upright thickness); use a mortise gauge for accurate marking up.

Place the upright flat in a vice or clamp it to your work surface. Make two cuts with a tenon saw to the depth line, keeping the saw on the waste side (inside) of the line. Remove the waste from between the cut lines with a chisel; if the piece of timber is very wide, you will need to use a paring chisel.

Apply woodworking adhesive to the inside of the housing and insert the crosspiece, securing the joint by pinning, or screwing, through the upright into the end of the crosspiece. Wipe off excess adhesive with a clean dampened cloth.

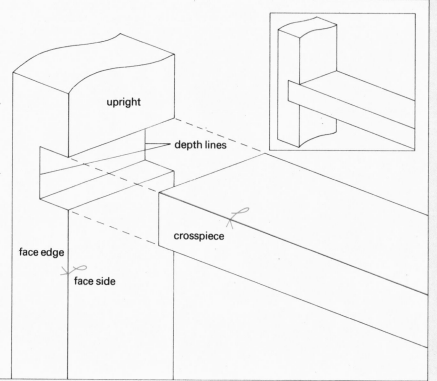

Stopped housing

Mark out the housing on the upright in the same way as for the simple housing joint but stop the lines the same distance short of the front edge as the length of the recess in the crosspiece.

Mark out the recess on the crosspiece, taking care to make it the correct size so the front edge of the two pieces of timber will be flush when joined. The width of the recess must never be more than one fifth of the total width of the timber in which it is cut and its depth must be equal to the depth of the housing. Cut out the recess with a tenon saw.

Place the upright flat in a vice or clamp it to your work surface and make two cuts with a tenon saw to the depth line, keeping the saw to the waste side (inside) of the line and at an angle to avoid removing the wood from the front edge where the housing stops. Remove the wood from this area by chopping down to the depth line with a chisel held vertically, bevel edge inwards. Apply adhesive to the inside of the housing and to the recess and bring the two pieces of timber together, securing the joint as before.

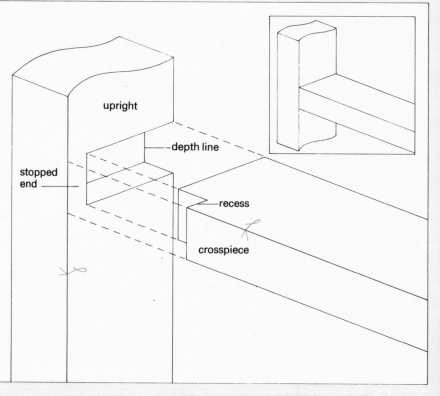

Joining wood end to end

These joints enable you to use up scrap wood and are therefore important for the economical use of timber. But they are never as strong as one complete length of timber and should not be used for load-bearing structures. The timbers should be of equal width and thickness; if the width of a piece of timber is more than twice its own thickness, these joints should not be used.

Lapped joint
Check the timber is square and mark the cutting lines on both rails, marking the depth of the recesses exactly half the thickness of the timber and the length of the recesses the same as their width. Use a marking gauge for accuracy. Place each rail in a vice and cut off the waste with a tenon saw, keeping slightly to the waste side of the line. Check the joint for fit (all edges should be flush) and, if necessary, remove more wood with a chisel or flat file. Apply woodworking adhesive to the fixing surfaces of both recesses and bring the two rails together, securing the joint with screws through one face. Wipe off excess adhesive with a clean dampened cloth.

Splayed joint
Check the timber is square and mark the cutting lines on both rails; make the length of the recesses the same as their width and their greatest depth exactly two-thirds the thickness of the timber, tapering to one-third the thickness at the end of both pieces. Place each rail in a vice and cut off the waste with a tenon saw, keeping slightly to the waste side of the line. Check the joint for fit then glue and screw together, securing it with screws in the same way as for the lapped joint.

'V' joint
Check the timber is square and mark a line squarely across the width of each rail the same distance back from the square end as the width of the timber. Draw a line centrally along the length of both rails and draw two more lines on each to mark the shape of the recess on one rail and the point on the other. Place each rail in a vice and remove the waste with a tenon saw, keeping slightly to the waste side of the line. Check the joint for fit then glue and screw together through each edge.

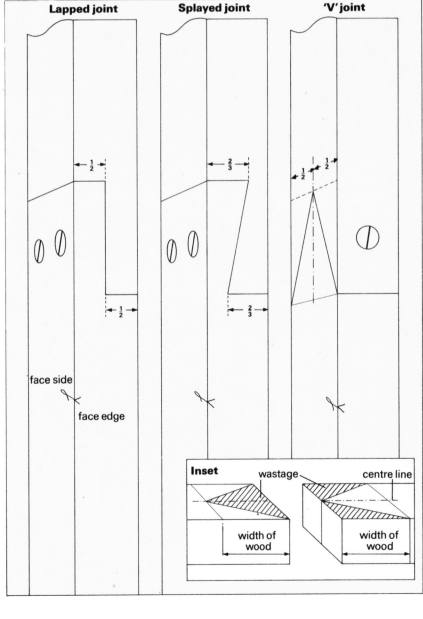

Through dovetail joints

Dovetail joints are widely used for box and drawer carcases and upright frames in furniture construction. They provide a strong corner joint which is resistant to pulling stress, indicated by their widespread use between the front of a drawer and its two sides. There are many variations of dovetail joints; in general, the wider the pieces to be joined the more tails and pins required. You can use dovetail joints to join timber of different widths; always form the tails in the thinner piece and the pins in the thicker piece. The length of the tails must be equal to the thickness of the piece they are to fit into, except when the joint is stopped (which will be covered later in the book). The angle on the tails and pins should be about 80 degrees. Mark out the tails first,

ensuring they are all the same angle by using a sliding bevel or dovetail template and spacing them evenly across the width of the timber. Measure the thickness of the thicker piece of timber and mark this distance in from the

end of the other piece. Add 2mm to this depth line for waste, which can be planed off afterwards, and lightly score round all four sides with a sharp cutting knife (**see 1**). The order and spacing of the recesses and tails and the

half-recesses at both ends is all important. For example, on a three-tailed joint the order of tails and recesses should be half-recess, tail, full recess, tail, full recess, tail, half-recess (**see joint assembly**). Decide the

Joint assembly
(dimensions in millimetres)

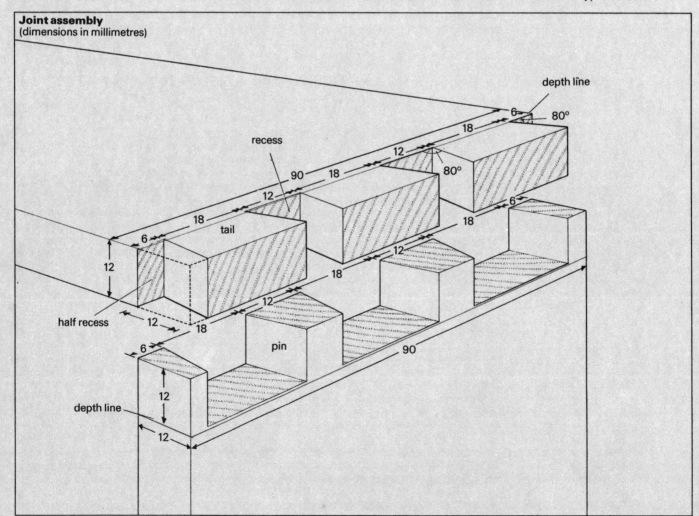

1 Marking depth line

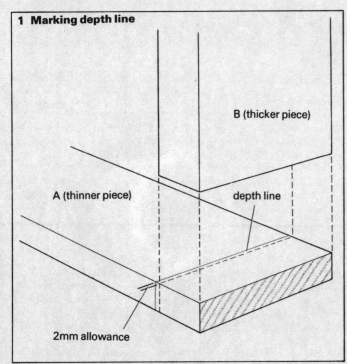

B (thicker piece)

A (thinner piece)

depth line

2mm allowance

2 Marking tails

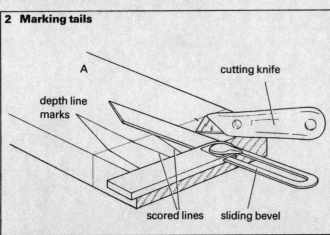

A

cutting knife

depth line marks

scored lines   sliding bevel

3 Making template

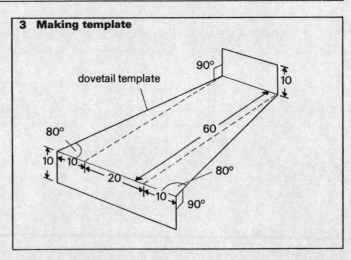

dovetail template

90°

10

80°

10

10

60

20

80°

10

90°

4 Marking pins

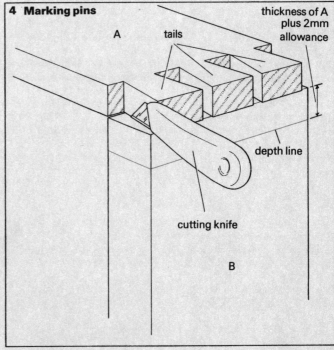

A

tails

thickness of A plus 2mm allowance

depth line

cutting knife

B

number of tails you require and divide this number into the width of the timber; for example if you want three tails and the timber is 90mm wide, the figure you will get is 30. Divide this by five to find the basic unit of measurement, that is 6. Double the basic unit to find the length of the full recesses (12) and treble it to find the length of the tails (18); the half-recesses are always one unit wide (6). Therefore, in this example, the figures are 6, 18, 12, 18, 12, 18 and 6, making a total of 90mm (see joint assembly). Mark out each of these measurements along the base line and use a sliding bevel or dovetail template to mark an 80 degree angle from each point in alternate directions, working across the timber

from left to right (see 2). After marking out the first half-recess, measure across its narrow end; this dimension should not be less than about 4mm. If it is between 3 and 4mm, reduce the width of all the tails by 1mm on each side (thus increasing the width of the recesses); if it is less than 3mm, reduce the number of tails until the minimum dimension is reached. A scale drawing of the joint will help. Make a dovetail template from a thin sheet of aluminium or stainless steel marked out to the dimensions shown (see 3). Bend over each end to 90 degrees in opposite directions. One of the upstands is held against the end grain of the timber on which the tails are to be cut and the tails are marked out

along the angled sides. Mark these lines squarely across the end grain and repeat the markings exactly on the reverse side. Cut out the tails with a dovetail or tenon saw, keeping to the waste side of the line; remove the waste with a coping saw, leaving the last 2mm which is removed with a bevel-edged chisel – always chisel only halfway through the timber from both sides. Save time when making several joints by nailing the pieces together through the waste timber, clamping the pieces in a vice and cutting all the tails at once. Use the cut piece as the template for the timber in which the pins will be cut. Hold the two at right-angles, with the cut tails across the end grain of the other piece,

and score accurately round the tails with a sharp marking knife (see 4). Mark the waste wood with a pencil. Mark on the base line in the same way as for the first piece and mark squarely along the grain from the corners of the marked pins down to the base line. Cut out the pins and chop out the waste as for the tails. Don't clean up the joint before assembly because this may make it loose; offer the parts together and check for fit. If the joint seems too tight, you will have to ease it; if it is too loose, pack it with wafer-thin offcuts. Apply woodworking adhesive and tap the pieces together, driving any packing pieces firmly into place. Check with a try square for accuracy and cramp until dry. Clean up the joint with block plane and abrasive block.

Lapped and secret dovetail joints

The variations in dovetail joints do use some of the basic principles of the through dovetail.
The three types of dovetail joint mentioned here should only be used with hardwood and on 'L' shape or carcase-type constructions.

Lapped dovetail
The effect of this type of joint is to conceal it from the front view and help prevent it moving out of square, both of which are particularly important in drawer construction. The lap feature is essentially a rebate and comprises not more than one third – and not less than one sixth – the thickness of the timber in which it is formed.
When marking out, remember the side of the construction with the tails in will still show when the joint is made; the hidden parts of the joint are in the other piece, which should be the thicker piece if you are joining timber of different thicknesses.
As with the through dovetail joint, the tails are made first and should be marked out to not less than two-thirds the thickness of the other piece of timber – and not more than five-sixths. They are then cut out in the usual way.
When marking out the other piece, score the depth line with a sharp cutting knife across the inside face of the timber. The depth line should be the same distance from the end of the timber as the

length of the tails.
Hold the tails in position over the end of the piece of timber in which the pins are to be cut and score around them with a sharp cutting knife. Shade in the waste wood at this stage to save confusion. Square down from the marked lines to the depth line on the inside face. With a dovetail or tenon saw, carefully cut the sides of the pins diagonally until the sawcut reaches from the depth line at one end to the bottom of the pin recess at the other.
Always cut to the waste side of the wood. Remove the remaining waste carefully with a sharp bevel edge chisel.
To ensure a straight joint line on the inside face when chiselling out the waste, clamp a square piece of scrap wood against the depth line to act as a guide for the chisel. This helps to ensure a square, flat-bottomed recess. Take care not to cut the recess too large or the joint will be weakened.

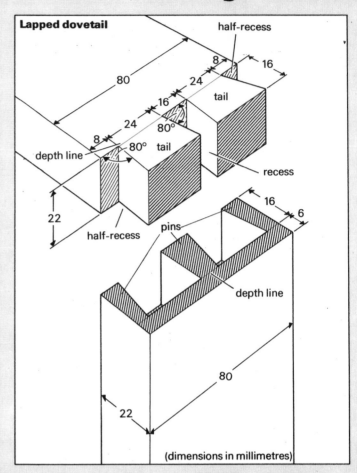

Lapped dovetail

half-recess

80

8

16

24

tail

16

16

24

80°

depth line

8

80°

tail

recess

22

half-recess

pins

16

6

depth line

80

22

(dimensions in millimetres)

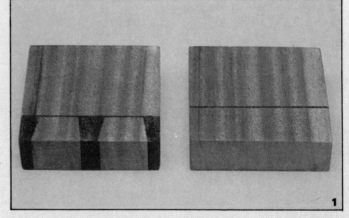

1

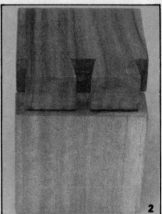

2

3

4

5

Double lapped dovetail
This joint demands particular accuracy since there is no allowance for error. It is a very strong joint and leaves only a small amount of end grain exposed; but it should only be made with pieces of timber of the same thickness. First cut out a rebate in the pieces of timber which will form the front and back (or top and bottom) of your construction. The rebate should be marked out to a depth of not less than two-thirds (and not more than five-sixths) the thickness of the timber and a width of not more than one-third (and not less than one-sixth) the thickness of the timber.
The recesses are cut on the inside faces of the timber; mark out the depth line for the recesses, which should be the same distance from the end of the timber as the thickness of the timber. These pieces of timber will be used for cutting out the pins and, contrary to previous dovetail joints, these are marked and cut out first. Mark out the pins on the sawn surface of the rebate. When chiselling out the waste, use the scrap wood guide as before. When you have cut out the pins, hold the piece in which the tails are to be cut in position in the rebate and mark round the pins, preferably with a sharp veneer cutting knife. Again shade in the waste wood.

Mark the depth line on the piece of timber in which the tails will be cut from the piece in which the pins have been formed (equal to the width of the rebate). Cut out the tails with a sharp bevel edge chisel as before.

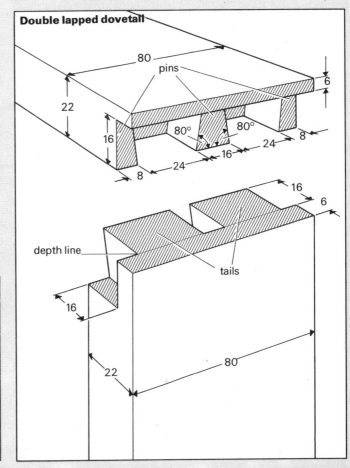

Double lapped dovetail

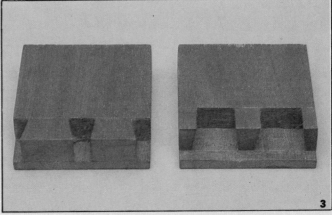

1

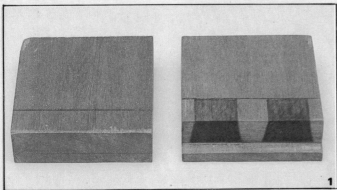

2

4

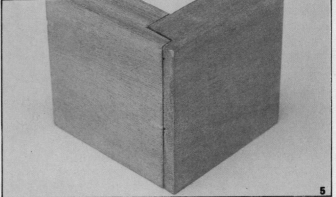

3

5

Secret (mitred) dovetail

The greatest accuracy in marking and cutting out is required to make a secret or mitred dovetail joint. The external appearance of the joint is the same as the normal mitre joint, since you cannot see the tails; but the secret dovetail joint has the advantage of being much stronger. The thickness of the timbers being joined must be the same throughout.

First cut your pieces of timber to the exact overall dimensions of the required carcase.

Mark out and cut a rebate at each end of each piece as described earlier for the pieces in which the pins are cut when forming a double lapped dovetail joint.

Mark the mitres on each side edge of each end with a sharp cutting knife, using a mitre square or a sliding bevel set to a 45 degree angle. Score the depth lines on the inside face across each end of each piece of timber at the point where the mitre lines reach the inside edge, again using a sharp cutting knife.

Mark out the pins as described for the double lapped dovetail joint, allowing between one fifteenth and one twenty-fifth the timber width for the shoulder each side and adjusting the dimensions of the pins and recesses accordingly. Cut them out, but remember the outside recesses must be cut very accurately to the scored mitre line – and not at right-angles as in the double lapped dovetail.

Rest in turn each piece of timber in which the tails are to be cut so the rebate nests in with that in the piece of timber in which the pins have been cut.

Mark out the tails as described above and cut them out, again remembering to cut very carefully to the scored mitre lines for each shoulder. You must now very carefully trim the rebate upstands all the way along the joint to form a 45 degree angle from the depth lines. Preferably use a sliding bevel as a gauge to chisel to and work with a long, very sharp paring chisel. There should be no evidence of tails when the joint is finished.

Warning When gluing the joint together use adhesive sparingly, since it can form a hydraulic lock and prevent the joint from closing properly.

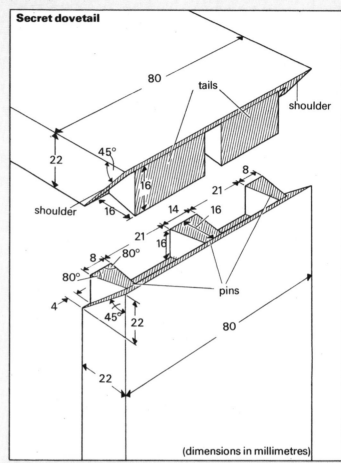

Secret dovetail

(dimensions in millimetres)

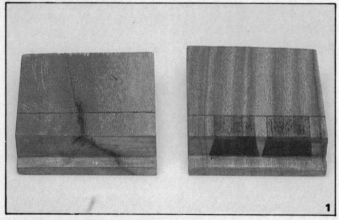

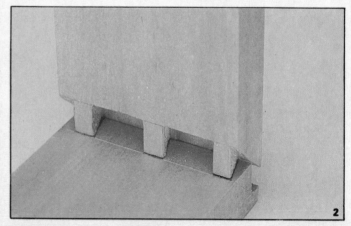

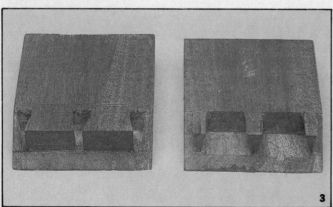

'T'dovetail joints

Dovetail joints can be used to form a 'T' joint in a frame structure. When forming joints in the timbers face-to-face, a dovetailed halving joint is used. When joining the timbers end-to-face, the through or stopped dovetail joint is used. You can simplify the joints by cutting the dovetail angle on one side only; these are known as barefaced dovetail joints.

Dovetailed halving joints

You can use this joint to join timbers of different thicknesses, provided the tail is cut in the thinner timber which forms the stem of the 'T'.

To mark out the joint, score the depth line with a sharp cutting knife all round the timber in which the tail is to be cut. This line should be marked from the end of the tail piece 2mm more than the width of the timber in which the pin is to be cut; the 2mm allowance can be trimmed off when the joint is formed. Set a marking gauge to half the thickness of the timber in which the tail is to be cut, place the stock against the front face of the timber and score across the end of the timber and down both edges as far as the depth line. With the gauge at the same setting, hold the stock against the front face of the timber in which the pin is to be cut and score along the top and bottom edges of the timber.

The width of the half-recesses on each side of the tail should be one sixth the length of the tail at the depth line. Mark the half-recesses on the front face of the timber in which the tail is to be cut. Join these marks by scoring with a knife to the outside edges of the tail at the end of the timber; this automatically gives the correct dovetail angle. Cut the halving joint in the same timber. Cut out the tail with a tenon or dovetail saw, making sure you keep to the waste side of the cutting lines. Rub the tail

smooth with medium fine, then fine, glasspaper and position it on the front face of the other piece of timber; score carefully round it with a sharp cutting knife. Mark the waste wood and, with a knife and try square, continue the pin lines down both edges as far as the depth line already marked. Carefully saw down to the depth line, keeping to the waste side of the cutting lines, and remove the waste with a bevel edge chisel. Clean up the bottom of the recess with a router.

To make a barefaced joint, omit the dovetail angle on one side of the timber in which the tail is cut.

When glued and clamped, the joint may be additionally strengthened by the use of pins or screws.

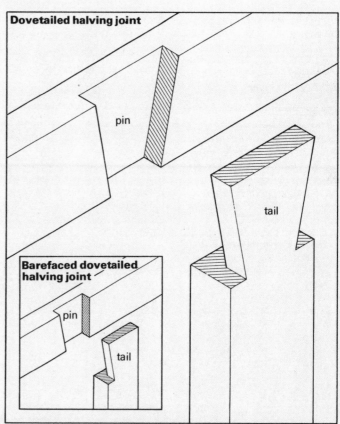

Dovetailed halving joint

pin

tail

Barefaced dovetailed halving joint

pin

tail

1

2

3

4

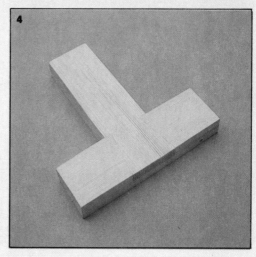

Single through dovetail

This joint is used when fixing timbers end-to-face to form a 'T'. The pieces of timber must be the same width, but the stem of the 'T' can be thinner.

First mark out the tail; its length must not be more than one third or less than one half the thickness of the timber in which the pin is to be cut.

The joint is formed in the same way as for the normal through dovetail, except the waste wood must be removed from the pin recess with a bevel edge chisel and the bottom of the recess finished off with a router.

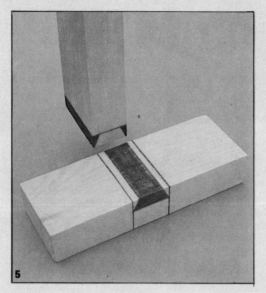

5

6

Single through dovetail

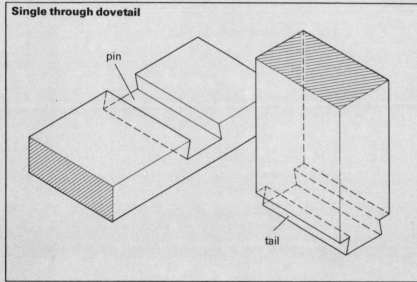

pin

tail

7

Single stopped dovetail

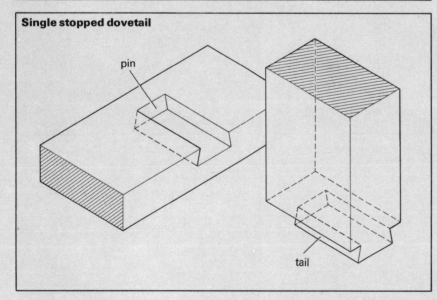

pin

tail

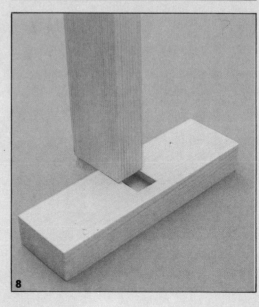

8

Single stopped dovetail

This joint is made in a similar way to the through dovetail, except the pin recess is not cut right through the timber and the tail is cut shorter to fit. This gives the appearance of a butt joint. The waste wood in the pin recess has to be removed almost entirely with a bevel edge chisel and so the joint is a difficult one to make accurately.

The length of the stop (or the amount of tail to be cut off) is normally the same as the thickness of the tail piece timber.

Single stopped barefaced diminished dovetail

This joint is used for shelves in cabinets, where the shelf helps to hold the sides of the cabinet together. The barefaced side usually forms the top of the shelf and the tail tapers from back to front on the shelf; this makes it easier to insert the shelf from back to front and ensures a close fit for the barefaced side of the joint.

Warning This joint is one of the most difficult of the dovetails to make and requires a great deal of skill and patience. Always practise on scrap pieces of wood before starting the work.

9

10

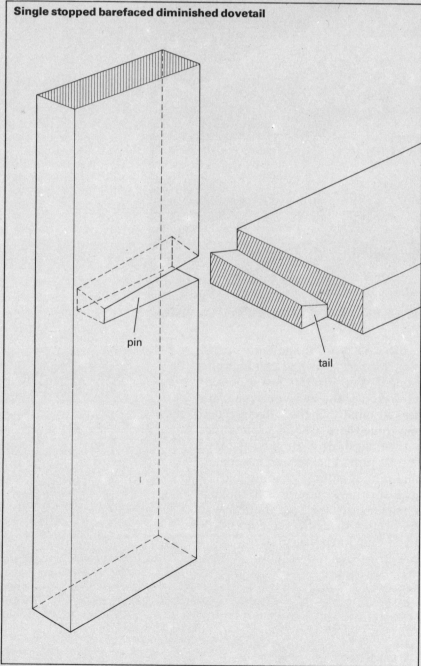

Single stopped barefaced diminished dovetail

pin

tail

11

12

Turning wood

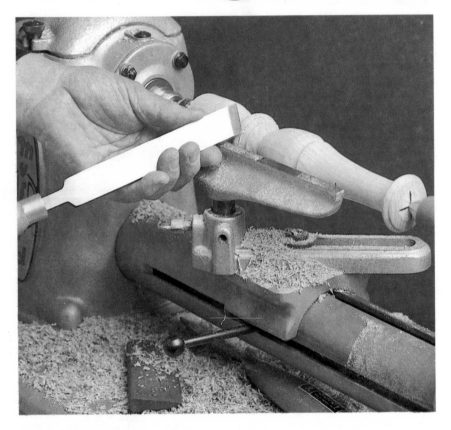

For the enthusiastic woodworker, the lathe opens
up whole new ideas for projects and can be well
worth the investment. You can buy just a power
drill attachment or go for the more professional
lathe, although bear in mind that the latter will need
a permanent home somewhere. Check on the range
of accessories you will need, depending on the type
of work you want to turn. This section covers all
the basic techniques of cutting, shaping and
finishing work and also shows you how to make a
range of projects, such as rings, wheels, hollow ware
and goblets. There is also advice on using up offcuts
of wood you may have lying about.

Introducing woodturning

By shaping wood with the help of a lathe you can make a range of items including bowls, platters, egg cups and chair and table legs. Woodturning is not difficult to learn, provided you use the correct tools and techniques.

The basic requirement for woodturning is the lathe. **1**
This can be a simple power drill attachment, a more
substantial semi-professional machine or even a
multi-purpose woodworking machine (where a
woodturning lathe forms the basic unit); the latter
is ideal when you do a lot of work but are restricted
by space. There are a number of different lathes
available; apart from deciding what you want to
pay, you should look for a reputable manufacturer
who will provide whatever additional accessories
and attachments you might need, as well as an
after-sales service.

Basic lathe parts

There are four main parts to a woodturning lathe
– the headstock, lathe bed, tailstock and tool rest.
All parts should be strongly constructed and rigid
enough to allow for vibration-free turning.

Headstock The headstock carries the main spindle
(sometimes called the mandrel) and the drive
pulleys which allow you to select a suitable turning
speed in keeping with the size and weight of the
work being turned; large diameter work is turned at
a slower speed than small section work.

A pronged driving centre is fitted into the headstock spindle to provide a positive drive for the
wood when turning between the centres, as with
chair or table legs. You can also mount face plates
or chucks onto the headstock spindle for work
which is held only at one end, such as plates and
bowls. On some lathes both ends of the headstock
spindle are threaded to allow extra large diameter
work to be turned.

The headstock is mounted on the lathe bed,
which should be rigid and strong and preferably
made of machined cast iron; on some lathes the bed
is round, solid or tubular with either single or
double bars. It is essential components such as the
tailstock and the tool rest are able to slide freely
along the lathe bed when required.

Tailstock At the opposite end of the lathe bed is the
tailstock, which is used to support the other end of
the wood when turning long work between centres.
It should be strongly constructed and able to be
quickly positioned and securely locked anywhere
along the length of the lathe bed. The barrel or quill
of the tailstock should be simple to operate and
have a positive locking arrangement and conveniently placed controls.

There are various types of dead centre available
for supporting the wood on the tailstock; the best
are of the Morse taper type which maintain a firm
hold on the work and can be easily removed. This is
done either by a metal drift through the hollow
centre of the quill or, on some machines, by a
simple self-ejecting device.

Tool rests The tool rest is fitted to the lathe bed and
is free to be moved along its length; the hand-held
turning tool is placed on top of it to shape the
rotating wood. Some lathes have provision for a
second tool rest. The rest should be rigid and strong
with conveniently placed locking controls, and it
should be possible to adjust the height of the rest to
suit the particular type of work being carried out as
well as the height of the operator. Rests vary in
shape from one manufacturer to another and
should be chosen for their comfort when using the
turning tools; there should be no rough ends or
corners and preferably a level surface; remember
the side of the forefinger or thumb is used to guide
the turning tool on the work.

Accessories Most woodturning lathes are supplied

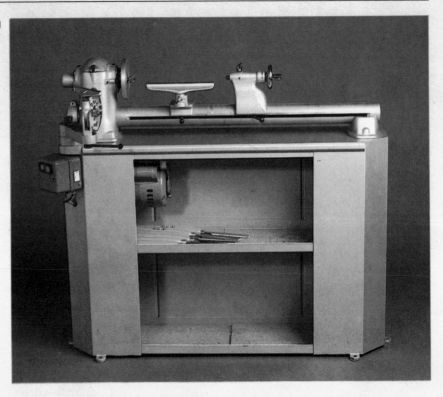

with basic accessories such as a face plate (used for
turning bowls, for example), a pronged driving
centre and a cupped or a dead centre which is fitted
to the tailstock. But for turning a range of work
between centres you will need a number of additional accessories to simplify your work and add to
the lathe's flexibility.

A Woodscrew chuck is invaluable for turning
small jobs such as egg cups, knobs, pepper mills
and small bowls where the work is held at one end
only. Specialized chucks, such as a combination
chuck, are available which greatly simplify the
turning of long vases and goblets – and any deep
boring work. Although the woodturning lathe is
mainly for shaping wood, it can be turned into a
versatile horizontal boring machine, which uses a
normal three-jaw chuck and suitable bits held in the
headstock; the work is advanced onto the boring
tool by the tailstock.

Lathe size

The length of work you can turn on a woodturning
lathe is determined, as on a metalworking lathe, by
the maximum distance between the centres. The
height of the centres above the lathe bed is half the
swing of the lathe; this is the maximum diameter of
work which can be turned without interfering with
the lathe bed.

On many woodturning lathes provision is made
for turning large diameter work held on a face plate
by using an extension of the headstock spindle at
the left-hand end or by having a gap bed. Some
headstocks can be rotated 90 degrees to the lathe
bed, which is ideal when working space is restricted.
An ideal lathe for the small workshop or garage
should have a centre height of about 112mm (4½in),
which allows for work up to a maximum diameter
of 225mm (9in), and a distance between centres of
about 750mm (30in), which would allow a complete table leg to be turned, for example.

When using a power drill attachment, the size of
work is restricted by the limited power of the drill.
The drill, in effect, forms the headstock.

1 Standard woodturning
lathe suitable for cabinet
mounting to make it a self-
contained unit. The lathe has
a capacity for hard work at
high speeds and should have
a long and trouble-free life

8

7

15

Turning tools

Having chosen a suitable lathe, you will need a number of turning tools; these are divided into two basic types – those with a scraping action and those with a cutting action. All have long handles with longer blades than the conventional chisel. Although they can be bought in sets, it is often better to buy them separately as you gain experience; it is easier to master a few tools of your choice than try to cope with sets made for the professional.

Scraping tools These are used to scrape the wood to shape; they require little skill and are most suitable for beginners since they are safe to handle and allow you to become familiar with the lathe. Although the overall appearance and finish will not be as good as that achieved with a cutting tool, you can turn a piece of wood to a reasonable shape with very little skill or effort. Scraping tools are obtainable in various shapes and sizes and you can grind them to any shape to suit particular jobs.

Cutting tools These tools, which consist of gouges and chisels, are used to cut through wood cleanly. As with conventional tools, cutting tools give a perfectly clean finish when working with the grain or cutting across it; more skill is, however, necessary for the latter operation. When cutting just by hand, the wood is held while the chisel moves; with woodturning the wood moves while the cutting tool stays still. When using turning tools – and especially cutting tools – work with the direction of the grain whenever possible to avoid lifting the wood fibres.

Turning gouges Used for general shaping, those with a large cross-section are used for the initial rough shaping of the wood to get the workpiece into balance before final shaping and finishing. A gouge of about 25mm (1in) cross-section is ideal for

Selection of turning tools:
2 Round-nosed scraper
3 Gouge
4 Skew chisel
5 Diamond scraper
6 Parting tool
Lathe accessories:
7 Woodscrew chuck
8 Coil grip chuck
9 Face plate
10 Combination chuck
11 Chuck tools
12 Bowl chuck (grips the bases of bowls and platters without screws)
13 Reducing jaws for the combination chuck
14 Chuck tool
15 Gouge

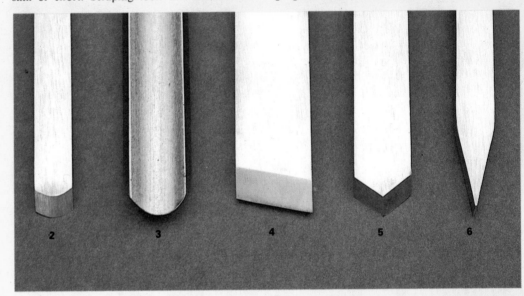

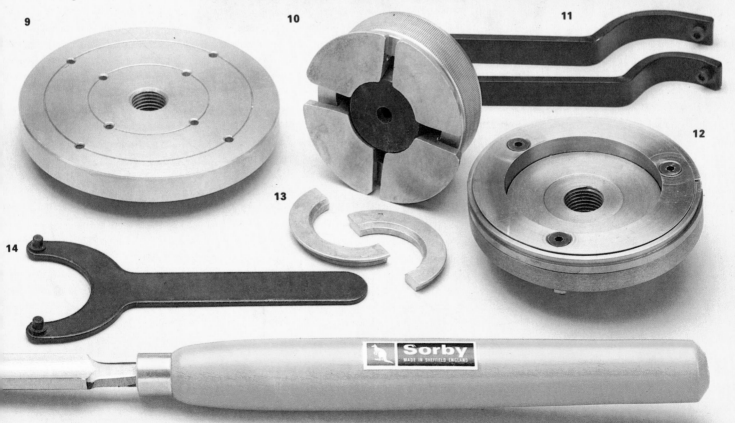

rough turning operations. For general shaping, the turning of bowls and pots, and work between lathe centres (often called spindle turning) a 6mm (¼in) and 12mm (½in) gouge will do. All turning tools are usually supplied with the cutting edges roughly ground to shape; it is up to you to provide the sharp cutting edge, but there should be only one bevel and this must be flat. Generally gouges for rough turning (a roughing cut) are ground square across the end while those for shaping are ground to a rounded or finger nail shape. You will find you develop a personal choice as you gain experience.
Turning chisels Available in a wide range of sizes from 6mm to 50mm (¼–2in), these are perhaps the most difficult turning tools to use. They differ from conventional tools in that they are bevelled on both sides of the cutting edge, which you either grind to a skew or square across as you require. Bear in mind that whereas chisels for hand work have two bevels on one side, those for turning have only one bevel on each side and that must be flat. Chisels are used to turn clean, cylindrical surfaces and form beads and corners where a clean cut is essential. Although the turning chisel is needed by the professional craftsman, you should use it carefully as a beginner; only use the extremities of the cutting edge, referred to as the heel and toe, until you gain experience.
Parting tool An essential part of the woodturner's kit, the parting tool is very simple to use. It is used to clean up the ends of cylindrical work, to form tenons and dowels and to cut away the finished work from the rest of the wood.

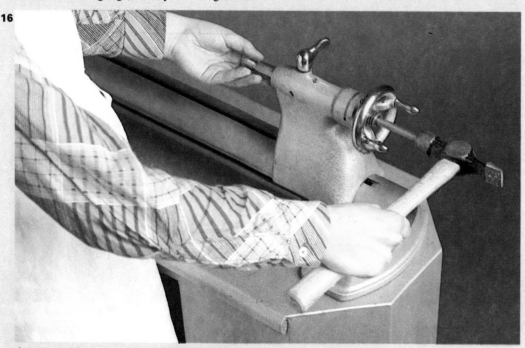

16 To remove a dead centre of the Morse taper type, drive a metal drift through the hollow centre of the quill
17 Position of the tool when cutting work on the lathe
18 Position of the tool when scraping work

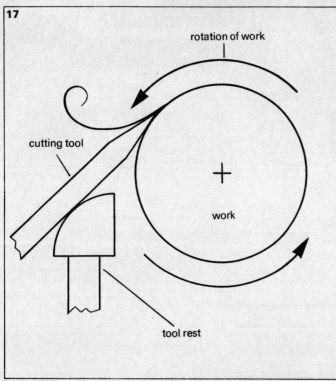

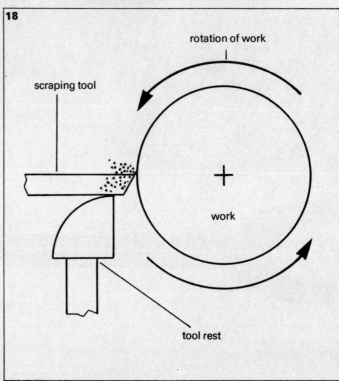

Cutting wood on the lathe

Although your turning tools may look sharp and in good condition, they will need to be ground and whetted to suit your particular requirements and sharpened frequently during use, since some timbers have a rapid blunting effect. A well-sharpened tool with a polished bevel helps to produce a smooth finish since the bevel rubs after the point of cut. A small powered grinding wheel is an essential part of a woodturner's kit; you will also need carborundum stones or oilstones (both fine and coarse grit), small carborundum slipstones and a can of fairly thin lubricating oil.

Sharpening tools

The method of keeping a good, sharp edge on cutting tools, including chisels and gouges, has already been covered earlier in the book. But even if you start off by using a scraping tool, which will give you a reasonable cutting edge, some attention must be paid to keeping it in good condition.

Scraping tool As described on page 73, this tool is very easy to use; it requires a cutting angle of 70–80 degrees. When using a powered grinding wheel to sharpen the tool, it is essential to have a supply of water to quench the tool since considerable heat is produced in the grinding process. Place the tool rest close to the grinding wheel and tilt the rest to a suitable grinding angle or, with a non-tilting rest, adjust the height. As you are grinding the scraping tool, keep its edge moving to prevent overheating and use the whole perimeter of the grinding wheel so it will wear evenly. Frequently inspect the cutting (or scraping) edge of the tool and stop grinding when you see a slight burr forming; if the tool becomes discoloured, it is overheating. To complete the sharpening process, the blade of the scraping tool should be placed flat on an oilstone and any burr removed by rubbing it over the stone. Finally, use a hardened steel rod (called a ticketer) to curl the cutting edge of the scraping tool slightly.

Turning methods

As previously described, there are two basic turning methods and you must understand the essential difference between the two before you turn work on your lathe.

Scraping This is carried out with the tool blade supported on the tool rest and sloping into the work; the cutting edge should be on, or slightly below, the centre line of the work and the handle must be higher than the cutting edge. Push the blade into the work so it scrapes the wood. To make satisfactory use of the tool, it must be sharp and you must move its blade in a side-to-side sweeping action across the surface of the timber, taking only light cuts. Timber cut in this way will always have a fairly rough finish, requiring the use of abrasive papers.

Cutting The tools used for cutting – gouges and chisels – pare the timber to shape. Just as a hand chisel used by a carpenter is brought into contact with the work at a slight angle to produce a slicing (or paring) cut, so the turner's chisel or gouge is used, depending upon the required profile.

Place the blade of the gouge on the lathe tool rest at an angle to the work so the bevel rubs the work. Again, position the tool rest slightly above centre

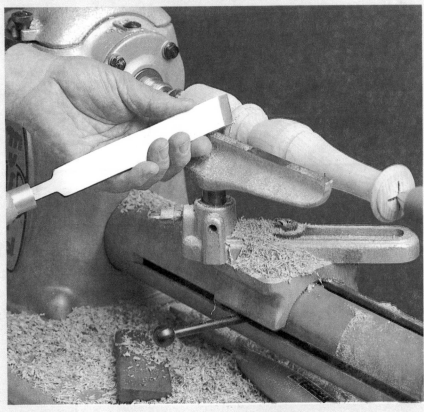

when working between centres and slightly below on face plate work. The cut is achieved by raising the right hand to bring the cutting edge into contact with the wood. Used in this way, a gouge will produce a slicing cut which requires very little finishing with abrasive paper.

You can form various intricate shapes with a gouge by placing the tool slightly on its side to the left or right. Again, keep the bevel of the blade in contact with the work so you produce a clean slicing cut.

One important rule for a woodturner is to produce wood shavings wherever possible; this is a good indication the timber is being cut to shape. Scraping, on the other hand, will produce shavings which break up into small chips or dust.

Of all the turning tools, the skew chisel is the most difficult to use. It has two cutting areas – the point (or toe) of the chisel and the opposite end known as the heel; most turning operations require you to use only the centre to heel, keeping the toe clear of the work. Place the tool rest above the centre line of the work so only the heel touches the work; to prevent cutting problems, the bevel must always remain in contact with the work. Lift the handle of the chisel slightly and advance the blade along the rotating workpiece to produce a cut. You can use both the heel and toe of the skew chisel to make various decorative cuts or to clean up the end of a piece of timber.

Grain direction All turning operations on a wood lathe require the cut to be made in the direction of the grain of the timber being turned; this ensures a clean finish. Working against the direction of the grain will always produce a rough finish. To ensure you are cutting in the correct direction, always

Above When making intricate cuts such as to decorate a chair leg or lamp standard, use the heel of the chisel

Lathe turning speeds

Work diameter (mm)	rough turning (rpm)	general shaping (rpm)	finishing (rpm)
Under 50	1000–1500	2200–2800	2800–3500
50–100	600–1000	1500–2200	2400–3000
100–150	500–800	1000–1500	1800–2400
150–200	400–600	800–1200	1200–1800
200–250	300–500	500–1000	800–1200
over 250	300	300–750	500–1000

Top Sharpening a scraping tool on a grinding wheel; when working, always wear protective spectacles and make sure all safety guards are in place
Top right Finish the sharpening process by placing the tool on an oilstone and rubbing it over the stone to remove the burr
Above Chart giving a range of lathe speeds for cutting different diameters of timber

work from the larger diameter of the work down towards the smaller, never the opposite way round.
Warning All cutting faults or mistakes are very difficult to remove; if possible practise first.

Lathe speed
To turn correctly, your work must rotate at the right speed; this is determined by the diameter of the work and its size. The lathe speed can be changed according to these dimensions, often simply by changing over a drive belt. Whenever possible, you should turn work at a speed which creates the minimum amount of vibration; use a slow speed for the initial rounding-off operation,

until your work is balanced. If you use a power drill and lathe attachment, the lathe speed will be governed by the type of drill you own; again, vibration must be kept to a minimum.

The chart shows approximate lathe speeds for different diameters of timber. The exceptionally low lathe speeds suggested for rough turning apply only when your work is extremely out of balance because of its shape, weight and general grain formation. Generally softwoods should be turned at a higher speed than hardwoods.

Timber for turning
Most woods can be used for woodturning; the more expensive types such as walnut, rosewood, teak and mahogany are best, although they are often difficult to obtain. Most timbers grown in Britain, both softwood and hardwood, also make ideal turning materials. In particular, the common fruitwoods such as plum, cherry, apple, pear and holly are often easily obtained in country areas at reasonable prices. You can also make some very interesting projects from simple offcuts obtainable from your local timber yard. Certain local timbers – such as cherry, plum, pear, holly, box, laurel, laburnum, sycamore, walnut and yew – have attractive natural colouring which will require little finishing.

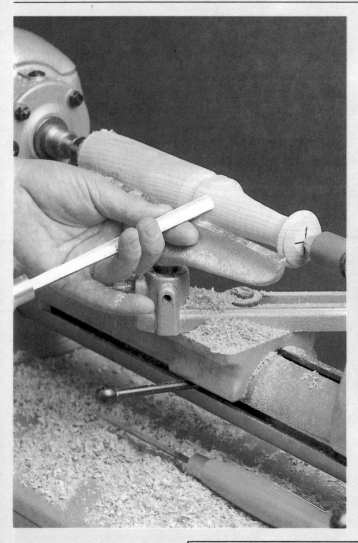 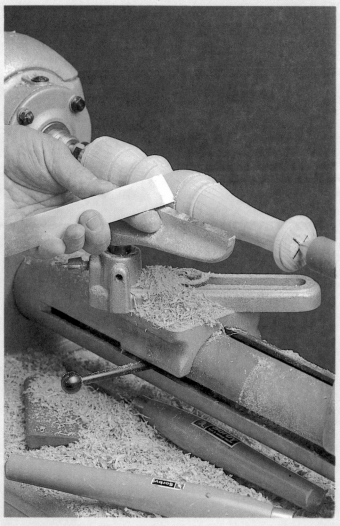

Above When turning wood on a lathe, always work from the larger diameter of the workpiece towards the smaller **Above right** You can use the toe of the chisel to make decorative cuts in the work **Right** Chart showing timbers suitable for turning

British timbers suitable for turning

Species	Colour	Qualities
apple	cream/yellow	hard, turns well
beech	cream/light brown	hard, turns well
box	cream/yellow	very hard, turns well
cherry	yellow/orange/pink	soft/hard, turns well
elm	cream/brown/dark brown	hard, difficult to turn
holly	white	very hard, turns well
laburnum	cream/brown/chocolate	very hard, turns well
laurel	yellow/brown	very hard, turns well
oak	cream/yellow	hard, turns well
pear	cream/yellow/grey	hard, turns well
plum	yellow/orange/pink	soft/hard, turns well
walnut	cream/brown/chocolate	hard, turns very well
yew	cream/orange/pink/brown	moderately hard, turns well

Shaping wood on the lathe

Forming a cylinder and producing simple decorative effects such as beads, coves and shoulders are all cuts which the beginner should master. Ideally, when you are just beginning to learn the techniques of wood turning, you should use a piece of hardwood, preferably beech or sycamore or a fruit wood such as cherry or apple; all these woods have a fairly even grain formation and cut well with turning tools. Avoid softwoods at this stage since they require careful cutting techniques.

Forming a cylinder
First cut the timber to a square section – 75 × 75mm (3 × 3in), for example – and draw diagonal lines from corner to corner at each end of the block to provide the exact centre for the work. Remove the pronged centre from the lathe and, using a copper hammer or mallet, make an indentation with the centre in the end of the workpiece so the driving point is secure. If you do not have a copper-headed hammer or mallet, you can use diagonal saw cuts to locate the pronged centre.

Make a pilot hole at the centre of the opposite end with a bradawl to provide a good support for the tailstock centre. Remove the corners of the timber by planing or sawing; this is not, however, necessary for small section work – below 50 × 50mm (2 × 2in) – being turned at high speed.

Replace the pronged centre, with the work attached, in the headstock spindle and bring the tailstock into position; secure it on the lathe bed and advance the tailstock centre into the piece of timber. It is a good idea to smear a small amount of grease or paraffin wax between the centre and the wood to avoid overheating and damage to the work; timber rotating at high speed on the centre can easily burn.

Positioning tool rest Position the tool rest along the lathe bed with the mandrel roughly on a line with your elbow; the top of the tool rest should be slightly above the centre line of the work. Turn the work by hand to ensure a reasonable clearance between it and the edge of the tool rest; always keep the tool rest as close to the work as possible, since this helps maintain a steady cutting action, and make sure the top edge is perfectly straight and without blemish. It might be difficult to have the tool rest in the ideal position on projects where part of the work has to be left 'in the square' such as a pummel to receive a mortise; but you will learn to cope with this by experience.

Holding tool Most turning tools are supplied with fairly long handles. Hold the handle in one hand and with the other hold the blade on the tool rest with the palm down and the side of the fist against the tool rest; this will deflect the shavings away from you. Alternatively you can have the palm uppermost with the side of the forefinger against the tool rest; this position has the advantage of allowing you to watch the cutting action and progress of the work.

Cutting The standard 18mm (¾in) gouge is the most suitable tool for cutting a cylinder. With the lathe running at a speed compatible with the cross-section of the workpiece (1000–1500rpm in this case), place the gouge at the extreme right-hand end of the

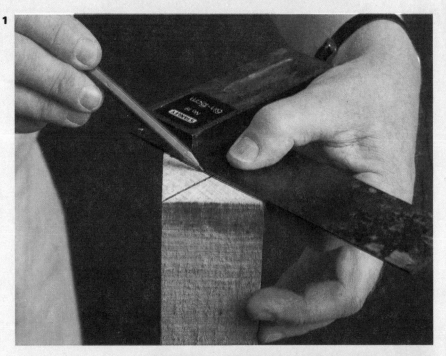

tool rest with the cutting edge just clear of the work. Bring the handle of the tool over a little to your left and at the same time twist it slightly to the right so the blade is at an angle to the tool rest.

Let the bevel of the tool rub the work and raise your right hand to bring on the cut. Make a second cut about 25mm (1in) along from the first cut and repeat the operation, this time moving the tool along the tool rest and joining the two cuts into one. Repeat this method of cutting along the length of the work, working from right to left, forming a cylinder to a point about 50mm (2in) from the left-hand end of the work. Reverse the position of the

1 Finding the centre for the work; make sure the wood is square and draw diagonal lines from corner to corner at each end of the workpiece
2 Securing the pronged centre to the workpiece; tap it into place with a copper-headed hammer or mallet

3

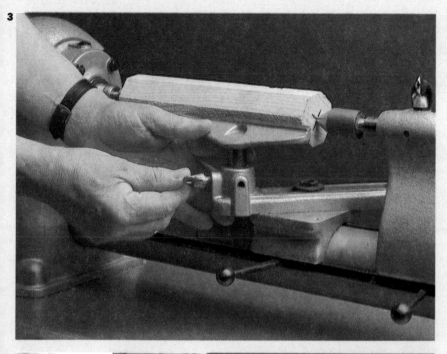

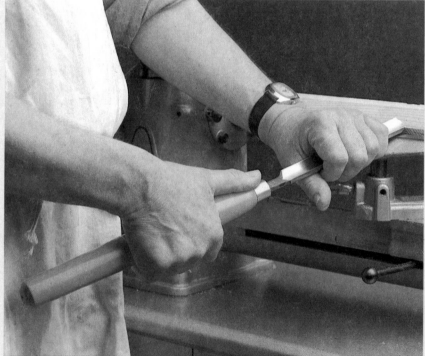

3 Positioning the tool rest
4 Holding the tool; hold the handle in one hand and with the other hold the blade on the tool rest with your palm down and the side of your fist against the tool rest

requires skill and care, but does produce work of quality. For most work between lathe centres (often called spindle turning), the 12mm ($\frac{1}{2}$in) gouge ground to a finger nail end, with its bevel ground to an angle of about 35–40 degrees, is perhaps the most versatile. As with all turning methods, always cut with the direction of the grain of the wood and work from the larger diameter to the smaller.

To form a simple hollow or cove with the small gouge, keep the bevel of the tool in contact with the wood and rest the blade on the tool rest at an angle of about 45 degrees to the tool rest. Lift the handle slightly so the blade cuts a small cove or depression in the wood, but don't push too far into the work. With the handle rolled slightly to the left, make a cut on the right of the hollow. Withdraw the blade and reverse the hold on the handle by rolling it to the right and making a cut from the left-hand side of the hollow.

Work in this manner by making alternate cuts from each side of the hollow to form the required shape; don't attempt to cut from the bottom of the hollow outwards. Move the tool further along the work and repeat the cutting operation, keeping the bevel in contact with the wood and making sure the cutting edge is sharp; some woods such as teak or elm can quickly blunt the sharpest tool.

You can produce interesting decorative effects by using the extreme end of the small gouge and rolling the handle. To produce a small step or fillet, lay the edge of the blade on the tool rest so the cutting edge is vertical; by rolling the blade and keeping the cutting edge in contact with the wood, you can form a clean-cut bead. A step can be formed or the end of the work rounded over in the same manner.

Using scraper When scraping, first position the cutting edge of the scraper so it is on or slightly below the centre line of work. Place the blade of the scraper on the tool rest and, holding it with one hand, raise the handle and trail the tool to allow the 'hooked' edge to bite. Always work from the larger diameter down to the smaller (cut inwards). Simple beads and steps are formed by using a scraper of the appropriate shape.

When using the scraper for shaping wood, reposition the tool rest so the cutting edge of the tool is on or slightly below the centre line of the work and the blade of the tool is held at a slightly downward rake. Don't allow the cutting edge of the scraper to work above the centre line of the work and keep it inclined slightly downwards for safety. To produce a shape with the scraper, place the blade of the tool on the tool rest and lightly push it into the rotating work; then swing the handle from right to left to open the cut and produce the required shape. Make these cuts, as with the gouge, working from the larger diameter down to the smaller diameter. Small beads and other decorative effects are produced in the same way, although great care must be taken to avoid tearing out the wood fibres; always keep the scrapers very sharp for the best results.

Using skew chisel This is generally used for smoothing off cylinders, but it has many other useful applications. Beads, grooves, coves and other intricacies found in traditional furniture designs can be easily and safely made using the heel or toe (tip) of the chisel.

To produce a bead, make a vee cut into the work, with the heel of the tool in the correct position and the handle slightly lifted. Make a similar cut to the required depth a short distance from the first and

gouge on the tool rest; place the blade at the extreme left of the tool rest at an angle to the work with the cutting edge just clear of the left-hand end of the work. Repeat the cuts, this time working from the left until you meet up with the partly turned cylinder. If you are holding the tool correctly, you will get shavings; this means the timber is being cut cleanly. Scraping produces chips and dust.

Shaping the wood
To shape the wood, you can either scrape it to shape or cut it with gouges. The same results can be obtained with both scraping or gouging tools; but although scraping tools are easier to use, they do not give such a good finish. Scraping methods are not satisfactory on soft or stringy woods and are best reserved for cleaning up.

Using gouge Shaping wood with a cutting tool

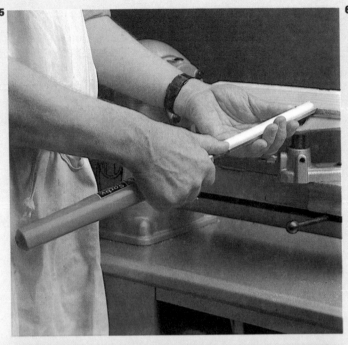

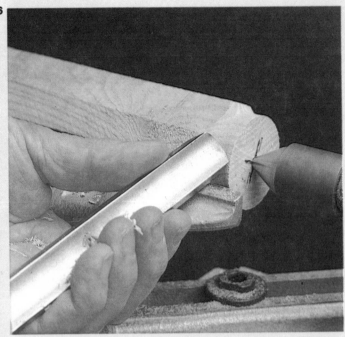

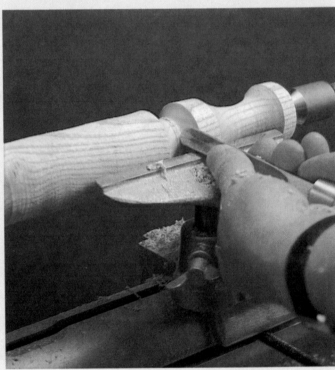

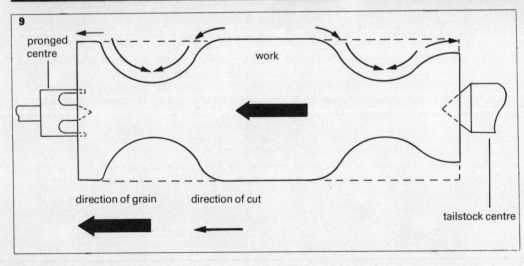

5 You can hold the tool with your palm uppermost and the side of your forefinger against the tool rest

6 Making the first cut into a cylinder with a gouge

7 To make the second cut, move the tool along; then join the two cuts into one

8 When forming a hollow, first cut a small depression in the wood then make alternate cuts from each side

9 When shaping wood always work from the larger diameter to the smaller and make all cuts with the direction of the wood grain

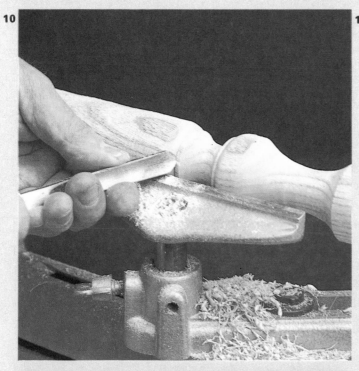

complete the cut by placing the bevel of the tool flat on top of the work with the heel just clear. The bead is then formed by rolling the handle of the tool while lifting it slightly so the blade cuts one side. The position of the blade is then reversed and a second cut made in the same way to complete the operation.

You can also use the chisel for rounding over the end of a turned cylinder; the bevel rubs and the centre of the chisel does the cutting. Place the blade of the chisel on the work, with the point well clear and lift the handle slightly so the centre of the chisel is brought into contact with the timber to start the cut; always keep the bevel of the blade rubbing the work to ensure you maintain a smooth cutting action.

The point or toe of the chisel is invaluable for jobs such as squaring up the end of partly turned wood or cutting and squaring shoulders. Position the tool rest so the cut is made on the centre line of the work, holding the blade of the chisel on its edge with the toe pointing downwards; remember always to keep the bevel of the blade in contact with the work.

Finishing off Finally, sand the work to a smooth finish, starting with medium glasspaper and finishing off with fine or flour glasspaper; always remove the tool rest before you begin sanding. In all lathe sanding operations, it is essential to keep the paper moving over the surface of the work to prevent the formation of sanding rings, which can be difficult to remove. For perfect control and safe sanding, always hold the abrasive paper underneath the workpiece.

10 Making a small shoulder or fillet with a gouge

11 Shaping the wood with a scraper; position the tool rest on or just below the centre line of the work with the blade at a slightly downward rake

12 Using a skew chisel to round over the end of a turned cylinder

13 For complete control when finishing off the workpiece, hold the abrasive paper underneath; keep the paper moving along the surface of the work to prevent the formation of sanding rings

Turning wood between centres

Turning between centres, or spindle turning as it is often known, should present you with few problems as long as you make sure the work is secure between the centres, the tools are sharp and you use them in the correct manner and the tool rest is at a comfortable height. Using the basic woodturning tools, simple shapes and a reasonable cylinder can be made although they may be very rough and require considerable finishing with decreasing grades of abrasive paper.

It is often only necessary to part-turn a length of wood between lathe centres, leaving a section or two 'in the square'; this type of work is most common with antique and traditional furniture, in chair and table legs, stools, and stretchers for sofas and tables. The general increase in demand for period furniture and the repair of broken pieces has brought about a growth in demand for this work; mastering the art of part-turning a square section of wood without damage to the remainder which is in the square is a skill the home handyman turner is likely to want to acquire.

Preparing and positioning work
Usually for a proper job the wood must be cut and planed square, although often when working with very old pieces of furniture it is an advantage to have the wood a little off square to give an 'antique' effect of unseasoned wood which has subsequently shrunk a little.

Carefully mark the sections of wood which are to remain in the square, preferably on all four sides of the work, and clearly mark the true centre of the wood at each end by drawing diagonal lines between the corners of the wood. Make a small hole in the centre with a bradawl to ensure the lathe centres are accurately positioned and drive the pronged driving centre into the end of the wood to ensure a positive drive. Alternatively, if you require extreme turning accuracy, you can place the wood between lathe centres with the tailstock quill advanced into the work so the work can be spun freely on each centre without actually engaging the driving prongs. Check the wood for accurate centring; if it is slightly off, you will often be able to

1 Marking out sections of work which are to remain in the square
2 Making a register mark on the prong of the driving centre
3 Making the first cut with a chisel
4 Using a chisel to make alternate cuts from the right and left to produce a wide vee

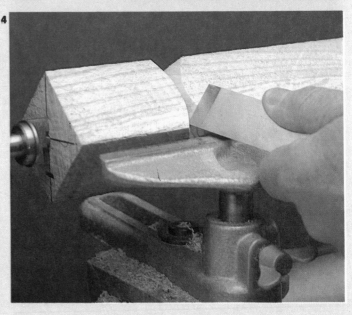

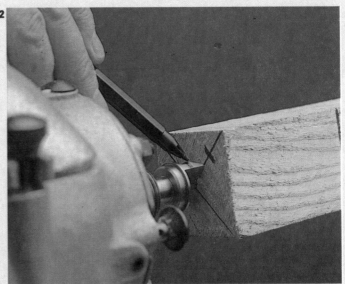

correct it by stopping the lathe and lightly thumping with your fist at the end which appears to be off centre.

In all turning work it is advisable to complete all the turning operations without taking the work off the centres. Often after a little use pronged driving centres cease to be accurate; before you begin it is always a good idea to mark one of the prongs of the driving centre with a triangular file to act as a register mark.

Turning work

With the wood mounted between lathe centres, the tailstock secure and a spot of grease on the point of the plain centre, adjust the position of the tool rest so when you rotate the work by hand it just clears the rest. Check the tool rest is secure on the lathe bed; sometimes in the initial stages of turning from square to round, vibration may cause the tool rest to work loose.

Carefully cut through the corners of the wood to the waste side of the indicated square sections; a skew chisel is suitable for this and it is best to choose an 18–25mm (or $\frac{3}{4}$–1in) tool. Hold the blade upright on its edge on the tool rest with the point of the chisel pointing under the centre line of the work.

Stand a little to the right of the point where the cut is to be made and, with the lathe revolving at a speed compatible with the cross-section of the wood, make a small cut into the wood to the right of the waste side of the marked section. Stop the lathe for a moment and inspect the cut; if the cut is accurately centred, the wood should be cut on all four sides. If correction is necessary at this stage to ensure accurate cutting, slacken off the tailstock slightly and give the work a light thump with your clenched fist at the off-centre point. Use the point of the chisel to make alternate cuts from the right and left to produce a wide vee; stop as soon as the cut appears all round the work.

Turning shoulders In some work the shoulders of the wood are left square cut; but it is more common to find these slightly radiused. To do this hold the chisel with the point slightly below the centre line of the work and the opposite edge of the blade on the tool rest. Using the point of the chisel and working towards the waste area, start to radius the work, making good use of the bevel of the chisel. Take only light slicing cuts to produce a neat clean finish. Any other square sections should be treated in a similar manner, working progressively towards the tailstock; check at all times the tool rest is clear of

5 Using the point of a chisel to radius the shoulders
6 Using a gouge to make the first cut for a cylinder
7 Making the final cut for a cylinder shape with the gouge reversed
8 Marking out the main features of a design

5

6

7
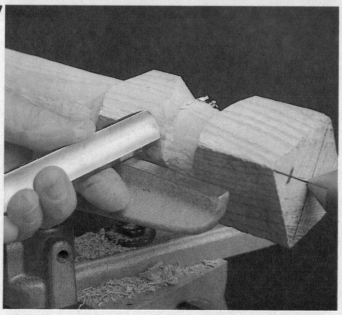

8
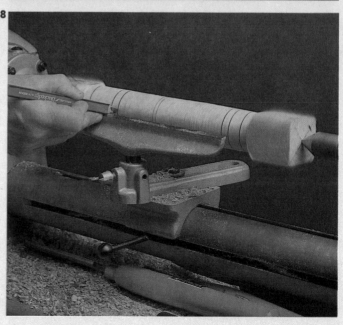

the rotating work on the lathe.

If you find difficulty in using a skew chisel, you can work with a gouge instead; use the same turning methods with the tool held on its edge and the cutting edge presented vertically to the work.

Turning cylinder shape To turn the remainder of the work to a cylinder without damaging the squared sections you will need to use a fairly wide gouge of about 25mm (or 1in), ground and sharpened to a fingernail end section. You should hold the gouge at about a 45 degree angle to the wood with the bevel in contact with it and work progressively towards the squared section. The final cut towards the square should be made with the blade of the gouge reversed. You can then turn the remainder of the work in a similar manner, taking care not to touch the clean cut end grain of the squared shoulders. At this stage the wood should be turned to the maximum diameter which the cross-section of the wood will allow.

Forming details Carefully mark out the essential details of the design required; where repetition work is to be carried out you should make up a template or pattern. Use a parting tool to mark out the main features in the design, in particular the position of beads and coves.

You can use a small skew chisel to form a bead by rolling it alternately from the right and left, always keeping the bevel of the tool in contact with the wood. It is a good idea to raise the height of the tool rest slightly; hold the blade of the tool between the fingers and against the tool rest while you roll the handle to form the shape required.

To ensure clean-cut lines when you are turning a hollow, cove or fillet, it is a good idea to cut through the surface wood fibres slightly with the point of a skew chisel before actually turning the work to shape. You can then complete the remainder of a cove, for example, using a round-nosed gouge. Always cut alternately from the left and right to obtain the desired shape; work from the larger diameter to the smaller to produce a clean cut without any tool handling problems.

Warning It is important to take light cuts and avoid working with blunt tools, which may cause damage to the adjacent design features.

Final turning After all detail work has been completed you can carry out the final turning of the main part of the work; use a gouge and, for detail work, the point of a skew chisel. Always work from the larger diameter down to the smaller and with the direction of the wood grain.

9 Scoring the details of the design on the work with a parting tool
10 Using a small skew chisel to shape a bead
11 Using the point of a skew chisel for the start of a cove
12 Finishing a cove using a round-nosed gouge

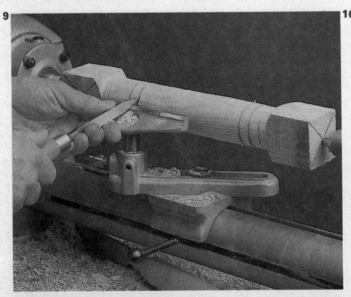

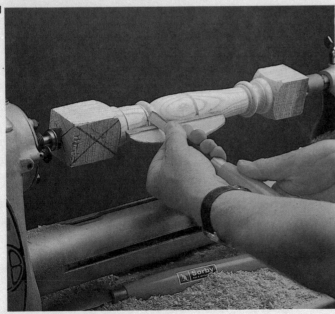

Basic woodturning using face plate

Using a face plate is an entirely different technique from spindle or centre-turning where the work is supported at both ends of the lathe. Here all the work – turning, sanding and polishing – is carried out with the wood held on a face plate or similar chucking device screwed to the headstock mandrel. Many objects, such as bowls, cruets, fitments and knobs can be turned with this method.

Diameter of work Face plate work can be a lot larger than the normal swing of the lathe above the lathe bed allows. This problem is usually overcome by the actual design of the lathe, together with various additional attachments. With some lathes turning large diameter work is carried out to the left of the headstock spindle using a special tool rest. With others, a gap is cut in the lathe bed to accommodate large diameter work. On some machines the complete headstock assembly is made to rotate through 90 degrees so the work is parallel to the lathe bed which is particularly useful where space is limited.

On drill-powered lathe attachments, the maximum diameter of the work is restricted by the design of the lathe and the limited power of the drill. Don't attempt to increase the capacity of these lathes, since it could prove dangerous and costly. Ideally you should use a speed reducer to obtain the correct speed.

Attachments Various attachments can be used to hold the work on the headstock end of the lathe and their use depends on the size of the project undertaken. They include the standard face plate supplied with the basic lathe, woodscrew chucks used for turning smaller items such as knobs and small bowls, specialized chucks with various applications and wood chucks which you can make yourself to suit a particular project.

For most bowl turning the face plate – with the work fixed to scrap timber and screwed to it – is sufficient; you will learn more professional methods with experience. Various projects may require different methods of holding the work on the headstock, but the general principles of turning are very similar. To begin with, turn something simple but interesting, like a small bowl, using the standard face plate supplied with the machine.

Warning At all stages in any turning exercise, don't let technical considerations make you forget the importance of safety. Care should also be taken in the initial preparation, since it greatly simplifies any future work.

Preparing the face plate
The face plate has a number of holes through which screws can be passed to secure the work. Although the wood is often fixed directly, it is better to fit a timber sub-face to the plate. This allows you to work close to the plate without actually touching it and damaging the cutting tool.

Take a scrap piece of timber or blockboard about 25mm (1in) thick, true and flat on one side and cut it to the approximate diameter of the face plate. Screw it directly onto the face plate, making sure the screws penetrate to about half the depth of the wood. Mount the face plate, complete with timber sub-face, onto the headstock and true it to a circle, preferably using a small gouge on its side to give a smooth cut. Clean up the face side with a scraping tool, making sure the blade of the tool is held at a slightly downward angle to the work.

To make mounting of the work on the face plate easier in the future, use the point of a skew chisel with the blade held flat on the tool rest to scribe a number of concentric circles. At the same time,

1 Fitting a timber sub-face to the face plate; this allows you to work close to the plate without touching it
2 Scraping the sub-face to a flat surface

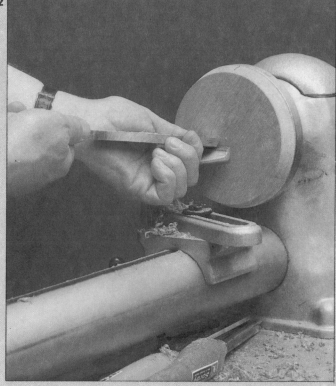

make a small register mark on the edge of the face plate and sub-face using a small triangular file or hacksaw blade; this will allow the two items to be mated accurately should they have to be unscrewed.

A small brad point tapped into the centre of the timber face and protruding about 3mm ($\frac{1}{8}$in) is a further aid to chucking or mounting the work on the face plate.

Preparing the wood
To prepare the work for the project, check one side of the wood is perfectly flat. If it is not, plane or sand it to get a flat surface and ensure perfect fixing to the face plate. Using a pair of dividers, carefully scribe the diameter of the project and cut it to shape with a handsaw – or preferably a bandsaw. Try to cut accurately to the marked line, even though any imperfections will be quickly removed when you start turning.

Securing the face plate
Secure the face plate to the wood disc with four screws, with the centre brad point in the prepared face plate acting as a guide. The fixing screws should extend into the wood about 9–13mm ($\frac{3}{8}-\frac{1}{2}$in) to

3 Before mounting the work, check the surface is flat
4 To aid mounting or rechucking the work, fit a brad point to the centre; concentric circles will help you centre smaller work
5 Fitting a thin card washer between the face plate and the headstock spindle
6 Turning a bowl using the same mounting throughout

3
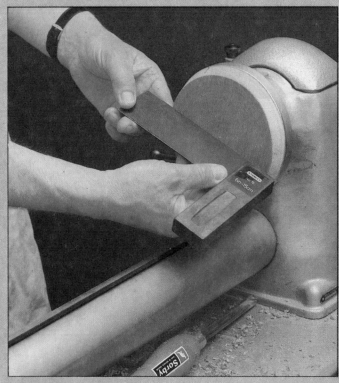

4
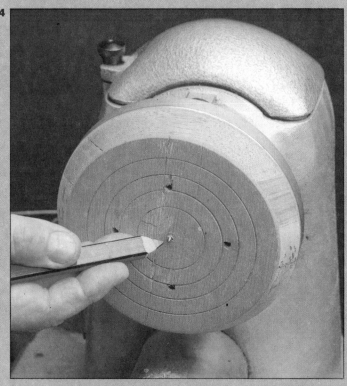

5
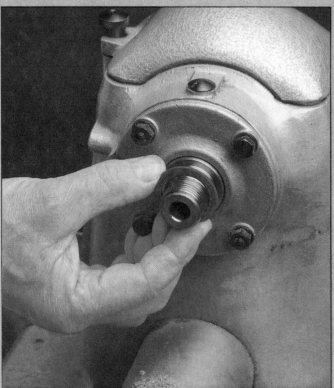

6

hold the wood secure. Finally, screw the face plate complete with the wood disc onto the headstock; use a thin card washer to prevent the plate becoming locked on the headstock spindle. Always check the face plate is secured before switching on the power; the back of the face plate must be against the shoulder of the headstock spindle. A loose face plate will tighten up on the threads of the headstock spindle, making it almost impossible to remove. Fitting a paper or card washer will minimize this problem.

For the initial shaping of the wood disc, use a fairly low speed; 1000rpm is ideal for a 150–200mm (6–8in) disc. If you are using a power drill, keep it at the lowest possible speed to reduce the effects of vibration, which may occur in the initial stage of turning, until the work is reasonably true and in balance. Before starting work, position the tool rest across the rim of the disc a little above the centre line of the workpiece so it just clears the edge when rotated by hand.

Methods of turning

There are two methods of turning the rough block of wood into a bowl. You can turn the bowl, both

7 Turning a bowl in two stages involves removing the work and remounting it on the face plate; you must ensure the remounted work is centred on the face plate
8 Cutting in the direction of the wood grain
9 Cutting against the grain
10 Using a gouge to give a smooth finish to the work

7

8

9

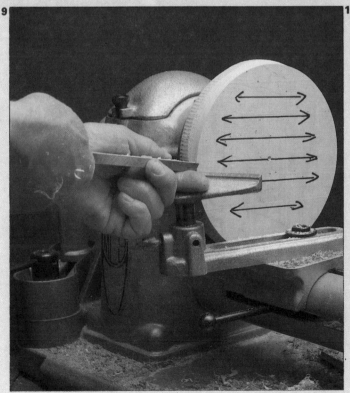

10

11 Truing up the face side of the work with a round nose scraper
12 Shaping the outside of the bowl with a gouge
13 After rechucking, make a small depression in the centre of the work with a square-ended scraper
14 Opening up the hole with a round nose scraper

inside and out, using the same face plate mounting throughout. Once you have secured the block of wood, this method has the advantage of allowing you to do all the turning and finishing without removing the work. Although the underside of the work might prove difficult to shape, this method is recommended for beginners since it will boost confidence and help you understand the general techniques of face plate turning.

Alternatively you can first turn the outside of the bowl to shape, remove the partly turned work and remount what is now the base of the bowl on the face plate and turn the inside of the bowl. This

method allows for greater flexibility in design, but it does call for accuracy when remounting the block on the face plate. To overcome this you can use a 6 in 1 chuck with expanding collet; when the work is reversed it is automatically recentred.

Shaping the work
The first stage in turning the bowl is to true up the block of wood so it will revolve free from vibration, although this can be exaggerated by the make-up and grain formation of the wood.

The simplest method is to use a scraping tool held square on to the edge of the work and to work slow-

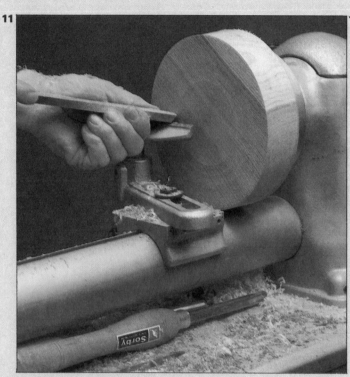

ly across the periphery until a perfect disc is turned. Although this is a common method, it has the disadvantage of damaging the grain fibres and making it almost impossible to obtain a reasonable finish. The importance of cutting the wood in the direction of the grain, which has been discussed earlier, is further complicated when shaping a wood disc. The grain more or less runs across the face of the disc, so a different direction of grain is presented to the cutting edge of the tool as the disc rotates. This results in some areas being rough and others smooth. To avoid this use a cutting tool (gouge), making the cut at about 45 degrees across the work edge with the bevel rubbing. This gives a smooth finish since you are, in effect, cutting with the grain. Continue in this way across the edge of the work, working from the face side of the disc.

To put this method into practice, position the tool rest fairly close to the edge of the disc and a little above the centre height. Holding a 12mm ($\frac{1}{2}$in) round-ended gouge (finger-nail end) with the blade on its left side on the tool rest and the bevel rubbing the work, make the first cut across the corner of the disc, continuing across the rim of the wood to produce a smooth finish.

Face side True up the face side of the block with a round-nosed scraper. Position the tool rest across the face of the disc and at a height which will allow the cut to be made on the centre line of the work with the handle of the tool held slightly upwards. This will give the blade a negative rake and prevent the tool digging into the work.

Use the scraping tool with a light sweeping action across the face of the work from the rim to the centre. Avoid taking large cuts since this will damage the grain formation and make it difficult to obtain a satisfactory finish later. Should you have trouble getting your scraping tools to cut well, check the edge is curled or 'ticketed' to bite the work.

Outside The general shaping of the outside of the bowl is similar to the first operation of truing up the edge of the block. Use the gouge on its edge with the bevel rubbing against the work to prevent any cutting problems. Never hold the gouge flat on the tool rest and square to the work. When you have shaped the block on the outside, make a small pin hole in the centre of the base to assist rechucking.

To rechuck, remove the partly turned disc from the face plate and reverse it, screwing what is now the base of the bowl onto the face plate. With the face plate secure on the headstock, not forgetting the paper or card washer to prevent it becoming locked, you can begin the final stage of hollowing out the work.

Hollowing out

Here again you have the choice of scraping or cutting. If scraping, place the tool rest across the face of the work and position it to allow the scraping tool to cut at around centre height. Make a small depression in the centre of the block with a square-ended scraper and, using the scraper as a boring tool, push it straight into the centre of the revolving block. Then, using a round-ended scraper, open up the hole with a series of adjacent cuts until the desired shape is formed.

If cutting, cut a small groove with a parting tool near the rim of the block. Then use a gouge with the bevel rubbing the wood and work towards the centre; the cut is brought on by raising the handle of the tool. Work in this manner until you obtain the desired shape and depth. Finally, sand the work down to a smooth finish using decreasing grades of abrasive paper held between the fingers and with the work rotating at a fairly fast speed. Work underneath when sanding the outside, and between 'half past' and 'quarter to' when sanding the inside.

15 Sanding the work to a smooth finish; use decreasing grades of abrasive paper
16 On this lathe large diameter work is turned to the left of the headstock spindle using a special tool rest; on others a gap cut in the lathe bed accommodates the work

Advanced woodturning using face plate

When you are using scraping tools to shape a bowl or platter you may find it extremely difficult to obtain a perfectly smooth finish in certain areas of the workpiece, in particular in the end grain section of the wood. If you inspect the work closely, you will find the grain fibres have been pushed to one side rather than cut cleanly through; this means even after considerable sanding with various grades of abrasive paper a perfectly smooth finish is often impossible to obtain. To solve this problem you will have to use cutting tools – gouges – and sever the wood fibres cleanly.

Carrying out the basic turning methods using the face plate as previously described ensures a certain degree of accuracy during the initial turning exercise and will allow you to build up confidence in handling tools and machines. But another problem which arises with this type of work is the unsightly screw holes left in the workpiece after it is removed from the face plate. You can camouflage the blind screw holes with plastic wood or a covering of cork or baize; as you become more practised you can aim for a higher standard of work.

Using cutting tools

To turn a bowl or platter, first mount the disc of wood on the face plate in the usual way, either directly screwed to the face plate or using a prepared face plate fitted with a wood sub-face. True up the outside of the disc using a scraper or gouge and turn the general outside shape of the bowl with the gouge, keeping the bevel in contact with the work throughout. If you are using a round-nosed gouge, the blade should be held on the tool rest on its side and at about 45 degrees to the work. Where you are using a gouge with the end ground straight across, you should use the side of the tool with the cutting edge at an angle to the work to present a slicing or paring action to the wood; sometimes the gouge can be inverted to obtain a clean cut, but never square on to the work.

Forming base Use a scraping tool to form the base and the tip of a gouge to form a clean cut edge which is slightly radiused to assist in the next chucking operation, the hollowing of the bowl. Thoroughly sand the outside of the bowl, including the base, using decreasing grades of abrasive paper, then wax or polish using clear or white French polish. For a truly professional look there should be no visible marks of chucking when the work is completed.

Making hollow chuck After you have removed the partly turned bowl from the face plate you should make a hollow wood chuck in which the base of the bowl can be fitted and held for the final hollowing out. To do this, screw a disc of softwood about 25mm (1in) thick to the metal face plate, mount the face plate on the headstock and use a scraping tool to trim up the rim and face side, checking with a try square the surface is true. Using a pair of dividers set to the radius of the base of the bowl, scribe a circle on the face of the prepared disc and use a square-ended scraper to turn a recess; starting in the centre of the disc, form an opening about 3–8mm (or $\frac{1}{8}-\frac{5}{16}$) deep which will accept the base of the partly turned bowl. Make frequent tests as you work to ensure a perfect fit.

It is important to make the sides of the opening with a slight inward taper. You can use hardwood for a chuck, but softwood is preferable since it will

1 Shaping the outside of a bowl with a round-nosed gouge; the blade should be held on the tool rest on its side and at about 45 degrees to the work
2 Forming the base with a scraping tool

give a little if the base of the bowl is slightly oversize for the turned recess. If the bowl base is a slightly loose fit in the chuck, sandwich a piece of paper between the work and the inside of the chuck or slightly dampen the inside of the chuck so it expands to hold the work securely.

Hollowing bowl Before switching on the power, rotate the work by hand to check it is centralized; if it appears to be slightly off centre, check it is firmly seated inside the wood chuck. To correct the position, knock the centre of the work with your clenched fist.

To clean up the face side of the disc for an even surface use a round-nosed scraper with the tool rest placed across the front of the work at a height which will allow the cutting edge of the tool to work on, or slightly below, the centre line of the work; the blade of the tool should point slightly downwards. To start hollowing, use the end of a gouge with the blade held on its side or a square-ended scraping tool to make a fairly deep 'V' cut about 25mm (1in) in from the rim of the disc; work from this direction since a bowl which is worked from the centre outwards is likely to become slightly out of shape before the work is completed – due to the general make-up of the grain fibres of the wood.

Using a round-nosed gouge no wider than 12mm (or ½in) start to open up the 'V' cut; make a cut on the left of the 'V' with the blade held on its right side on the tool rest and the bevel in contact with the side of the 'V' cut, followed by a similar cut on the right of the 'V' with the blade of the tool resting on its left side. Continue in this manner, taking alternate cuts from each side of the 'V', until most of the inside of the bowl has been removed, with each cut going deeper into the bowl to obtain the desired internal shape. Make sure you do not use the gouge square onto the work with the back of the blade resting on the tool rest; it must always be used on its side.

Cutting the wood to shape in this way where the tool is making a slicing or paring cut across the wood should produce shavings and a smooth finish. Also very little strain is placed on the mounting of the bowl base within the wood chuck, retaining it securely within the chuck. Any turning difficulties due to misuse of tools or using blunt ones can quickly force the wood off centre, making it almost impossible to complete the turning operation satisfactorily.

As the hollowing of the inside of the wood nears completion, a small cone of wood is formed in the centre of the work; this is impossible to remove completely with a gouge. For the final operation and to remove any slight imperfection in the rest of the inside of the bowl, use a round-nose scraping tool. With the blade of the tool held flat on the tool rest pointing downwards, move the blade across the surface of the wood with a light sweeping action. Avoid taking heavy cuts and check the tool is really sharp to obtain a perfect finish.

Finishing bowl A bowl or platter turned in the manner described should require very little sanding to obtain a good finish. Use a medium or fine abrasive paper, keeping the paper moving across the surface of the work; don't apply excessive pressure in one particular area since this could form scratches which may be difficult to remove. Use fine steel wool to complete the sanding process.

Most wood bowls or platters are given a coat of clear or white French polish, prepared wax or synthetic lacquer while the work is still mounted on the lathe; this will be described in detail later in the book.

To remove the work from the wood chuck, give a slight knock with your fist; don't use anything hard since this may damage the wood.

Warning Some species of timber such as elm and teak often have extremely hard resinous crystals embedded in the grain fibres which are difficult to detect with the naked eye; these will blunt the keenest edged tool very quickly. If the cutting

3 To make a hollow chuck, scribe a circle of the same radius as the base of the bowl onto the timber sub-face
4 Use a square-ended scraper to turn the recess

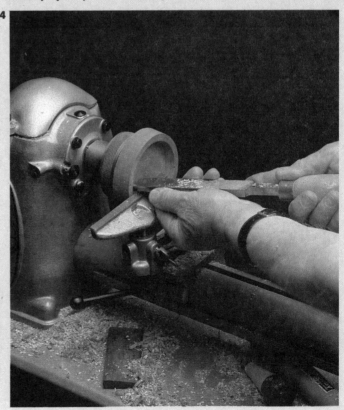

action of your tools becomes ineffective, stop the lathe and inspect the wood closely; there may be small areas of grain which are causing the problem. In this case you will have to sharpen your tools frequently or use some of the high speed steel-tipped tools which are becoming more widely available.

Using paper sandwich method

When you are turning bowls or platters from thin stock where normal screw-fitting to the face plate cannot be used, the wood should be stuck to a prepared wood face plate with a thick sheet of paper sandwiched between the work and the face plate. This is known as the paper sandwich method. Often the project is completed with only one mounting on the face plate, with both the front and back being completed without changing the position of the work on the face plate.

The paper sandwich method of chucking or holding work on the lathe has many applications in both large and small projects. Throughout the turning operations, however, great care must be taken not to force the work off its adhesive mount-

5 Check the hollow chuck for fit against the base of the bowl
6 Begin hollowing the bowl by making a deep 'V' cut with the end of a gouge
7 Open up the 'V' cut with a gouge
8 Take alternate cuts from each side of the 'V' until most of the inside of the bowl has been removed

5

6

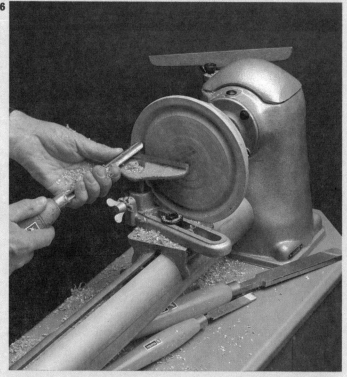

7

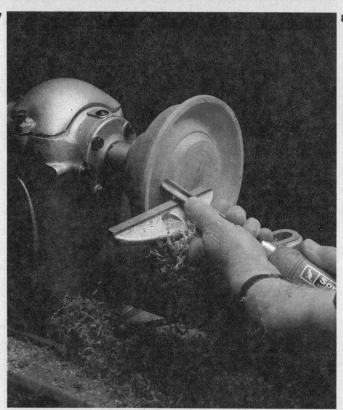

8

ing; wherever possible all turning stresses should be towards the face plate.

Preparing face plate and workpiece The face plate is prepared in the usual way by screwing a disc of 25mm (1in) stock to it, mounting it on the lathe and truing up the rim and the face side with a scraping tool as previously described. Check the face side with a straight-edge or try square to make sure it is perfectly flat and true. Prepare the wood you are going to use with one side planed flat and true for mounting on the face plate. Apply a thin coat of PVA adhesive (not the impact type) to the wood sub-face on the face plate, followed by a reasonably thick disc made of blotting paper or similar material. Apply a coat of adhesive to the face side of the workpiece and place the workpiece on the sub-face, sandwiching the paper in between. To make sure the wood is centrally placed on the face plate, use the tailstock as a vice to hold the sandwich together while the adhesive sets; this will normally take one or two hours. Where the wood is soft – and anyway to prevent damage to its surface – place a wood pad between the centre of the tailstock and the work.

9 As the hollow nears completion a small cone will be formed in the centre
10 Removing the cone with a round-nosed scraper
11 With the paper sandwich method of chucking, use the tailstock as a vice to hold the sandwich together while the adhesive sets
12 Shaping the underside of a platter

13 Start to hollow out the platter with the tool on its side for safety and a clean finish
14 Continue shaping the work, still using the tailstock for support
15 With the tailstock removed, complete the shaping with a scraping tool
16 Removing the finished work from the face plate

Shaping workpiece Turn the back of the platter to shape with the tool rest positioned behind the work; for this, it is often an advantage to use sharp scraping tools and a card template if carrying out repetitive work. Position the tool rest across the front of the disc and part-hollow the work with a round-nosed scraper, still using the tailstock to apply pressure to the work throughout the turning operation to make sure it is not levered off its paper mounting. When the rim and a fair amount of the inside have been shaped, withdraw the tailstock and complete the remainder using scraping tools.

Gouges are not suitable for this type of turning. As with all operations using scraping tools, it is essential the tool rest is at the correct height with the cutting edge of the tool on or slightly below the centre line of the work and pointing slightly downwards.

Removing workpiece To remove the finished work from the face plate, tap the edge of a thin-bladed knife or chisel into the joint to break it, taking care not to damage the workpiece at the same time. You should then sand the base of the work to remove any remaining paper and adhesive.

13

14
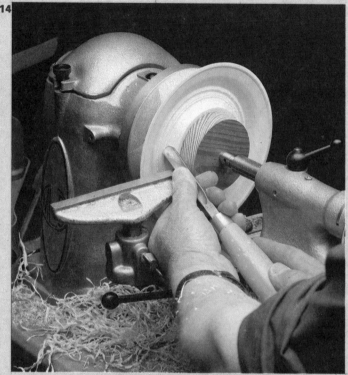

15
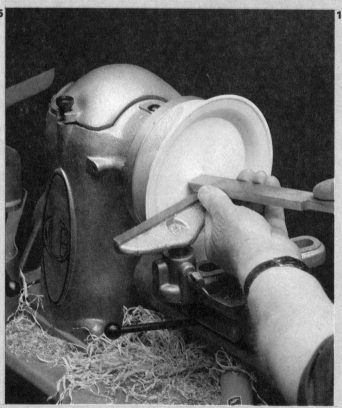

16
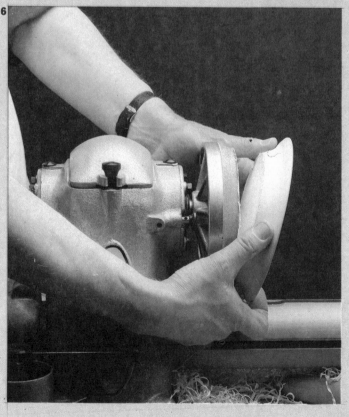

Using the woodscrew chuck on the lathe

Much of the pleasure and satisfaction you can gain from using a lathe can come from turning small, decorative items such as powder bowls, boxes with lids, egg cups, vases and goblets. You can often make these from offcuts of rare timbers which are not large enough for full size salad bowls and platters. These smaller items usually require special turning techniques and alternative methods of chucking at the headstock.

The standard face plate supplied with the lathe is often too large for this type of work and you need to use your ingenuity to adapt it to suit your requirements. You can buy various chucks and accessories to increase the flexibility of the lathe; for small items you will probably find the simple woodscrew chuck the most useful.

This small chuck will enable you to turn fairly large bowls as well as the smaller items; in its basic form it has an adjustable centre screw or it can be part of a combination chuck. The larger woodscrew chucks can be used as conventional small face plates if you use two or more securing screws.

Small projects You can turn many interesting items using one or more contrasting timbers glued together to form the basic timber; alternatively you could use a dark timber for the main body and a lighter piece for the lid. It is always best to choose timbers of the same characteristics and density; a hardwood bowl with a softwood lid, for example, could cause many expansion and contraction problems (softwood usually shrinks more).

With a woodscrew chuck you can utilize the odd ends of boards for small items when the grain runs across the diameter of the timber; this usually provides a good screw hold for the chuck. For even smaller items, such as drawer pulls, knobs and chessmen, use sections of timber which have the

grain running from end to end; these items often cause problems in chucking, however, since the woodscrews never hold too well in end grain and alternative chucking methods may have to be used.

Making a lidded bowl

For most turning operations of this type you will only need to secure work to the woodscrew chuck with the centre screw; additional screws are often provided in the back plate to give added support. This enables bowls in excess of 250mm (10in) diameter to be turned with the chuck.

Mounting work
For the simplest form of lidded bowl, the timber is cut with the grain running across the disc to provide a good screw hold. Plane or sand one side of the work perfectly flat and make a small centre hole with a bradawl; cut the work to a rough disc and screw it onto a woodscrew chuck. Make sure the work is bedded down flat against the face of the chuck back plate; if there is a gap, there could be turning problems later on. To be sure, slightly recess the centre of the work around the screw hole to give a flush fitting. Alternatively you could fit a timber ring, made of thin plywood or hardwood or a folded piece of abrasive paper or cloth, between the back of the work and the chuck to provide a non-slip mounting.

Rough turning
The initial operation is to turn the bowl roughly to size to provide a symmetrical shape; this will reduce the amount of vibration during the later stages of turning. With the tool rest positioned

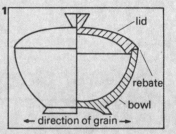

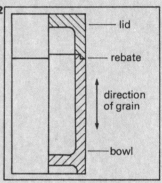

1 Shallow bowl and lid turned from separate wood discs
2 Deep bowl and lid turned from the same piece of wood and separated
3 Hardwood ring fitted between the work and the chuck to provide a secure mounting
4 Cleaning up the wood with a gouge; the bevel should be in contact with the work

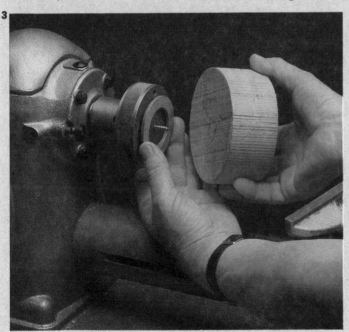

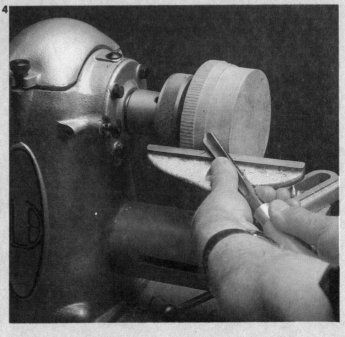

across the rim of the work at roughly centre height, set the lathe to run at the required speed for rough turning as described in Week 74. Clean up the edges of the work with a 12mm ($\frac{1}{2}$in) gouge which has an end ground to a finger-nail shape. Hold the tool with the side of the blade on the tool rest and the bevel resting on the work and pointing upwards at an angle of about 45 degrees. Cut from the face side of the work and move towards the face plate or woodscrew chuck; this will give a clean slicing cut. In all turning operations, remember any grain fibres damaged by dull or badly used tools can never be repaired with abrasives; it is therefore vital to keep your equipment in top condition.

You may prefer to use a scraping tool for the rough turning; hold the blade so it points down slightly to give a trailing action to the cut. Position the tool rest to produce a cut just below the centre line of the work.

Final turning
To clean up the rough cut, position the tool rest across the face side of the work and use a round or straight-ended scraping tool. Start from the outside of the work and make light cuts towards the centre; take a final finishing cut to produce an even surface.
Outside You can now turn the outside of the bowl to the desired shape with a 12mm ($\frac{1}{2}$in) gouge. You

5

6

7

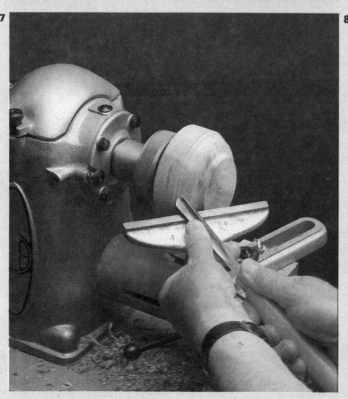

8

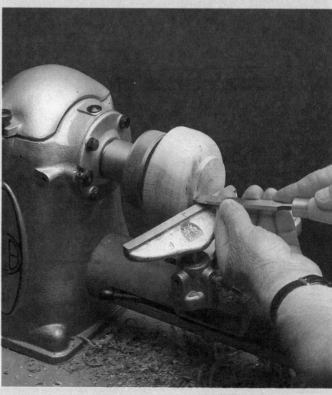

will find this tool useful for most shaping operations, on work either mounted between centres or held at the headstock. Keep the bevel of the gouge in contact with the work while you hold the blade on its side at a slight angle on the tool rest. Don't attempt heavy cuts; as with any wood-cutting operation on a machine, it is best to take a number of light cuts instead of one heavy one.

Base Turn the base of the bowl to shape using the 12mm (½in) gouge and a small square-ended scraping tool. At this stage you must decide which chucking method you will use to hollow out the partly turned work.

Hollowing out work

As you are already using a woodscrew chuck, the simplest method is to make a short blind hole in the centre of the base with a bradawl. Put the bradawl blade on the tool rest at a slight angle to the work, carefully advance the point into the work and bring the bradawl handle to a position at right-angles to the base; this will give you a perfectly central hole. Remove the partly turned work from the chuck, reverse it and remount it on the centre screw fixing. Alternatively turn a hollow timber chuck from a piece of scrap timber to accept the rim of the bowl base; fit the wood chuck to the woodscrew chuck as before. A third method involves using a combination chuck to hold the work; this accessory can be adapted to hold different work in a variety of ways.

Whichever chucking method you choose, hollow out by making a small depression in the centre of the base with a small round or square-nosed scraping tool. Open out the hole and deepen it with a series of sweeping cuts from the side of the work towards the centre until you form the required shape. Again it is essential to use sharp tools and at the correct angle to the work, taking light cuts. Take a final light cut with a newly sharpened edge, working from the outside to the centre of the hollow.

Checking for true

At this stage it is a good idea to stop the lathe and inspect the work. You may well find the surface of the bowl is still quite rough inside, especially where you have made cuts into sections of end grain. This is a common turning fault in hollow ware; you can usually repair the damage quickly by using a newly ground small-nosed scraping tool, taking light sweeping cuts. Alternatively use a small 12mm (½in) gouge ground to a finger-nail edge; hold the tool on the rest on its side at about 45 degrees to the face side of the work. Start the cut by letting the bevel of the tool rub the work and bringing on the cut by moving your right hand; as the cut proceeds, the bevel of the blade will follow the inside profile of the bowl. By moving the handle slightly from left to right, you can make the tool follow the inside profile; once you begin the cut, this requires very little effort. Always keep the blade on its side, never on its back or square on to the cut.

You will find in many hollowing jobs there is one small section where the walls of the work meet the bottom; this requires special attention. You may find it worthwhile to grind a special scraping tool to suit this particular profile. Finally sand and polish.

Shaping lid

Place the prepared block for the lid onto the wood-screw chuck or face plate and turn it roughly to shape and balance as already described. Using a sharp parting tool, form a small rebate in the lid which will allow the bowl to fit tightly over it. Take light cuts and a number of test fittings to avoid cutting the rebate oversize and to give a good finish. The lid and bowl fitting together properly depends very much upon the next stage.

Turn the underside of the lid to shape, using a round-nosed scraping tool; take light cuts to avoid damage to the grain formation. For shallow hollowing such as this you should not use the gouge. Sand and polish the underside; it is best to sand and polish each component as it is finished.

5 Alternatively clean up the wood using a scraping tool with the blade sloping slightly downwards
6 Cleaning up the face side of the work with a round nose scraper; keep the blade down
7 Using a gouge to shape the outside of the bowl
8 Shaping the base with a square-ended scraping tool
9 Using a bradawl to mark the centre of the base for rechucking
10 Hollowing out the bowl with a scraping tool

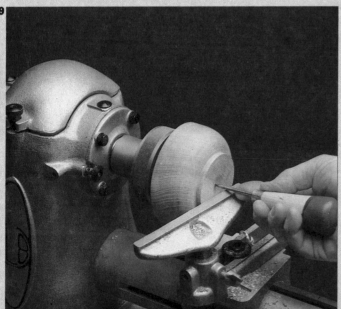

Finishing lid

Remove the lid and place the turned bowl on the woodscrew chuck or face plate; place the partly turned lid in the opening of the bowl (it should be a tight fit if you turned the rebate correctly). Advance the tailstock to give added support to the work. It is an advantage to use a live centre in the tailstock in this case; if you do not have one, use a spot of grease on the plain centre to prevent overheating and burning. Using the small gouge and scraping tools, turn the outside of the lid to shape. Also turn a small centre knob, removing the tailstock to complete the very centre of the knob. Finally sand the lid to shape, as always using decreasing grades of abrasive paper.

Using alternative methods

You could turn the lid from thinner timber and fit a separate small knob; this will use up scrap timber and the woodscrew chuck will prove invaluable. Turn the main bowl section and sand and polish it as described above. Mount a disc for the lid onto the woodscrew chuck and shape the underside and the rebate as before. Sand and polish the underside and reverse the partly turned lid in the chuck so you can turn the outside; you will not require the tailstock for this operation. Remove the lid and bore a central hole to accept the knob. Turn the knob from a small piece of scrap timber, preferably one which matches the bowl.

Same block It is often an advantage to turn both

11 Using a sharp parting tool to form a small rebate in the partly turned lid

12 Checking the bowl fits tightly with the lid; make several tests to avoid cutting the rebate oversize

13 Shaping the underside of the lid; take light cuts to avoid damaging the grain formation

14 Shaping the outside of the lid with a scraping tool; use the tailstock to give added support to the work

11
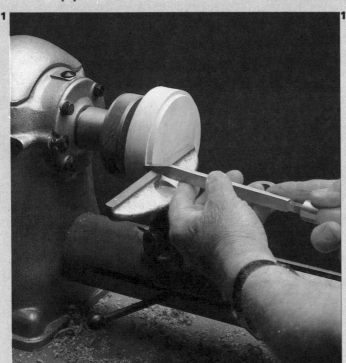

12
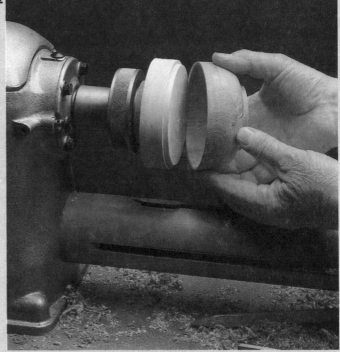

13
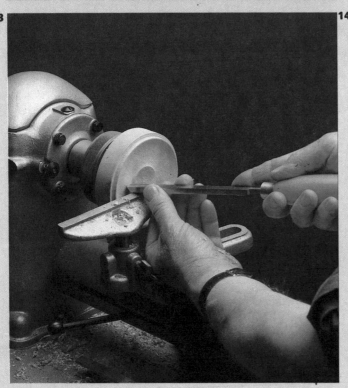

14
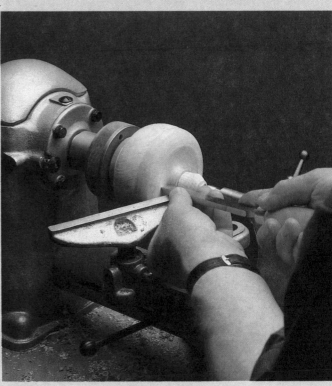

15 Shaping the knob with a 6mm gouge; remove the tailstock to complete the centre of the knob

16 Forming the base and the lid from one block of wood; shape the inside of the lid and the rebate with a parting tool

17 Separating the lid section from the base with a parting tool

18 Hollowing out the inside; check regularly to ensure the components are a good fit

components from the same block of timber, especially with small-lidded projects. Prunings from fruit and ornamental trees can provide materials for some attractive items which have colour and grain matching perfectly. Use a block of timber suitable in length for both lid and base (plus extra for waste), mount it on a woodscrew chuck and turn it roughly to a cylinder. Again it is often an advantage to advance the tailstock for support. With the tool rest across the end of the work, turn the inside of the lid to shape. Pay particular attention to the forming of the small rebate around the rim of the lid as before; use a small sharp scraper or parting tool for this and take light cuts only.

Use the parting tool to part-cut the lid from the

remainder of the block; sand and polish the lid and finally part it off completely. Bore out the base section and cut a small rebate around its rim to match that turned on the lid. Take light cuts with sharp tools and make test fittings with both sections as before. If the base section is to be quite deep, it is an advantage first to bore a blind hole down the centre of the block with a drill chuck and small bit mounted at the tailstock end. Place the lid on the hollowed base section; it should be a tight fit. Complete the remaining turning operations as before.

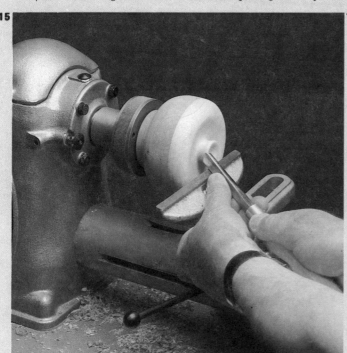

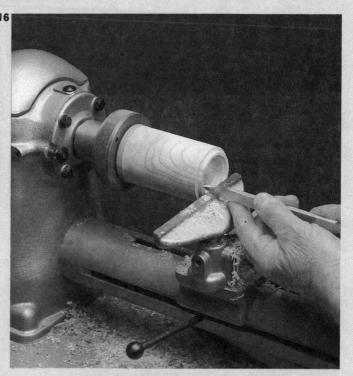

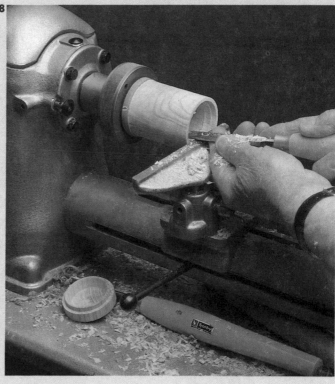

Boring and shaping on the lathe

Many interesting items can be turned using unlikely pieces of wood such as small branches from garden prunings, a log from the winter fuel store or a piece of driftwood collected during a seaside outing. The wood must be left to season before it is turned and often you will need to use special turning and chucking techniques if the work is to be completed satisfactorily.

Problems are likely to arise concerning the method used to hold the work securely on the lathe when it is to be bored or hollowed and held at one end of the lathe only. The standard face plate and woodscrew chuck are often inadequate in this situation since much of this work is carried out in end grain materials which are always difficult to secure with a conventional woodscrew. You should always consider the various stresses on a woodscrew fixing of any type where the work is over 75mm (3in) long. Again, a turning tool working on the extreme end of the work produces considerable leverage which can force the work off centre or even completely off the chuck.

Turning the work

You can produce attractive and useful items such as vases, spill and cigarette boxes, pepper mills and shakers and wine goblets by holding a pre-turned cylindrical piece of wood around its periphery at one end while hollowing and turning is carried out. Various chucks are available for this type of work; alternatively you can make up a chucking device using the standard face plate.

Shaping the cylinder A 6 in 1 combination chuck with its various attachments is most useful and can be used to hold small pieces of wood for turning and also for holding large diameter work or long lengths of wood which are to be bored and turned. The wood requires minimal preparation prior to mounting on the lathe. When using the chuck for boring and shaping work, the wood should be centred on the lathe in the same way as for basic spindle turning. Roughly turn it to a cylinder of a suitable diameter to fit within the chuck, allowing a small amount of waste for the eventual parting off. If the wood has a few burrs or the ends of small branches showing, you should take particular care with the initial setting of the lathe, rotating the work by hand to ensure it clears the tool rest.

Use a gouge about 25mm (1in) wide to shape the wood to a cylinder, taking the first cut about 13mm ($\frac{1}{2}$in) from the tailstock mounting. Hold the tool at a 15 degree angle to the workpiece with the blade tilted slightly on its right side on the tool rest, making sure the bevel is rubbing; bring on the cut by raising your right hand. Make the cut towards the tailstock and continue the cutting process along the work to a point about 50mm (2in) from the headstock end of the lathe. At this point you should reverse the hold of the tool so the blade is reversed and the gouge is resting on its left side pointing

1 Checking the roughly shaped workpiece clears the tool rest
2 Taking the first cut with a gouge
3 Reversing the blade of the tool to work from left to right for the final cuts
Using a 6 in 1 chuck:
4 Cutting a groove in the work at the tailstock end with a parting tool; the groove allows the work to be secured in the chuck
5 Checking the groove for fit against the split rings of the chuck
6 Fitting the work into the chuck

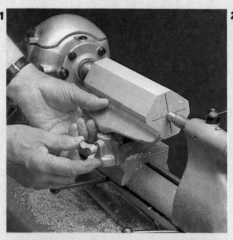

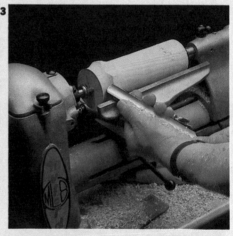

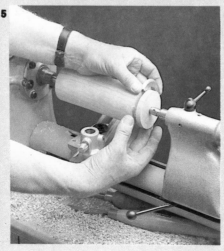
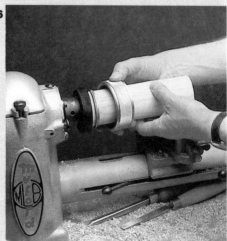

upwards and to the left at about a 15 degree angle; holding the gouge in this manner will produce a slicing action which gives a clean cut.

Securing work for hollowing You should now decide on the type of chuck you are going to use for the rest of the turning operations. If you will be using a commercial chuck such as the 6 in 1 universal, you should cut a small groove at the headstock end to allow the workpiece to be secured within the chuck. If, however, you are using a home-made chuck utilizing the standard face plate, a method used on a power drill lathe attachment, you will have to turn a small tenon or dowel at one end to fit within the prepared chuck.

To prepare a standard face plate to hold the work, screw a 25mm (1in) thick disc of wood such as laminboard or thick ply to the face plate in the normal manner; make sure the outside is trued up with a scraping tool to a perfect circle and the face side is made perfectly flat with a square-ended scraper. Use a small scraping tool to bore a centre hole to accept the partly turned cylinder which you then glue in position; you can use the tailstock as an end-to-end clamping device while the glue sets.

It is worth pointing out at this stage that securing work with a home-made chuck as described is quite suitable for many one-off jobs; but where you are undertaking repetitive work it is better to use a commercial chuck.

Hollowing out work With the work secured within the chuck and the face plate secure on the headstock, you can begin to hollow out the work. For this you can use standard turning tools, a boring bit held in the tailstock or a combination of both. To bore with the turning tools, first position the

tool rest across the end of the work at a height which will place the cutting edge of the scraping tool on a line with the centre of the work when the blade is held flat on the tool rest. Use a small round nose scraping tool to make a small depression in the centre of the revolving wood – which should be turning at about 1500–2000rpm – to serve as a starting point for the hollowing. Using a square-ended scraper about 12mm (½in) wide start to bore out the centre applying a steady forward pressure to the tool. Continue boring until the desired depth is reached; while you are working you should withdraw the tool frequently to remove the waste.

If you use a woodboring bit mounted in a drill chuck held in the tailstock, you will be able to produce a starting hole much more quickly. With this type of work where you are boring into the end grain, it is best to use a saw tooth bit since this produces a clean hole and does not wander; flat bits should be fed slowly into the work otherwise they can run off centre. Conventional twist bits are not suitable.

Saw tooth bits should be used at the correct speed to produce a good cutting action with the minimum of overheating. Suitable speeds are:

Bit diameter	Speed
10mm (⅜in)	1000rpm
12mm (½in)	750rpm
19mm (¾in)	500rpm
25mm (1in)	400rpm
38mm (1½in)	250rpm
51mm (2in)	200rpm

Sometimes it may not be possible to choose the correct speed on the lathe; to help prevent over-

7 Tightening the 6 in 1 chuck with a chuck spanner
8 Making a small depression with a round nose scraping tool in the centre of the work
9 Boring out the centre hole with a square-ended scraper
Using home-made chucks:
10 Turning a dowel at one end of the work to fit within the chuck
11 Using a scraping tool to bore a hole in the chuck to accept the part-turned work
12 Securing the work; use the tailstock as a support while the adhesive dries

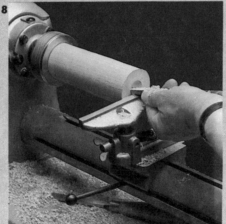

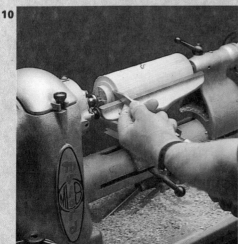

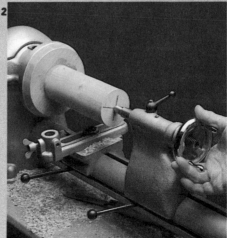

heating and remove any build-up of waste at the same time, you should withdraw the bit from the work frequently when you are carrying out any boring operations.

To keep the saw tooth cutters in good condition sharpen them with a few strokes from a small file or carborundum slipstone; make sure you sharpen both cutters on the underside, maintaining the manufacturer's angle. The saw teeth should rarely need attention; if they do, sharpen them sparingly on top – never file the rim.

After the initial boring you can enlarge the centre hole by making a series of light cuts on the left side of the hole with a square-ended scraper; don't cut heavily since the best results will be obtained with light cuts.

Where you are going to use a glass or plastic insert as a liner, such as a small test tube in a vase for single flower blooms, you should make frequent tests for fit when the lathe has stopped; never do this, however, when the lathe is moving.

Final shaping Turning the outside of the work is carried out in the normal manner using a gouge and chisel; the tailstock is used to support the free end of the work and a small tapered wood plug inserted in the open end of the work on which the tailstock centre can bear. Work progressively from the tailstock end of the lathe towards the headstock, leaving a small section as waste to be parted off when the project is completed. Take light slicing cuts with the gouge; the blade should be held at a slight angle to the work with the bevel of the tool in contact with it.

Wood with the grain running along its length can be used to produce interesting tall boxes with the grain matching on both the lid and body. Turning and boring procedures for this type of project are the same as described above, but the wood for the lid must be parted off from the rough cylinder in the early stages of turning. The lid must be shaped on its inside and a rebate formed using a hollow wood chuck fitted to the face plate; the partly turned lid is then placed on the bored-out block and turned to shape with the rest of the project.

Finishing the work

Where the beauty of the wood grain is a particular feature you should use non-staining polishes for finishing. After a good sanding with progressively finer grades of abrasive paper you should rub fine steel wool over the surface of the work as it rotates to remove any sanding rings which may have formed. Apply a coat of clear or white French polish or other type of non-staining polish with a brush or cloth pad and allow it to dry; then apply a second coat. Where French polish is used, the first coat may have raised the grain slightly; if so, rub lightly with fine steel wool before applying the second for a good satin finish.

Where a matt finish is required you can burnish the work with a handful of shavings. For a high shine, apply a light application of clear or white French polish while the work rotates at speed; keep the polishing pad moving quickly over the surface of the revolving work and don't allow it to stop in any one position. Many items can be completely polished while on the lathe, with a small waste area left at one end for the final parting off. You should take great care when you are using the parting tool so you do not damage the finished surface.

13 Using a woodboring bit mounted on a drill chuck for hollowing out
14 Shaping the outside of the work with a large gouge; use a turned plug inside the bored hole so the tailstock can be used for support
15 Making a detail cut with a small gouge
16 Burnishing the work with coarse shavings
17 Parting off the work after finishing; take care not to damage the surface
18 The finished article after French polishing on the lathe

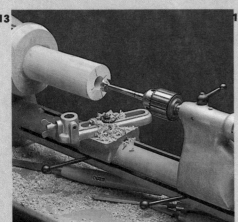
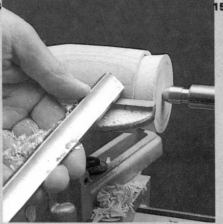

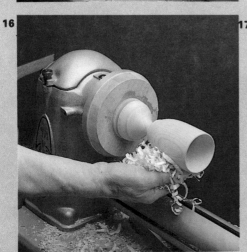

Turning rings, wheels and frames on the lathe

Many woodturning projects appear to be quite simple until you begin to put theory into practice. The best method of tackling the work is not always immediately obvious, but as you become more experienced in the art of woodturning you will be able to analyse the job in hand and decide which means of holding the work, which tools and which turning procedures will produce the best results.

Turned rings, model wheels and rebated circular frames are typical of a range of items which, although basic in appearance, require some consideration of the methods of chucking and general turning procedure. Like the lidded bowl described earlier, these objects are examples of work which cannot be turned between lathe centres or where the use of the standard face plate would be unsatis-

factory. Here an alternative method of holding the work is necessary and, although there are several proprietary holding devices available, the simple chuck made from offcuts of wood is often the best choice.

Making a ring

The first stage in making a wood ring is to mount a roughly cut disc of wood onto a woodscrew chuck, preferably using a backing disc of hardboard or folded abrasive paper to prevent slipping and damage to the work. Position the tool rest close to the edge of the disc at a height which will allow a small gouge, about 12mm (½in) wide, to cut a little above the centre line of the work. Holding the blade of the gouge between the fingers of your left hand

1 When turning a ring, make the first cut on the outside edge with a small gouge
2 Continue with the gouge on its side, making a clean cut at each stage
3 Reverse the direction of the cut to remove any roughness from the rear edge
4 Clean up the face side of the work with a scraper

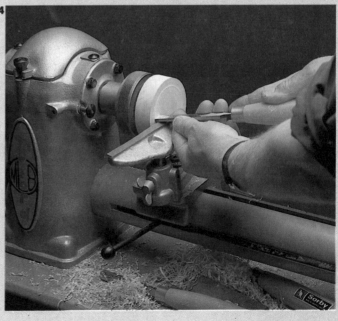

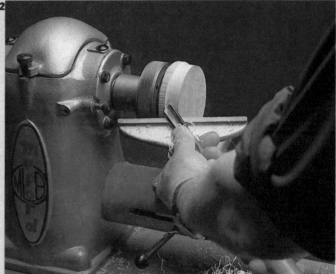

and the handle in your right, start to make a light cut on the outside edge of the disc; the blade of the tool should be on its left side at about 60 degrees to the tool rest and the bevel should be in contact with the surface of the wood.

Cutting wood in this manner and advancing the tool from right to left across the periphery of the disc will ensure a good clean cut with shavings coming away from the cutting edge; this is particularly useful when working with softwood or timber which has a difficult grain formation. You can, of course, use a scraping tool, in which case the blade should be held almost horizontally to the work; but bear in mind the general finish may not be wholly satisfactory.

When making the first cut with a gouge it is often an advantage to reverse the hold on the tool to make a light cut from left to right of the edge of the disc; this will remove any roughness at the rear edge and ensure the back of the disc is not frayed or split. Where repetitive work is envisaged, you should check the diameter of the work frequently with calipers; this will simplify the making of a suitable chuck in which the partly turned work will eventually be completed.

General shaping Using a round or square-ended scraping tool you can now true up the face side of the disc to the required dimensions; remember to raise the handle of the tool so the cutting edge is pointing slightly downwards but still cutting on the centre line of the work. Mark out the depth of the ring, which should be equal to the thickness of the disc of wood, with a pair of dividers and use a thin parting tool to cut a deep groove on the inside of the scribed mark. The tool should be square on to the work and the cut should be made on the centre line; withdraw the blade frequently to clear the waste and prevent the end of the tool overheating.

The face side and part of the rim of the ring can now be turned to shape with a 9–12mm ($\frac{3}{8}$–$\frac{1}{2}$in) gouge. Again the blade should be held on its right side when cutting towards the centre of the disc and on its left side when cutting towards the outside. In all cases the bevel of the gouge must be in contact with the wood. To ensure the ring is an even shape, it is a good idea to draw a pencil line round the centre of the periphery.

Using form tool Where the wood is reasonably hard a shaped scraping tool, called a form tool, can be used. This is ground to the profile required, used as

5 Use dividers to mark the depth of the ring, which should be the same as the thickness of the disc
6 Cut a deep groove inside the scribed mark with a parting tool
7 Continue shaping the inside with a small gouge
8 Use the same gouge to shape the outside of the ring

5

6
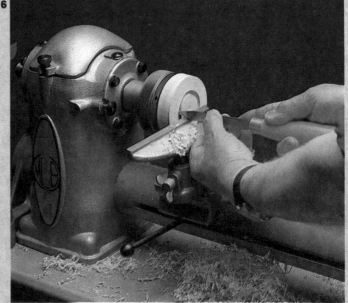

7
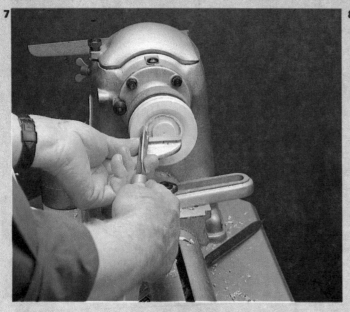

8
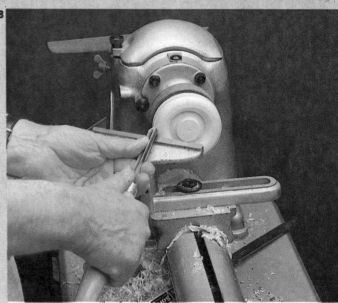

a normal scraping tool and pushed into the wood to form the shape; as with any scraping tool, never use force since a rough finish will result.

To shape the remainder of the ring you can either reverse the disc on the woodscrew chuck or use a hollow wood chuck. Using the woodscrew chuck is probably the simplest method and is quite satisfactory provided the centre screw is accurately mounted. Mark the centre of the partly turned ring with a bradawl, remove it from the chuck then reverse and remount it. Turn the remaining part of the ring as already described, after scribing the face side of the reversed disc. Shape the outside of the ring before tackling the inside and parting off; clean up the outside of the work as you progress.

Using hollow wood chuck After parting off the ring from the centre disc there is always a small area on the inside which requires further finishing; here you will find it helpful to use a hollow wood chuck turned from a piece of hardwood and mounted on a face plate. Use a square-ended scraper to form a recess on the face side which will accept the diameter of the ring, making frequent checks to ensure a perfect fit. If you find the wood chuck is very slightly oversize and the ring can be withdrawn easily, a little water applied to the inside of the chuck should make it expand for a perfect fit; alternatively you can place a piece of newspaper between the work and the chuck.

With the partly turned work held in the chuck you can complete the remainder of the turning and finishing.

Making a wheel
Turned wood wheels can be made in a very similar manner. The outside is shaped first as already described and is reversed on the woodscrew chuck; but the ring or tyre of the wheel is not parted off from the centre boss.

Making circular frame
The technique of turning a rebated circular frame is similar to turning a ring, except a mandrel chuck is used; in this case the work fits over the chuck rather than inside it as with the hollow wood chuck.

With this type of project, you can achieve good results by using wood recovered from an old piece of furniture; but bear in mind the wood is likely to be extremely hard and you will need to sharpen

9 Remove the partly turned ring, reverse it and remount it on the woodscrew chuck
10 Shape the ring with a form tool; use the tool gently for a smooth finish
11 Remove the ring after parting off
12 Remount the ring on a hollow wood chuck and finish inside with a scraper

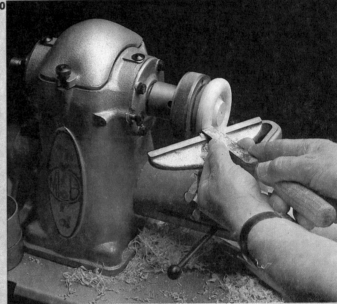

13

14

15

16

17

your turning tools frequently to obtain a satisfactory finish. Plane the wood on one side and mount it on a woodscrew chuck; turn it to the required overall diameter and true up the face side with scraping tools. On the face side of the disc use a small square-ended scraper to turn a recess which will accept the item to be framed, first scribing the area to be removed. Again if you intend to turn several frames, check the diameter of the work frequently.

Now turn a chuck from a scrap disc of wood, mounted on the woodscrew chuck or a face plate, over which the partly turned frame will fit; there is no need to be too particular about the finish of the chuck since a slightly rough surface can often be an advantage. If the frame fits loosely on the chuck, apply a little water to the outside or use a piece of newspaper to provide the necessary adjustment.

The final shaping of the frame can now be carried out. Using a small gouge or scraper turn the outside to shape, paying particular attention to the position of the tool rest to ensure a good cutting action. If using a gouge, make sure you hold it at a slight angle to the work with the bevel of the tool in contact with the wood to prevent any cutting problems.

13 When turning a circular frame, form a recess in the disc to accept the item to be framed
14 Check the item fits snugly in the recess
15 Fit the partly turned frame onto a mandrel chuck
16 Use a small gouge to carry out the final shaping
17 The finished articles: (from left) a ring, a circular frame and a wheel

Turning hollow ware

Many projects can be made by turning and polishing a rough piece of wood on the lathe using the same face plate or woodscrew chuck. This is a particularly useful way of using up offcuts of wood which accumulate in any woodturner's workshop. Other articles, because of their shape, will probably require two or more separate operations on the lathe and for these you might need specially prepared home-made chucks or holding devices to avoid spoiling the work. Whichever method you use, make sure screw holes and external bruises caused by chucking are not visible after the work is completed.

We describe below how to make a simple salt and pepper shaker set; wine goblets, spill vases and egg cups can all be made in a similar fashion. These popular items of tableware do present a few problems and are not the straightforward pieces of turning they might at first seem. When working on any project which entails boring a hole, think carefully about the method of turning and bore the hole while the wood is rough, before you start shaping. For example, when making a candle holder always bore the hole for the candle first; use this hole to centre the work for the remainder of the turning. Even with turned legs the holes for the stretchers should be bored while the wood is in the square – before final turning. If you attempt to bore the hole after shaping the outside, it will be difficult to centre it in the work.

1 Side elevation and section of salt, pepper and mustard pot set
2 Plan view of set
3 To make salt shaker first mount turned cylinder on woodscrew chuck and bore centre hole to required depth; counterbore hole to take base disc
4 Reverse and remount work using tailstock for support and turn external shape
5 Complete shaker by drilling holes in top for salt

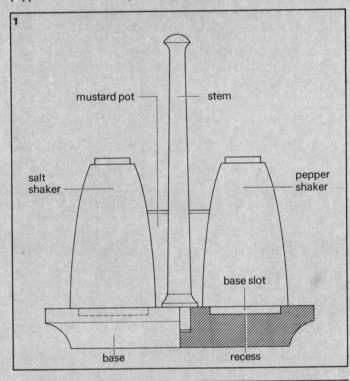

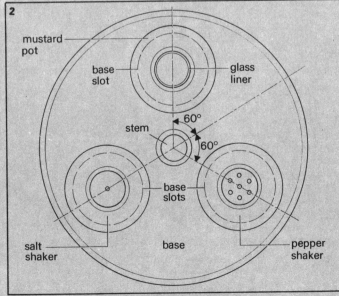

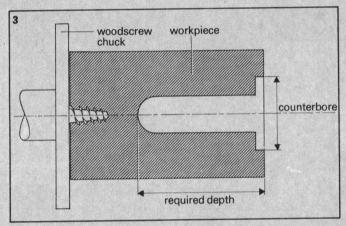

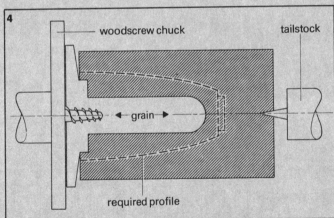

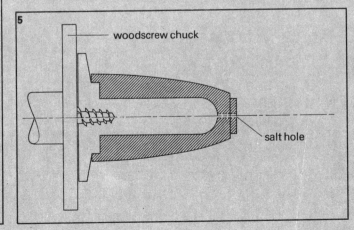

6 Using gouge to turn piece of wood to cylinder slightly larger in size than finished project

7 Using parting tool to shape end to be mounted on woodscrew chuck

8 Screwing workpiece onto woodscrew chuck; place abrasive paper between chuck and workpiece to prevent wood slipping

9 Marking on shank of saw tooth bit depth of hole to be drilled

Preparing the wood

Prepare the rough blocks of wood for mounting on the woodscrew chuck or similar holding device. Square the blocks with a saw or plane and mark the true centres with diagonal lines in the usual way; use a bradawl to make a small hole at these points to help mounting on the lathe between the centres. Check the tool rest for height, making sure the work clears the edges of the rest when rotated by hand.

Using an 18–24mm ($\frac{3}{4}$–1in) gouge, roughly turn the wood to a cylinder a little larger in diameter than the finished size of the project. Start at the tailstock end of the block and make a series of adjacent cuts, holding the blade of the tool at an angle to the work. You do not need a smooth finish at this stage since the object is to remove the corners of the wood to produce a cylinder which is reasonably in balance.

Clean up the tailstock end of the wood with a parting tool on edge to produce a slightly concave base for mounting on the woodscrew chuck. Remove the prepared block from between the lathe centres and, after boring a small centre hole with a bradawl or twist bit, remount the cleaned end of the block on the screw of the woodscrew chuck. Always take great care when mounting a wood-screw into end grain. It is preferable to have a prebored centre hole about half the diameter of the woodscrew of the chuck rather than driving the screw into the wood with brute force.

To ensure the work does not slip while mounted on the woodscrew chuck, fold a piece of abrasive cloth or paper (abrasive on the outside) and place it between the face of the chuck and the end of the wood to be turned.

Boring the hole

The first stage in making the project is to bore a centre hole of about 19mm ($\frac{3}{4}$in) diameter. Do this by using a saw tooth or flat bit mounted in the jaws of a drill chuck fitted in the tailstock. The lathe

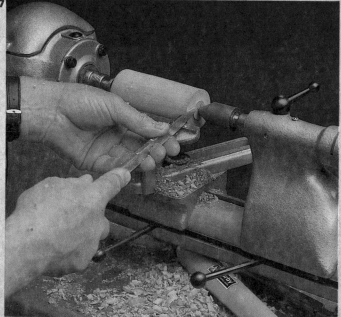

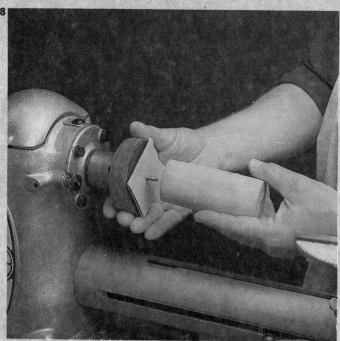

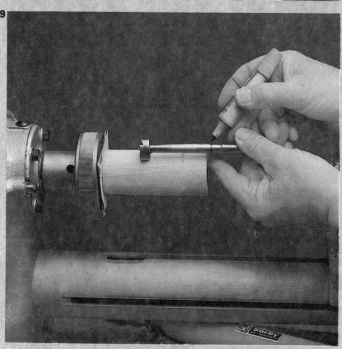

should be running at a speed of about 1000rpm; any higher speed will cause the bit to overheat. To bore the hole to a predetermined depth, make a mark on the stem of the bit with a pencil or a piece of adhesive tape. The bit should be frequently withdrawn from the hole to clear the waste and prevent the bit clogging or overheating.

Position the tool rest across the end of the bored block and, using a parting tool or a small square-ended scraper, form a recess or rebate to take a small, turned wood disc in which a further small hole is bored to accept a small cork or rubber bung. Remove the bored block from the woodscrew chuck and repeat the process with the other shaker; use a scrap piece of wood of dimensions which allow it to be turned to a diameter so it can fit snugly inside the partly turned block. Take care when doing this and use a pair of calipers or a sizing tool set to the diameter of the boring bit to ensure a perfect fit.

If you make a slight error when turning this small

mandrel chuck, wrap adhesive tape or thin twine round the wood to provide a positive hold; even a dampened cloth will often expand the wood sufficiently to provide a perfect fit.

Shaping the wood

Mount the prebored block on the prepared chuck using the bored hole; use the tailstock to support the free end of the work. To avoid damaging the work use a live or ball-bearing centre mounted on the tailstock in place of a normal plain centre. To minimize the possibility of cutting through from the outside to the bored inside, make a pencil mark on the outside corresponding to the depth of the internal hole.

Using a small round-ended gouge, turn the outside to shape; leave a small area as waste at the tailstock end. Take light cuts with a sharp tool to avoid separating the work from the chuck. If the extreme end of the work is end grain, shape it with a skew chisel; place the blade on its edge on the tool

10 Boring centre hole with saw tooth bit
11 Making rebate in base of block to take wood disc
12 Mounting block on prepared mandrel chuck
13 Shaping outside of block using round-ended gouge

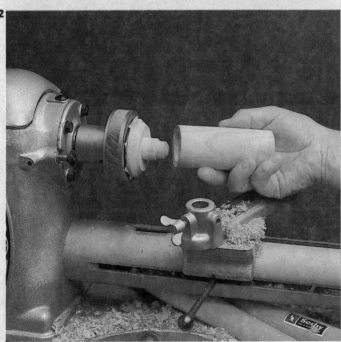

rest and, with the bevel rubbing the work, use the centre, or just below the centre, of the blade to cut through the grain fibre. When the outside turning is almost completed and a little waste is left at the tailstock, remove the tailstock completely from the work and carefully remove the waste with the skew chisel to produce a clean rounded end.

Bore the necessary small holes in the end – for the salt shaker a single hole of about 2mm (or $\frac{1}{16}$ in) and for the pepper a number of much smaller holes. To do this remove the woodscrew chuck from the headstock and mount the drill chuck in its place; this will allow the lathe to be used as a horizontal boring machine. Hold each shaker by hand and use the tool rest for support. After boring the holes, remount the work on the woodscrew chuck mandrel and sand and polish it to a smooth finish.

To make the small wood inserts to fit into the base of the rebate of the shaker, mount a small piece of wood on the woodscrew chuck and turn it to a cylinder of the right diameter to fit snugly into the

base of the shaker. Next, with the drill chuck mounted in the tailstock, bore a 13mm ($\frac{1}{2}$in) hole a short way into the end of the block. Using a parting tool, cut off the discs from the turned wood.

Turning the base
You can either use the shaker on its own or mount it on an attractive turned base, which can serve as a further chucking and turning exercise.

Turn the centre stem of the base by taking a length of hardwood about $200 \times 25 \times 25$mm ($8 \times 1 \times 1$in), mounting it between lathe centres and turning it to a slender shape with both the gouge and the skew chisel. Since this is of small cross-section, use the highest speed on the lathe to obtain a good cutting action and clean finish; 2500–3000rpm is ideal. Using the parting tool, turn a small spigot or tenon at the headstock end of the stem to about 13–16mm ($\frac{1}{2}$–$\frac{5}{8}$in) diameter. Leave a small section as waste at each end; this can be removed later with hand tools. Sand the workpiece

14 Removing waste at end of block with skew chisel
15 Boring small holes in end of pepper shaker
16 Using calipers to check diameter of wood plugs to fit in base of shaker
17 Parting off wood plugs

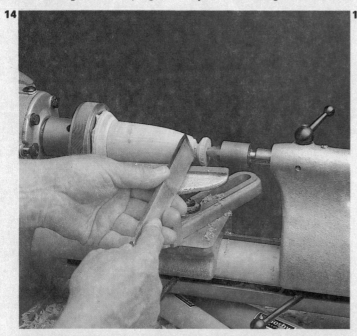

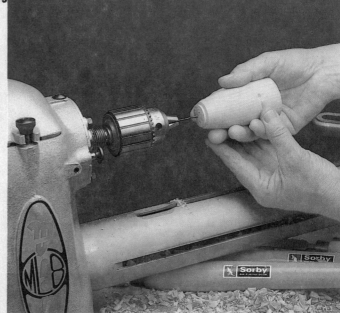

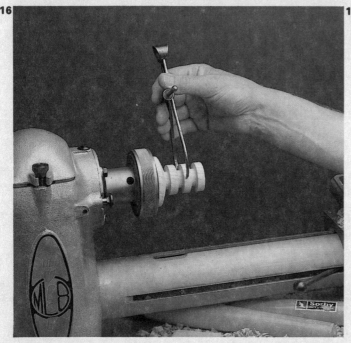

and polish with abrasive paper as you proceed.

The base is turned from a 150mm (6in) disc of 25mm (1in) stock, preferably planed true and flat on one side. This side is then mounted on a prepared face plate; use the paper and adhesive (paper sandwich) method since this will leave a perfectly smooth base after turning, with no unsightly screw holes. To do this, screw a disc of wood to the face plate; the workpiece is then glued to this with a piece of thick paper between the two items. Allow time for the adhesive to set before starting to turn.

Turn the disc to shape, first by using the gouge to true up the outside of the disc and then with the scraping tool to give the face side a perfectly flat finish. When using the scraper, don't forget to position the tool rest so the blade of the tool points slightly downwards when the cutting edge is on the centre line of the work. The rim of the disc should be shaped by using the gouge held well over on its side so the tip of the tool gives a slicing cut to the wood; this will ensure a smooth finish.

Using the parting tool or a small square-ended scraping tool, bore a blind hole in the centre of the turned disc; use the previously turned stem to test for fit. Take care in this operation since the centre-turned stem must fit exactly in the base.

After sanding and polishing, remove the base from the face plate and break the paper sandwich with a chisel. Sand off any paper adhering to the base to complete the project.

Making an egg cup

Egg cups are turned in much the same way, although some people prefer to bore and turn in one mounting. In this case the rough wood is mounted on the woodscrew chuck, hollowed out with a small round nose scraper, turned to shape on the outside with the gouge and parted off with the parting tool.

18 Using gouge to shape base stem while turning between centres
19 Shaping rim of base with gouge
20 Fitting stem into centre of base
21 Turned salt, pepper and mustard pot set

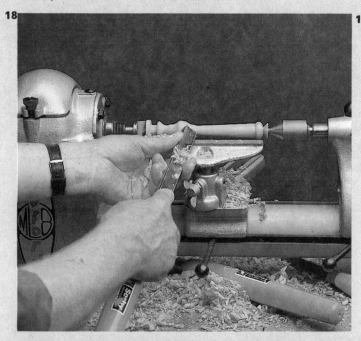

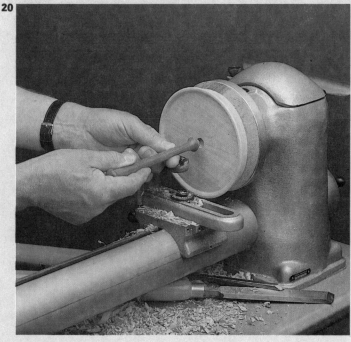

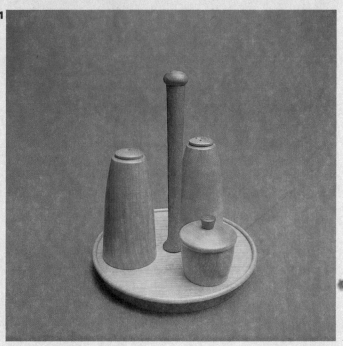

Off-centre turning on the lathe

The art of woodturning is often described as making wood articles on the lathe in the round; this refers to such pieces as hollow ware, table legs and lamp bases. With a little skill, however, it is possible to produce articles such as hammer handles, cabriole legs and oval table lamps which are not round. This work is called off-centre turning between lathe centres and often entails using more than one centre position at each end. In this article we explain how to turn an oval hammer handle, a cabriole leg and a foot.

Turning a hammer handle

In this type of work it is essential to choose your timber carefully; use a fairly long and straight, close-grained hardwood such as ash in which the grain runs from end to end. Avoid short grain wood where the grain appears to run diagonally since this type of wood is not strong enough.

Square the stock from which the items are to be turned in the usual way and carefully plot the true centre of the wood at each end. At both ends of the work mark two off-centres on opposite sides of the true centre and 4–6mm ($\frac{3}{16}$–$\frac{1}{4}$in) away from it; number these 'one' and 'two' at both ends. Mark the off-centre shape by sight or with a pair of compasses or dividers; if you use the latter, it will give you a fairly accurate idea of the final turned shape.

Draw ridge lines connecting the end axes as a guide during turning. A certain amount of vibration is unavoidable with this type of turning, so it is essential to select a suitable lathe speed which will keep it to a minimum and avoid turning work of a large diameter. If you are using a drill-powered lathe attachment, use the slowest speed of the drill and use wood of less than 63mm (2½in) cross-section.

Mounting work Mount the wood between the lathe centres using the number one off-centre position at both ends. Check the tailstock is secure on the lathe bed and, if using a plain centre in the tailstock, apply a small amount of grease to prevent the wood burning at that end. Check the pronged driving centre is secure in the end of the wood and provides a positive drive; position the tool rest at a suitable working height. It is a good idea at this stage to rotate the work by hand to ensure it clears the edge of the tool rest.

Roughing out Take a fairly wide gouge – 18–25mm ($\frac{3}{4}$–1in) is ideal – ground to a finger nail or rounded end. Ensure it is sharp by using a small, hand-held slipstone, first on the bevel of the tool and then on the inside of the blade. Switch on the lathe at a speed of about 1500rpm for the initial roughing out and start to round off the work. Make your first cut in the normal manner at the tailstock end of the

Turning a hammer handle:
1 Having marked the true centres, scribe the off-centre positions at both ends of the work
2 To act as a guide, draw ridge lines connecting the end axes
3 Using the number one off-centre positions, partly turn the work to the ridge line
4 Ensure you maintain the ridge line during the initial rounding off
5 Remount the wood on the number two off-centre positions
6 Turn the work to an oval shape with a gouge

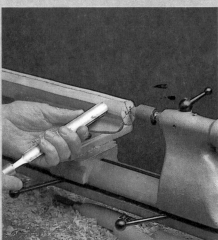

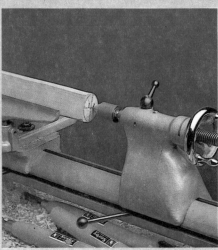

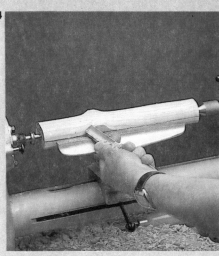

7 Remount the work on the true centres and turn the handle to the required shape
8 Finish off by smoothing the work with abrasive paper
Making a cabriole leg:
9 Using a skew chisel, cut a deep vee in the work at the point which is to remain in the square
10 Using a gouge, open up the vee on the right-hand side of the cut
11 Working on the true centres, form the foot base with a round nose gouge
12 Remount the tailstock end of the work on the second centre position and adjust the tool rest

work, holding the gouge slightly on its side and pointing upwards at an angle of about 45 degrees; keep the bevel of the blade in contact with the wood. You can use a round nose scraping tool if you prefer, although the finish will not be so good. Hold the blade of the tool flat on the tool rest and cut progressively along the work from right to left. Throughout the initial rounding off process take great care to retain the ridge line which runs from end to end of the work since it will assist you in making a true oval shape.

When turning near the headstock it is always best to reverse the hold on the gouge and make the final cuts towards the tailstock. Finally, using the gouge well over on its side, make a light cut from end to end of the work to produce a reasonably smooth finish, still keeping the ridge lines.

Remounting the wood Remove the wood from between the lathe centres and remount it on the number two off-centre positions. Repeat the turning process, beginning at the tailstock end of the work, and make a series of adjacent cuts with the gouge along the work, taking care to keep the ridge lines clean and uncut throughout.

Stop the lathe and inspect your work, which will not be quite oval at this stage. It is quite easy to produce a near-true oval with a little sanding, preferably with a length of abrasive cloth held on the work while it is rotating; always remove the tool rest before you begin sanding.

Most oval tool handles are shaped to fit a particular metal head and to provide a comfortable hand-hold. To do this remount the work on the

lathe using the true centres and turn the wood to the required shape with a gouge or scrapers. When shaping always cut from the larger diameter down to the smaller to produce a good clean finish.

Finally sand the work to a good finish, preferably using both the true and off-centre positions; keep the abrasive paper or cloth moving all the time to prevent unsightly sanding rings.

Warning Take care with your lathe speed when using this method of turning and keep it low enough to avoid excessive vibration. Also keep an eye on the oval shape of the piece; when turning any item there should never be more than 13mm ($\frac{1}{2}$in) between the normal centre of the workpiece and the off-centres.

Turning a cabriole leg

Another piece which is turned by the off-centre method and will be of particular interest to makers and repairers of furniture is the club-footed or cabriole leg. Here you will only need normal centres and one off-centre at the tailstock end. Square the wood carefully and mark the true centre at both ends; where a section of the wood is to be left in the square to make mortise joints, define the area clearly with diagonal pencil marks.

Place the wood between the lathe centres in the normal way, secure the tailstock and tool rest and carefully cut a deep vee into the work at the point which is to remain in the square using the point of a skew chisel. Using a 12mm ($\frac{1}{2}$in) gouge ground to a finger nail end open up the vee on the right side of the cut; keep the bevel of the gouge in contact with

the wood to produce a clean paring cut and make the cut towards the squared end. Round off the remainder of the leg with a gouge in the usual manner, working from the tailstock towards the squared end.

Forming foot Turn the end of the work to form the underside of the foot of the leg; you can use the heel of the skew chisel for rounding over the work, although a small round-ended gouge held well over on its side is best for this operation. Always keep the bevel of the gouge in contact with the wood. Remove the tailstock from the centre of the work and replace it in the second centre positioned about 13mm (½in) from the true centre; keep the normal pronged driving centre at the opposite end of the work in its original position. Move the tool rest further forward to allow for the extra movement created by the wood being placed off-centre at the tailstock end and check for clearance between the wood and the lathe and tool rest by rotating it by hand. When you are first attempting this type of work use a low lathe speed.

Using a small gouge or a round nose scraper, start to turn the toe and ankle of the leg. Begin the cut about 50mm (2in) from the end of the work and make a series of cuts from both sides to form a slight hollow, keeping the bevel of the gouge in contact with the work and always working from the larger diameter down to the smaller. Stop the lathe frequently to inspect the work. Once the general shape of the foot is correct, turn the remainder of the leg to a gentle taper.

While turning this type of work you can often see the outline or 'ghost' of the finished leg if you hold a plain or white background beneath it; this helps you to correct any turning errors.

Finishing off After the leg has been turned to the required shape sand it to a smooth finish, preferably using a length of abrasive cloth moved along the surface. Alternatively you can sand by hand with the abrasive cloth or paper held underneath the rotating work; finish off with the lathe at rest and sand along the length of the wood.

Turning a foot

When making floor lampstands or small stools, you will often need a small off-centre turned leg or foot to make the project more stable; to make this you can use a woodscrew chuck. First mount a short length of 50mm (2in) square wood on the centre of a woodscrew chuck and turn it to a rough cylinder with a small 12mm (½in) gouge as described earlier in the book. Use the gouge on its side, first rounding over the end of the partly turned block to form a base to the foot; keep the bevel of the tool rubbing against the wood. You can use a scraper here if you wish, although the finish will be rougher. Remove the partly turned work from the woodscrew chuck and make another centre with a bradawl about 9–13mm (⅜–½in) from the first. Remount the workpiece on the chuck using this second centre. Again, the work will be slightly out of balance so there will be a certain amount of vibration; you can reduce this by lowering the speed of the lathe.

To shape the toe and ankle follow the same procedure as for the cabriole leg; using the 12mm (½in) gouge, make alternate cuts from each side to form a slight hollow. Finally use the parting tool to form a small spigot or dowel. The completed work is then sanded and cut away from the waste to complete the project.

13 Shape the toe and ankle of the foot using a small gouge
14 Turn the remainder of the leg to a gentle taper
15 Sand the work to a smooth finish
Making an off-centre foot:
16 Turn the wood to a rough cylinder, using the true centres of the block
17 Mount the work on the second centre position and use a gouge to shape the toe and ankle of the foot
18 Form a small dowel or spigot at the top of the foot using a parting tool

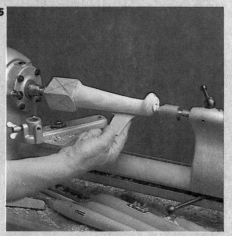

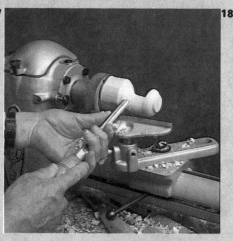

Turning offcuts on the lathe

One of the great advantages of woodturning is you can put even the smallest pieces of waste or offcut to good use. Here we explain how to make a napkin ring, which is a typical example of this type of work and particularly attractive when made from yew, walnut or elm. Other small items such as door or drawer knobs and chess pieces can also be turned from scrap wood.

Turning napkin rings

Although natural faults in the wood can often enhance the character of the work, choose wood which is free from splits and knots – and 18–25mm (¾–1in) thick. You must first decide upon the size of hole in the napkin ring since it will be necessary to make a simple jig on which the ring can be turned and finished; a 38mm (1½in) hole should be satisfactory. Since you will almost certainly be making several rings, it is most important to work in a definite order, using a production line method. Carry out all similar operations at the same time on each piece of wood; this will help to ensure all the rings end up the same shape and size.

Preparing the work

Roughly mark the centre of the centre hole on both faces of the work and, using either a power drill mounted in a vertical drill stand or the lathe as a boring tool, bore out the wood to the required size. To prevent the sides of the hole splintering where the drill bit leaves the wood, bore from both sides of the wood to produce a clean hole. When using the lathe as a drilling tool, mount the drill chuck in the headstock of the lathe with a flat or saw tooth bit secured within the jaws.

Mount a block of wood over the nose of the tail-stock to act as a drilling pad and, holding the work by hand, carefully start to bore through the wood; stop the action as soon as the point of the bit appears through the wood. Remove the bit from the wood by retracting the tailstock, reverse the piece of wood side for side and complete the boring action. The small centre hole you made in the first stage will ensure a correctly centred start into the second side and consequently a perfectly clean bore. Once the holes are bored remove the work from the lathe, cut off the rings with a saw and shape each piece roughly to a circle.

1 These attractive napkin rings are just one example of the many different objects you can make with pieces of scrap wood left over from another project

2 To turn a napkin ring, first bore holes in the wood block using a flat bit held in a drill chuck; place a piece of scrap wood over the nose of the tailstock to act as a drilling pad

3 Remove the block from the lathe, cut off the bored pieces with a saw and cut each piece roughly to the shape of a circle

4 Turn a slightly tapered jig on which the bored pieces can be mounted for shaping; the jig should be slightly larger in diameter than the holes in the block

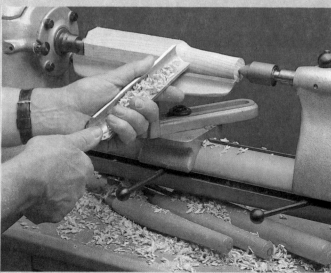

When using a saw tooth bit for boring, it is essential to keep a fairly low speed to prevent the bit overheating; otherwise the bit will jam in the wood and might damage the temper of the metal.

Tapered jig   The next stage is to turn a simple tapered jig on which the bored pieces of wood can be mounted for shaping; they must be held securely while the outside is turned to a clean circle. Mount a 250mm (10in) length of 50mm (2in) square hardwood between the lathe centres, having previously marked the true centres at each end in the normal way. Adjust the height and position of the tool rest to suit the work and, using a fairly wide gouge, start to round off the rough piece of wood.

Begin at the extreme right-hand end of the work and work progressively along to the opposite end, reducing the rough square length of wood to a long cylinder a little over the diameter of the holes bored in the scraps of wood. Using a scraping tool or chisel, carefully reduce the work to a gradual tapered cylinder; a reduction from end to end of about 1.5–3mm ($\frac{1}{16}$–$\frac{1}{8}$in) in diameter will be sufficient with the larger diameter at the headstock end. Don't be too particular about producing a perfectly smooth finish since the roughness obtained by scraping can help to hold the wood.

Shaping the rings
Move the tool rest away from the work and withdraw the tailstock so one of the pieces of bored

wood can be mounted on the tapered jig. Give the wood a couple of twists to make sure it is secure; should any slipping occur during the turning, a dampened cloth applied to the tapered jig will allow the wood to swell slightly to grip the wood blank more firmly.

Reposition the tool rest relative to the work to be shaped, turning the wood by hand to ensure the corners clear the rest. Using a small round-ended gouge, ideally 12mm ($\frac{1}{2}$in) wide and with the lathe running at a speed of about 1500–2000rpm, start to shape the outside of the wood. Keep the tool over on its right side and work from the tailstock towards the headstock – up the tapered jig – so the turning action does not move the wood off the taper. It is best to use a gouge because of its cleaner cut, although scraping tools can be used provided light cuts are made.

Check your turning frequently with a pair of calipers and keep all the items uniform in diameter since this will simplify chucking during final finishing. The ends of the wood rings should now be slightly radiused or rounded over to produce a clean edge, using the gouge on its side or a skew chisel. Design details can be turned in a similar manner, although it is still necessary to work from the larger diameter down to the smaller as in normal turning techniques. Where the wood has a positive grain and colour, external decoration should not be necessary. Turn all the items in the same manner

5 Fit one of the bored pieces onto the jig, tapping it gently with a wood bar to ensure a tight fit
6 Turn the outside to a round, working with the direction of the taper so the turning action does not move the ring off the taper
7 Check the diameter of the work with a pair of calipers
8 Shape the outside with a gouge, keeping the tool over on its right-hand side

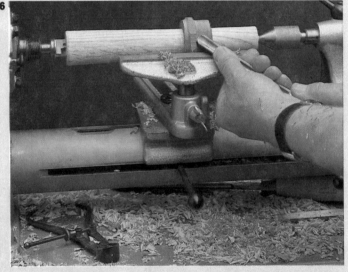

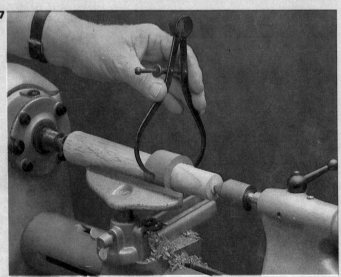

while the lathe is still set up for this operation and remember to check the overall diameters constantly. Lastly, rub the rings smooth with abrasive paper for a good finish.

Clean up the inside of the rings and radius the outside of the holes slightly to allow a napkin to be inserted easily; to do this you will need a hollow wood chuck to hold the rings. Mount a thick disc of softwood on the woodscrew chuck in the normal manner and turn the outside up to a clean disc using either the gouge or scraping tools. Clean up the face side with a scraper and, using a pair of dividers, carefully scribe the face to the diameter of the partly turned rings. Remove the inside of the disc with a parting tool or square-ended scraper, working to the inside of the scribed marks. The inside should be turned to a very slight taper to ensure the napkin ring fits neatly. The depth of the hole in the chuck should be equal to about half the thickness of the wood ring.

Continuing with the main turning operation, place one of the partly turned rings inside the hollow chuck; give it a slight tap in one or two places to make sure it is really secure and at the same time rotate it by hand to check it is evenly placed. If the work fits loosely in the chuck, a piece of newspaper will often produce the necessary grip; alternatively you can moisten the inside of the chuck which will expand the wood and provide a positive grip.

Position the tool rest across the face of the work and, with a square-nosed scraper or a chisel used as a scraper, lightly clean up the inside of the ring and radius the ends. Reverse the position of the ring within the chuck and repeat the operations. Sand and polish the inside of the ring and return the ring to the taper jig between lathe centres for further polishing if required, using a piece of paper to protect the inside if necessary.

Repetitive work

When making repetitive small projects such as chess pieces, it is a good idea to use a shape-tracer or contour gauge. With this type of work, first one item is turned to the required shape, using calipers and dividers to obtain an accurate model or pattern, and the shape-tracer is pushed into the pattern to obtain an identical outline of the shape. It is then a fairly simple matter to check the remainder of your turning with the shape-tracer.

Another aid when making many pieces of a similar cut or diameter or when copying is the sizing tool. Here the working pattern is turned to the required shape in the normal manner; the sizing tool is then set up and adjusted to cut the particular diameter required. The copying piece is roughly turned to a diameter a little over the diameter required and the sizing tool placed over it. The cut is made by lowering the sizing tool cutter into the wood to produce a set diameter.

9 Use a shape-tracer to record the shape of the ring; this will ensure each ring is exactly the same
10 Prepare a hollow wood chuck to accept the ring
11 Secure the ring in the chuck and clean up the inside with a scraper, radiusing the ends
12 When making several objects of the same size you can use a sizing tool to ensure each one is the same

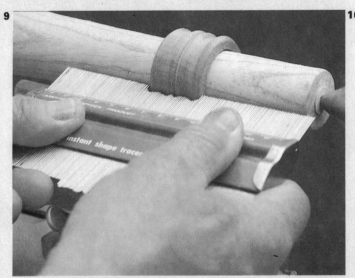

Turning goblets on the lathe

A wide variety of interesting projects can be made from small offcuts of timber or prunings from the garden or orchard. These include making goblets, a particularly suitable turning exercise using a small woodworking lathe or drill-powered attachment.

Before you begin work it is worth studying the general shape of a goblet to consider any special turning problems it will present. For example, the main body of the goblet is supported on top of a slender stem so it is important the wood you use has sufficient strength and the grain runs cleanly from top to bottom. Since the slender stem is the weakest part of the goblet it should not carry any end or short grain wood. Also, since the bowl will be hollowed out of end grain wood, it is essential the general hollowing out of the bowl and the shaping throughout is carried out in a systematic manner to maintain the strength of the wood at its weakest point – the stem.

Holding the work
You will have to make sure the wood is mounted on the lathe in a way which allows it to be hollowed out in safety; for example, if the wood is fairly long, it is particularly important the wood blank is held securely by a suitable chuck.

The simplest of all holding devices on the lathe is a standard face plate suitably prepared for this type of work. Alternatively there are various suitable proprietary devices such as a 6 in 1 chuck or a coil grip chuck. Where you are working with fairly small section wood, you can use a woodscrew chuck

– in particular for turning egg cups, which is a very similar exercise. Because in this case there is only a single screw holding the work, you should make sure the wood is hard and fairly close-grained to ensure a good hold.

Using standard face plate To prepare a standard face plate for this type of work you will have to fit a wood sub-face consisting of a planed piece of 18mm (¾in) timber cut to a rough disc. After mounting the sub-face on the face plate, it should be cleaned up with scrapers or a gouge.

Place a length of wood (which is suitable for the project) between lathe centres and turn it roughly to a cylinder in the usual way with a fairly wide gouge; it is not necessary at this stage to turn a perfect cylinder. Use a parting tool to clean up both ends of the rough cylinder and turn a small spigot or dowel at the headstock end of the work to a diameter of about 25–30mm (1–1¼in).

Replace the prepared face plate on the lathe and use a square-ended scraper to bore a hole in the centre which will accept the turned spigot; test for fit as you proceed to ensure the workpiece fits snugly within the wood face of the face plate. Glue the wood into the prepared face plate ready for hollowing and shaping.

Using proprietary chucks These are particularly suitable for use where repetitive work is being carried out. The general preparation of the wood blank is similar to that involved when using a standard face plate, but the processes involved in the initial setting up vary with the type of chuck

1 Turning the wood blank to a cylinder using a gouge
2 Using a parting tool to turn a small spigot at the headstock end of the work
3 Using a square-ended scraper to bore a hole in the centre of the prepared face plate to accept the spigot
4 Making a test fit to ensure the workpiece fits snugly within the wood face
5 Supporting the work with the tailstock while the adhesive sets
6 Turning a small shoulder at the headstock end of the work to provide a clamping area for a 6 in 1 chuck

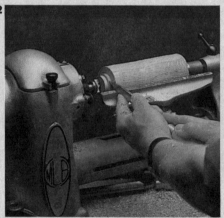

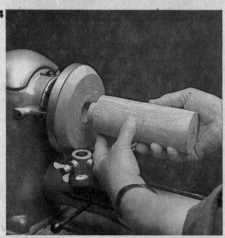

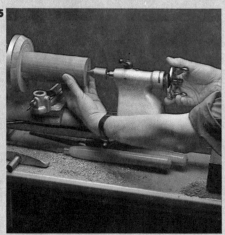

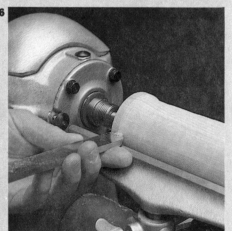

used. With a coil grip chuck, for example, it is necessary to turn a small flange at the headstock end of the work which will fit inside the chuck; although the size of the flange is not critical, it is advisable to use a pair of calipers to ensure a trouble-free fit. The prepared work is then placed within the chuck and secured by the outer clamping ring, using the spanner and tommy bar provided.

Another method of mounting the wood in either a 6 in 1 or a coil grip chuck is to use the outer ring of the chuck only where the overall diameter of the workpiece is slightly less than that of the inside of the clamping ring. A small shoulder is turned on the workpiece to provide a clamping area for the chuck. Where the work is of small diameter and you are using a 6 in 1 chuck, the split ring clamping arrangement means it is only necessary to turn a groove with a parting tool to ensure accurate mounting within the chuck.

Turning the work

Whichever method of chucking is used to hold the work, the general turning and shaping of the project remains the same and is carried out in a systematic order.

Hollowing out bowl You will first have to hollow out the centre of the wood block to form the bowl of the goblet while there is a maximum amount of support in the remainder of the wood; it is very difficult, if not impossible, to hollow this type of work after external shaping has been carried out. Use a round nose scraping tool with the tool rest positioned squarely across the end of the work at a height which will place the cutting edge of the tool in the centre of the wood. Push the tool into the end of the rotating work (which should be turning at about 1500–2000rpm), keeping the blade of the

tool flat on the tool rest. As the hole develops, swing the handle over in a right-hand direction to deepen and open up the hole in the end of the wood. Continue in this way, taking progressive cuts into the block and always working from the centre outwards; this will ensure the cut is made with the direction of the grain so a reasonably smooth finish is obtained.

To speed up the hollowing out process you can first bore out part of the inside of the goblet with a saw tooth bit held in a drill chuck mounted in the tailstock; then use a round nose scraping tool to turn the remainder of the inside to shape.

Where you are making a number of identical projects or a copy of an existing one, it is a good idea to use a card template of both the inside and outside. If, however, you have acquired a certain amount of experience, turning a project freehand to a required shape and size without the use of a template should present few problems.

Once you are satisfied the inside of the goblet is the required shape, give it a thorough sanding using decreasing grades of abrasive paper; hold the paper between your forefinger and thumb in a trailing action with the rotation of the wood.

Shaping outside of bowl Although the work can be completed using the single-ended chucking method, you will find it advantageous to use a support in the open end of the block. Place a tapered wood plug in the open end of the bored-out block and position the tailstock to support this end of the work.

Using a round nose gouge 12mm (½in) wide, you can begin to shape the outside of the bowl starting at the tailstock end of the work. The blade of the tool should be at an angle of about 45 degrees to the work and the first cut should be made towards the right-hand end of the work. Continue in this way

7 Fitting the workpiece into the 6 in 1 chuck
8 Using ring spanners to clamp the chuck firmly onto the workpiece
9 Using a round nose scraping tool to hollow out the bowl of the goblet
10 Using abrasive paper on the inside of the bowl to provide a smooth finish
11 Shaping the outside of the bowl with a 12mm round nose gouge; support the end of the workpiece with the tailstock
12 Forming a bead where the bowl meets the stem of the goblet using a skew chisel

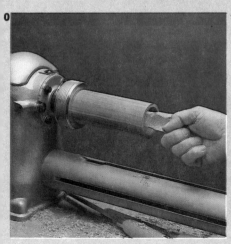

Left Attractive and useful goblets which have been turned on the lathe; some are small enough to use as egg cups

by making a series of adjacent cuts to obtain the shape you want. Throughout the turning, the bevel of the gouge must be kept in contact with the wood to ensure an easy clean-cutting action.

Reverse the hold on the gouge so it points at an angle to the left and start to form a hollow at the point where the stem of the goblet will begin. By making a series of cuts from alternate sides of this hollow you can form the base of the bowl. Make sure the cut is made from the larger diameter down to the smaller and never the other way round. Try to retain the maximum amount of wood between the cutting tool and the point where the wood is fixed by shaping progressively from right to left.

Where the bowl meets the stem you should form a small step or bead using the point of a turning gouge or the heel or point of a skew chisel. The outside of the bowl can be sanded in the usual way with the abrasive held under the rotating work.

Forming base and stem Use a parting tool to make a blind cut into the work to indicate the actual position of the base of the goblet. Place the parting tool on its edge on the tool rest, with the cutting edge resting on top of the work but not actually cutting the wood; lift the handle slightly so the tool begins to cut. To give the base a slightly concave profile you should hold the handle of the parting tool slightly over to the left.

To shape the rest of the stem, work from a point adjacent to the base of the bowl with a 12mm ($\frac{1}{2}$in) wide round nose gouge held on its right side with the bevel in contact with the wood. Since you will be considerably reducing the thickness of the wood to form the stem, it is most important you use sharp tools to avoid applying excessive pressure to the work otherwise the whole project can be ruined at this stage.

You should have few problems shaping the base, where most of the turning is carried out using the same small gouge. Where any small steps or fillets appear in the general shaping you should use the point of a skew chisel to give a smooth cut.

Finishing The whole project should be sanded to a smooth finish and given two or three coats of polyurethane lacquer. It can then be parted off using a parting tool and a small handsaw.

13 Shaping the stem of the goblet using a small round nose gouge
14 Using the same gouge to shape the base of the goblet
15 Types of chuck used to turn goblets: (from left) 6 in 1 chuck, coil grip chuck and woodscrew chuck

13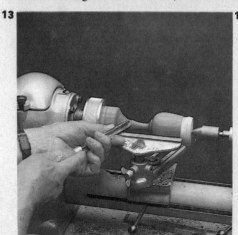

14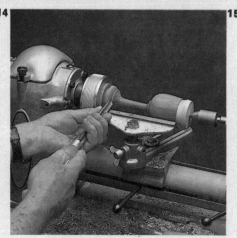

15

Finishing wood on the lathe

Once you have acquired the necessary experience with turning tools and the general method of working with a lathe, many of the projects you make will be greatly improved by an attractive finish. Final sanding is often insufficient to withstand wear and general handling; a good finish, although sometimes complicated, is most important.

Although certain projects such as kitchen ware can be left in a natural state, the application of polish, sealer or domestic wax polishes not only provides a more durable finish but also greatly enhances the natural grain formation of the wood. The problem of finishing work made on the lathe can often be simplified if all the finishing operations are carried out with the work on the lathe.

It is essential to use the correct turning methods in the first place to produce a good smooth surface on which to apply the polish; poor workmanship with incorrect or blunt tools can never be corrected with abrasives.

Before starting any finishing process take a close look at your work; bowls and hollow work are especially prone to rough areas. To make good these parts take a few light cuts with a freshly ground scraping tool. Hold the blade slightly down so the cutting edge of the tool is just below the centre line of the work; don't force the tool since this will only increase the roughness. Where possible use a sharp gouge with the end ground to a rounded or finger nail shape; for a perfect finish make light cuts with the tool held on its edge on the rest, taking care to keep the bevel in contact with the wood.

Centre work or spindle turning should be carefully checked to make sure the coves, beads and any other areas where there are abrupt design changes, such as from convex to concave curves, are cleanly cut. Use a skew chisel to clean these parts and always remember to cut from the larger diameter down to the smaller. When sanding such intricate pieces, however, great care must be taken not to damage the detail of the work.

Sanding

The first stage in any finishing operation is the general sanding which removes all trace of tool marks, provides an overall smoothness to the work and shows up any natural faults in the wood such as small knots and splits.

Use a medium abrasive paper or cloth, preferably garnet, and fold it into a pad which can be conveniently held between fingers and thumb. With the lathe running at a speed compatible with the diameter of the work, lightly move the abrasive across or along the surface of the work. Avoid excessive pressure with the abrasive and always keep it moving to prevent the formation of unsightly sanding rings. After you have removed all the tool marks, repeat the sanding process using decreasing grades of abrasive paper. Finally, rub over with a pad of medium grade steel wool to obtain a fine finish. Where there are intricate details, coves or beads, take particular care to retain the crisp cut edges; use the corner of a folded piece of abrasive paper where necessary.

Often after careful sanding you can find un-

1 With the lathe stationary, fill any cracks in the work with wax stopper
2 Go over the surface with abrasive paper so the wax forms a bond with the wood dust and fills the cracks
3 Use steel wool to give a satin-like finish
4 Make good any rough areas by taking a few light cuts with a sharp scraping tool

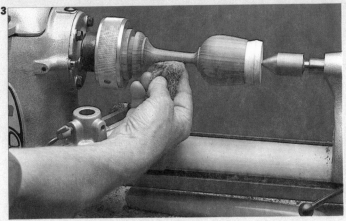

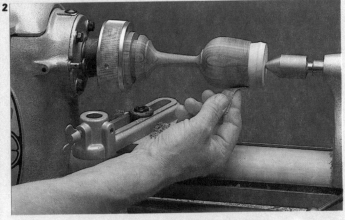

-sightly marks in the wood such as hair splits, small dead or loose knots or even the odd worm hole. After removing any dust or dead wood from around the fault, many of these blemishes can be treated with a commercially prepared wax stopping or a paste stopper available in various shades.

Staining

When staining wood take great care in the selection of the type of stain and in its application, remembering all turned work consists of a wide variety of grain formations. In the end grain areas stain will be absorbed in greater quantities than in others, making it considerably darker. It is essential to use a stain or dye which is easy to control and which will not be thrown out of the wood by centrifugal force when polishing; this often happens with oil or naptha-based products. Water soluble dyes or stains are best and can often be applied direct from the can or diluted; a slight raising of the grain may occur which will require a further light rubbing over with steel wool to remove any roughness.

All types of stain dry much lighter than when first applied and will change again when the finishing polish is applied; make a number of test stains on scrap wood similar to the project which is to be polished. It is also a good idea to make a number of applications with a weak stain solution rather than use a strong one.

The stain or dye should be applied with a brush or cloth while the work is stationary on the lathe and any excess wiped off with a cloth before it dries; the lathe bed should be protected with paper or a cloth while you are doing this. Although you may be tempted to switch on the power to speed up drying, the results can be disastrous since the centrifugal force set up by the fast revolving work will throw the stain all over the workshop.

Once the stain is completely dry seal it with a thin brush coat of French polish, cellulose sealer or clear polyurethane lacquer, although the latter does take a long time to dry and is liable to attract particles of dust and wood.

Filling grain

Timbers with a fairly open grain, such as elm and some oaks, will require a certain amount of grain-filling to provide a good polishing surface. Wax or French polish can also act as a perfect grain filler; the general polishing action on the lathe forces the polish into the grain fibres and produces a perfect finish. Where separate finishing is necessary, use a paste stopping of whichever shade you like, thinned with water until it is soft; allow it to dry, then seal it with a thin coat of sealer polish.

Waxing and polishing

Most woodturners prefer to use a species of timber which has its own distinctive colouring and grain formation which makes it almost unnecessary to add any further treatment other than a clear or white polish.

Beeswax This is perhaps the simplest finish of all; it is easy to apply and makes a perfect filler. Apply the beeswax directly to the revolving work and rub it into the grain of the wood with a worn piece of abrasive cloth or paper; the combination of wax and wood sandings makes the perfect grain filler and always matches the wood. You will find the abrasive becomes clogged with the mixture, but this all helps to achieve a satin finish. A thin sealer coat of clear French polish – or something similar – will retain the fillings.

Carnauba wax This wax is often used by woodturners and is obtainable from many lathe accessory manufacturers. It is applied directly to the revolving

5 For a perfect finish use a gouge ground to a rounded or finger nail shape; keep the bevel of the blade in contact with the wood
6 Clean up details such as beads and coves with a skew chisel
7 Take light cuts with the skew chisel to avoid damaging the detail
8 Give the work a smooth finish using abrasive paper; hold the paper under the work and keep it moving to avoid unsightly sanding rings

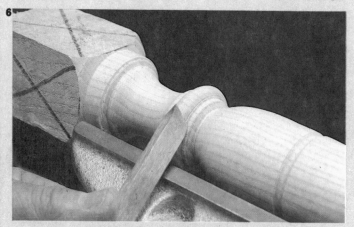

work and quickly produces a pleasant shine when buffed with a coarse cloth or wood shavings. Insufficient pressure when polishing will give an all-over frosty appearance, while excessive pressure will completely remove the wax. To obtain the best results with carnauba on its own, practise using a double thickness of cloth. Place your fingers behind the pad and work the wax into the wood; the resulting friction heat will give you an idea of the state of the wax and its temperature. When the heat becomes excessive, move the pad or cloth rapidly over the work surface to spread the wax film. For final burnishing hold a handful of shavings under the revolving work, remembering to keep the polishing action on the move.

Unfortunately a wax finish is not durable; it becomes dull with handling and requires a lot of attention to retain its shine. Also, exposure to moisture or water will produce unsightly white spots, although these can be removed by vigorous buffing with a coarse cloth.

Sometimes when working with extremely light wood or laminated work, where light and dark woods alternate, it is difficult to separate the various species and colours since the application of liquid polish often causes the colours to merge. This is caused by the transference of small particles of wood dust during sanding and can be quickly remedied by rubbing the lighter woods with carnauba wax.

French polishing

French polish has been used extensively over the years to finish many pieces of turned work, since it produces a beautiful finish and a strong shine. Although it requires considerable skill to apply over large areas using a polisher's rubber and linseed oil, the process is somewhat simplified when applied to items turned on the lathe.

First make a small pad consisting of a core of cotton wool, surrounded by a piece of lintfree rag, which can be comfortably held between the finger and thumb. Soak it in methylated spirits, keeping the outer surface of the pad free from wrinkles, and allow it to dry ready for use. With the lathe running at a slightly slower speed than used for turning the project, put a small amount of French polish on the pad and apply it to the rotating work; apply reasonable pressure and force a small amount of the polish out of the pad over the work area. Recharge the pad when it becomes dry and repeat the operation.

One great advantage of this method is it dries quickly. Where the work is porous or slightly open-grained, you will have to make several applications. The polish will also work as a grain filler. Always use clear or white French polish.

Oiling

An oil finish is usually applied to items which hold food, such as salad bowls or kitchen ware; it prevents moisture and food odours entering the wood. Materials used for finishing this type of ware must not be harmful and are usually of the vegetable type such as olive and coconut oil.

Application is very simple, the oil being applied to the prepared wood with a cloth pad; keep the lathe running at a low speed and replenish the pad frequently to ensure a liberal amount of oil enters the wood fibres. Several applications are usually necessary to build up a resistant finish; the wood is then left to dry out. Objects finished in this way should not be immersed in water for cleaning, but simply wiped clean and re-oiled.

9 When using French polish, apply it from underneath the work and protect the lathe bed with sheets of newspaper
10 Apply the polish to the rotating work, forcing a small amount out of the pad over the work area
11 If using wood dye or stain, protect the lathe bed with newspaper and keep the lathe stationary while you work
12 Any knots in the work should be dug out carefully and filled with paste stopper

Projects in wood

The projects included here cover some of the basic furniture requirements around the home, as well as a 'fun' item – a sandboat. Bear in mind, however, that these designs can be adapted to suit your specific requirements. With the skills that you have perfected by working on the information in the other sections, you will be able to make up your own projects. Apart from detailed assembly instructions, there are also tools, materials and cutting lists.

Garden bench

This slatted timber garden bench finished in teak-coloured preservative will look well in any setting and can seat three adults comfortably.

Tools and materials

timber (see cutting list)
measuring tape, pencil and try square
protractor, sliding bevel and marking gauge
medium fine and fine glasspaper
tenon saw and coping saw, block plane, 16mm chisel
hand or electric drill, 2, 5, 9 and 12mm bits
three sash cramps and two G-clamps
screwdriver, countersink bit, mallet
850mm of 9mm diameter dowel
No 8 brass countersunk screws 38mm long, sockets to fit
water-resistant woodworking adhesive and clean cloth
wood preservative and 25mm paint brush (for finish)

Cutting list for softwood

Description	Key	Quantity	Dimensions
Slats	A	16	1500 × 45 × 22mm
Back legs	B	2	830 × 70 × 44mm
Front legs	C	2	334 × 70 × 44mm
Horizontals	D	2	490 × 70 × 44mm
Brace	E	1	1250 × 73 × 33mm
Feet	F	2	556 × 70 × 44mm

stage 1

Measure and cut with a tenon saw all the pieces of timber according to the dimensions shown (**see cutting list**).
Cut off the waste with a tenon saw from the top end of both back legs B according to the dimensions shown (**see 1**), mark out the curve in the front edge of both back legs and cut out the waste with a coping saw. Using a protractor, sliding bevel and marking gauge, mark out the angled tenon at the bottom end of both the back legs according to the dimensions shown (**see 1**) and remove the waste from each one with a tenon saw; keep slightly to the waste side of the cutting line in every case.
Mark out the angled mortise in the front edge of both back legs according to the dimensions shown (**see 1**), drill out the bulk of the waste

from each one with a 12mm diameter bit and remove the rest of the waste with a sharp 16mm chisel.

stage 2

Mark out and cut the angled tenon at both ends of both front legs C according to the dimensions shown (**see 2**). Mark out and cut the angled tenon at one end of both horizontals D to the dimensions shown (**see 3**). Mark out and cut off the waste from the other end of both horizontals, then mark and chop out the angled mortise in the bottom edge of each one according to the dimensions shown (**see 3**). Mark out the 77 degree angle at the front end of both feet F (**see 4**) and cut off the waste from each one with a tenon saw. Mark and chop out the two angled mortises in the top edges of both feet according to the dimensions shown (**see 4**).

Assembly diagram
(slats removed)

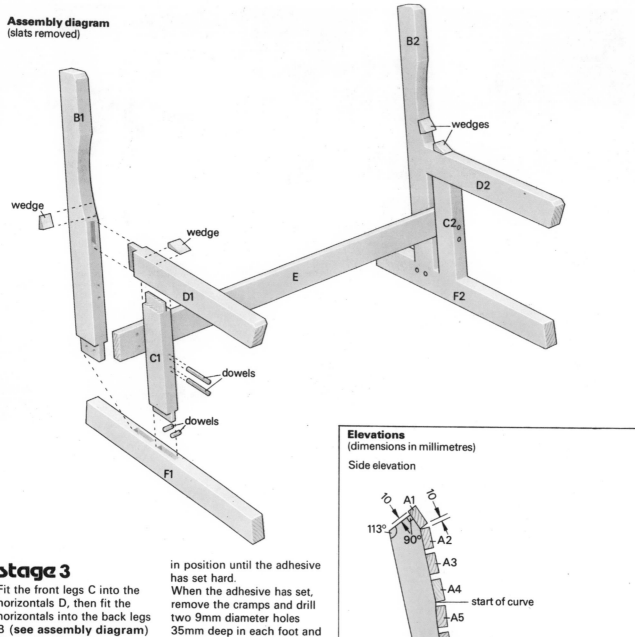

stage 3

Fit the front legs C into the horizontals D, then fit the horizontals into the back legs B (**see assembly diagram**) Fit the feet F onto the front and back legs and check all joints fit neatly and tightly together. Trim with a sharp chisel joints that do not fit. Rub smooth all surfaces of all pieces in the end frames (B, C, D and F) with medium fine, then fine, glasspaper. Apply water-resistant woodworking adhesive to all joint surfaces and assemble the end frames in the same order as before, tightening sash cramps over the joints and placing wedge-shaped pieces of scrap wood between the cramps and the timber both for protection and to keep the cramps in the required position (**see 5**). Wipe off all excess adhesive with a clean dampened cloth and leave the cramps tightly

in position until the adhesive has set hard.
When the adhesive has set, remove the cramps and drill two 9mm diameter holes 35mm deep in each foot and back leg tenon and in each back leg and horizontal tenon at the dimensions shown (**see side elevation**). Cut eight 35mm lengths of the 9mm diameter dowel, apply adhesive to the cut lengths and ram them firmly into the holes with a mallet. Wipe off excess adhesive and trim the dowels flush with the surface using a block plane.

stage 4

Using a block plane chamfer the top edges of all 16 slats A. Drill a 5mm diameter clearance hole 222mm in from both ends of each one (**see 6**), countersink them to take No 8 screws and hammer the brass sockets into the clearance holes.

Elevations
(dimensions in millimetres)

Side elevation

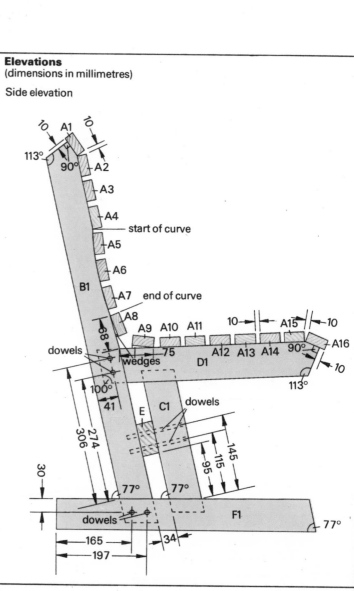

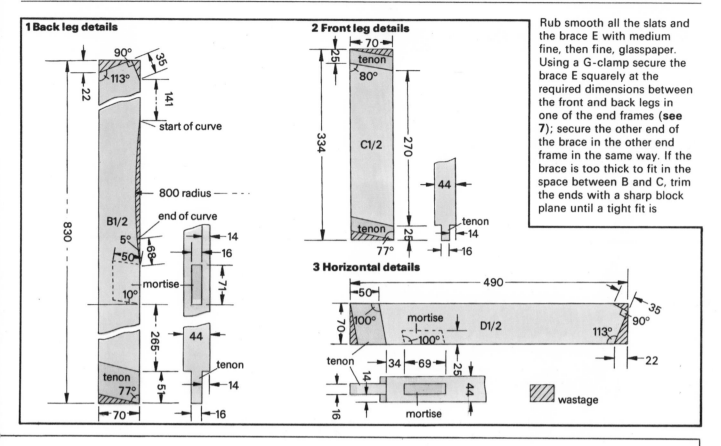

1 Back leg details

90°
35
113°
22
141
start of curve
800 radius
B1/2
end of curve
5°
50
68
10°
mortise
830
14
16
71
265
44
tenon
77°
5
tenon
70
16

2 Front leg details

70
25
tenon
80°
334
C1/2
270
44
tenon
14
tenon
25
77°
16

3 Horizontal details

490
50
35
70
100°
mortise
D1/2
90°
100°
113°
tenon
34
69
25
22
tenon
14
44
16
mortise

wastage

Rub smooth all the slats and the brace E with medium fine, then fine, glasspaper. Using a G-clamp secure the brace E squarely at the required dimensions between the front and back legs in one of the end frames (**see 7**); secure the other end of the brace in the other end frame in the same way. If the brace is too thick to fit in the space between B and C, trim the ends with a sharp block plane until a tight fit is

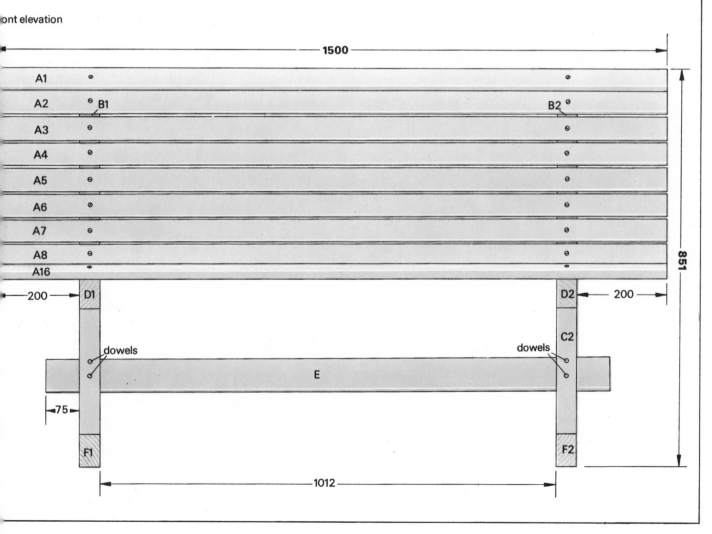

ont elevation

1500

A1
A2 B1   B2
A3
A4
A5
A6
A7
A8
A16

851

200 D1   D2 200

C2

dowels   dowels

E

75

F1   F2

1012

4 Foot details

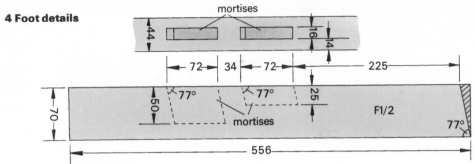

5 Cramping end frames

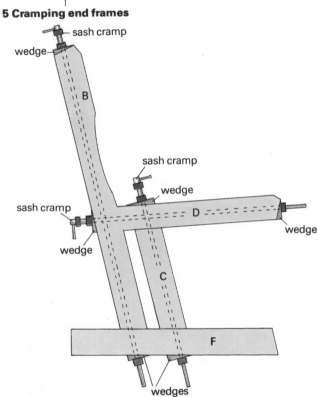

6 Slat details

chamfered edges

clearance hole
5 diameter
countersunk for
screw cup

A

222

45

22

inset

wedge for
slat A8

wedge for slat A9

15°

grain

grain

45

45

44

44

11°

11

9

7 Fixing brace

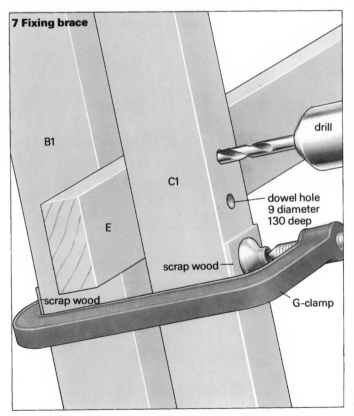

B1

C1

E

drill

dowel hole
9 diameter
130 deep

scrap wood

scrap wood

G-clamp

achieved. Check the brace is square to both end frames and drill the two 9mm diameter dowel holes, 130mm deep, at the dimensions shown (**see side elevation**).

Cut four 140mm lengths of 9mm diameter dowel, remove the G-clamps, apply adhesive to the areas of the brace which will be in contact with the front and back legs and clamp the brace in position in the end frames as before. Pour some adhesive into the dowel holes and push the cut lengths of dowel into position, ramming them firmly home with a mallet.

Cut the four softwood wedges out of a piece of scrap wood according to the dimensions shown (**see 6 inset**); these are used when fixing the slats A8 and A9 to create a smooth curve (**see side elevation**). Apply adhesive to the fixing area of the slats A1–8 and fix the

slats firmly and squarely in position, with the 38mm long brass screws, at the required dimensions (**see elevations**), remembering to drill a 2mm pilot hole for each screw and to place the larger wedges under the slat A8. Wipe off excess adhesive and fix the slats A9–16 to the top face of the horizontals D in the same way, placing the wedges under the slat A9.

When the adhesive has set hard, remove the protruding dowels in the front legs C with a sharp chisel and block plane.

For the finish, apply three coats of wood preservative; we chose a natural wood colour although there are many bright colours available if you prefer.

Double bed

Our double bed is very easy to make and is designed to take a standard size mattress (2000×1500mm). It has four spacious drawers which provide invaluable storage; the whole structure, except the drawers, can be taken apart and bundled up should you wish to move it. You could paint the bed to match your bedroom colour scheme – as we did – or leave it with a natural finish.

stage 1

Measure and mark all the cutting lines onto the sheets of plywood according to the dimensions shown (**see cutting list and cutting plans**) and score along these lines through the surface veneer with a sharp trimming knife held against a metal straight-edge.

Cut all the plywood pieces to size with a fine-tooth panel saw, keeping slightly to the waste side of the line. Cut all

Tools and materials

timber (see cutting list)
measuring tape, pencil, try square, metal straight-edge
tenon, coping and fine-tooth panel saws, trimming knife
medium fine, fine and flour glasspaper
hand or electric drill, 7, 8 and 19mm bits
four G-clamps, 12mm chisel, screwdriver, bradawl
block plane, flat file, hammer and nail punch
woodworking adhesive and clean cloth

For assembly

24 knock-down corner joints
4 tee nuts, 50mm long 6mm countersunk machine screws
oval nails 38mm long, panel pins 19 and 32mm long
16 plate fixing castors 46mm high and 19mm long screws
cellulose filler or matching plastic wood, primer, undercoat
and top coat or clear matt polyurethane lacquer, 25 and
100mm paint brushes (for finish)

Cutting list for plywood

Description	Key	Quantity	Dimensions
End panels	A	2	1524 × 397 × 12mm
Side panels	B	2	2000 × 170 × 12mm
Long cross piece	C	1	2000 × 365 × 12mm
Short cross piece	D	1	1524 × 365 × 12mm
Long drawer stops	E	4	321 × 100 × 12mm
Short drawer stops	F	4	227 × 100 × 12mm
Base boards	G	2	2000 × 750 × 12mm
Drawer fronts	H	4	990 × 170 × 12mm
Drawer backs	J	4	966 × 170 × 12mm
Drawer sides	K	8	460 × 170 × 12mm
Drawer bases	L	4	942 × 460 × 12mm
Castor mounts	M	16	50 × 50 × 12mm

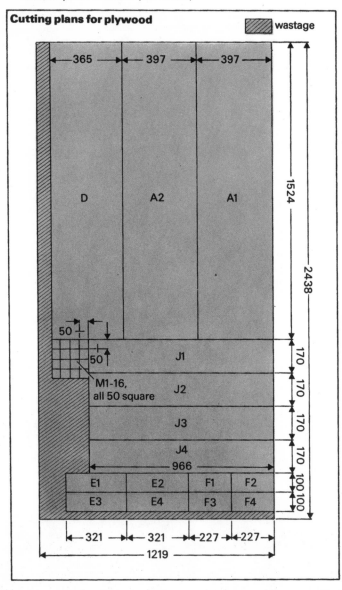

Cutting plans for plywood — wastage

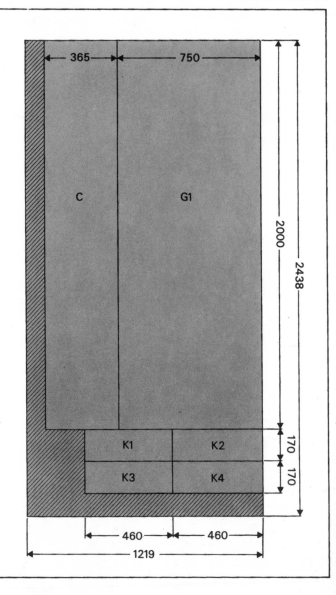

Cutting list for softwood

Description	Key	Quantity	Dimensions
End battens	N	2	1500 × 44 × 35mm
Side battens	P	2	2000 × 44 × 35mm
Long drawer battens	Q	8	898 × 22 × 22mm
Short drawer battens	R	8	460 × 22 × 22mm

the softwood pieces with a tenon saw and smooth all cut edges of all pieces with medium fine, then fine, glasspaper. To avoid confusion later on, label each piece with the appropriate code letter. Mark out the halving joint at both ends of the end battens N and the side battens P according to the dimensions shown (**see 1a and 1b**) and cut out the waste from each one with a tenon saw. Mark out the housing in the centre of each of these battens (**see 1a and 1b**) and remove the waste by making two cuts with a tenon saw to a depth of 12mm then chopping out the timber from between the cut lines with a 12mm chisel. Drill an 8mm diameter hole through the centre of the halving joint in both of the end battens N and hammer the tee nuts firmly into position in the bottom (uncut) face of the joint (**see 1a**). Drill a 7mm diameter

clearance hole through the centre of the halving joint at both ends of the side battens P and countersink them on the top (uncut) face of each batten to take the machine screw heads (**see 1b**). Mark with a pencil the required positions of the end and side battens N and P on the inside face of each end and side panel A and B according to the dimensions shown (**see 2a and 2b**). Apply woodworking adhesive to the fixing edge of N and P and fix them to A and B with G-clamps. You need at least four G-clamps to fix each batten so you may have to fix one batten at a time or screw each in position instead of merely clamping it. Don't forget to place pieces of scrap wood between the clamps and the plywood to prevent marking and don't remove the clamps from the work until

the adhesive has set hard. Cut the recess with a tenon saw in one corner of each of the four long drawer stops E according to the dimensions shown (**see 3**) and smooth the cut edges with medium fine, then fine, glasspaper. Apply adhesive to the fixing face of the drawer stops and fix them in position on the end panels A, so the recess is facing outwards in each case, at the dimensions shown (**see 2a**). Wipe off all excess adhesive with a clean dampened cloth.

stage 2

Mark out the slot in the centre of the long and short cross pieces C and D according to the dimensions shown (**see 4a and 4b**). Mark the cutting lines on both sides of the plywood and score along the lines through

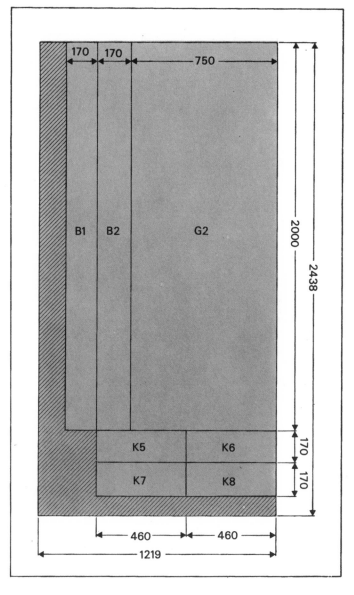

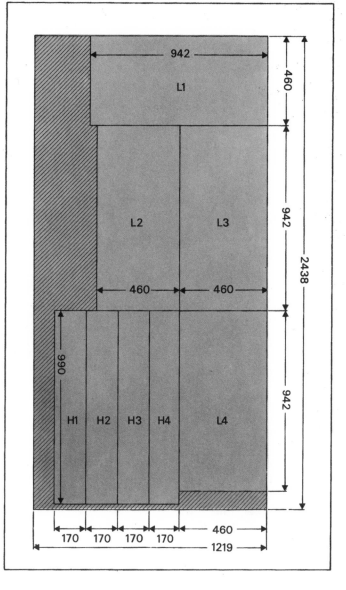

Assembly diagram
(drawers removed)

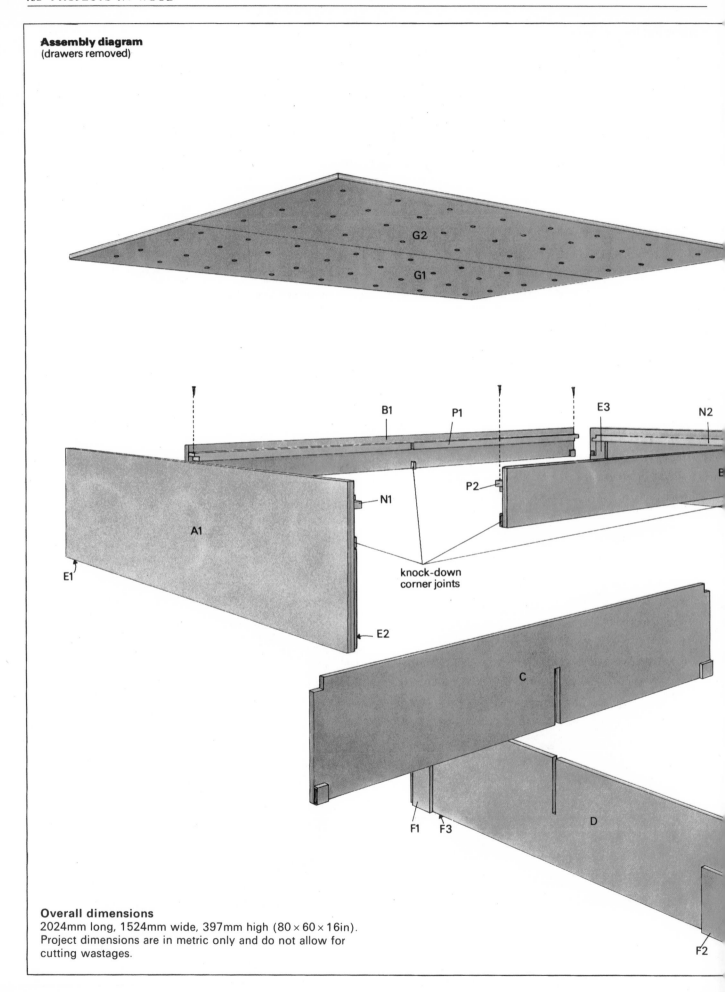

B1

P1

E3

N2

N1

A1

E1

P2

B

knock-down
corner joints

E2

C

F1

F3

D

Overall dimensions
2024mm long, 1524mm wide, 397mm high (80 × 60 × 16in).
Project dimensions are in metric only and do not allow for
cutting wastages.

F2

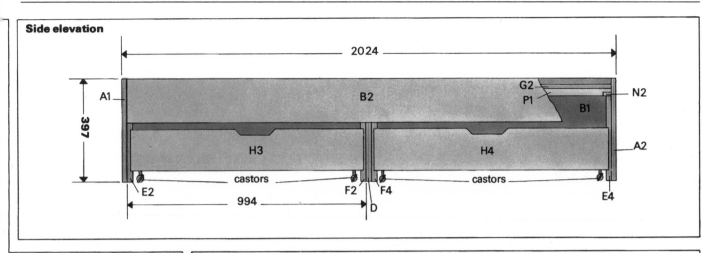

Side elevation

---

1 End and side batten details
1a End batten

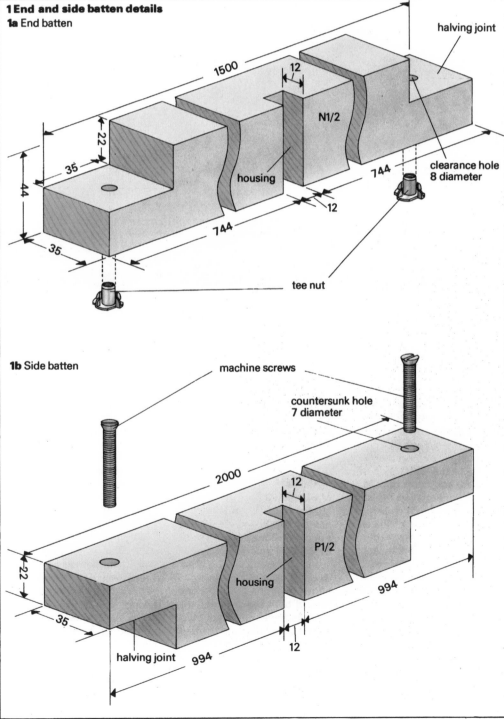

1b Side batten

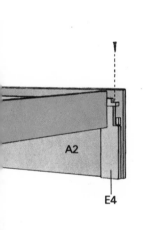

2 End and side panel details

2a End panel

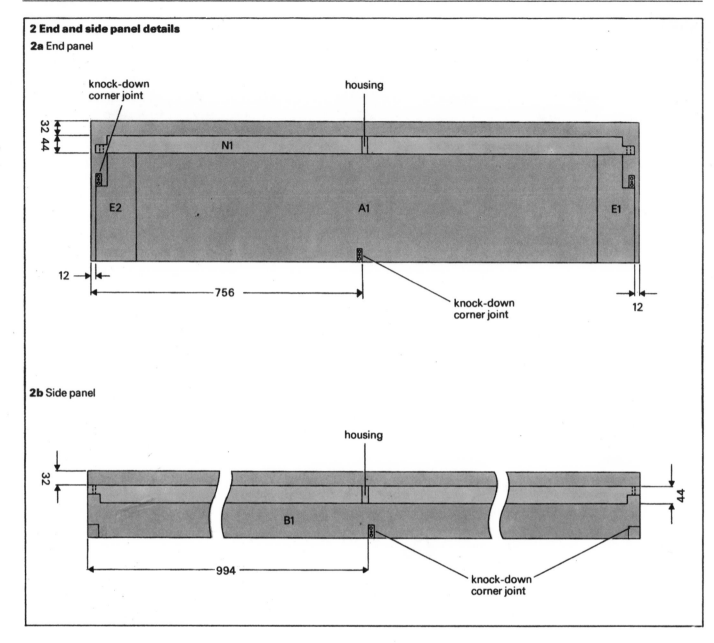

2b Side panel

the surface veneer with a sharp trimming knife held against a metal straight-edge. Cut out the slots with a fine-tooth panel saw, keeping slightly to the waste side of the lines, and chop out the waste from between the cut lines with a 12mm chisel. Smooth the inside of the slots and check the cross pieces fit snugly together; if they are too tight, trim the insides with a flat file. Mark out the notch in both top corners of C and D according to the dimensions shown (**see 4a and 4b**) and cut them out with a tenon saw.
Mark out the required positions of the short drawer stops F at both ends of the short cross piece D (**see 4b**). Apply adhesive to the fixing

face of the drawer stops and secure them on D with G-clamps. Wipe off excess adhesive.

stage 3

Mark out and drill all the 19mm diameter ventilation holes in the base boards G at the dimensions shown (**see 5**); place a piece of scrap wood under the drilling area in every case. Smooth the edges of all the holes on one face of both base boards; this ensures there are no splinters which could damage the mattress and bedding.
Screw the knock-down corner joints in the required positions at the ends and centre of the end and side panels A and B and at the

ends of the cross pieces C and D at the dimensions shown (**see 2 and 4**).
Fit together the slots in the cross pieces C and D and screw the corner joints together so the main frame is fully assembled (**see assembly diagram**).
Tighten the machine screws through the halving joints in the end and side battens N and P into the tee nuts already secured in the end battens N. Lower the two base boards G into position and check they fit neatly; trim any tight edges with a block plane.

stage 4

Mark out the cutting lines for the hand-pull area in all four

drawer fronts H according to the dimensions shown (**see 6**); use a small coin to mark the curves. Cut out the waste with a coping saw and smooth the cut edges with medium fine, then fine, glasspaper. Apply adhesive to the ends of the long drawer battens Q and fix these squarely to the short drawer battens R with the 38mm long oval nails (**see 7**).
Apply adhesive to one face of these frames and fix the drawer bases L in position with the 32mm long panel pins, making sure all edges are flush (**see 7**). Make certain the joints between the long and short drawer battens are square and punch all nail and pin heads below the surface with a

3 Shaping plan for long drawer stops

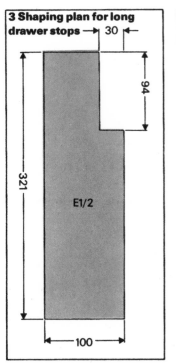

30

94

321

E1/2

100

4 Cross piece details

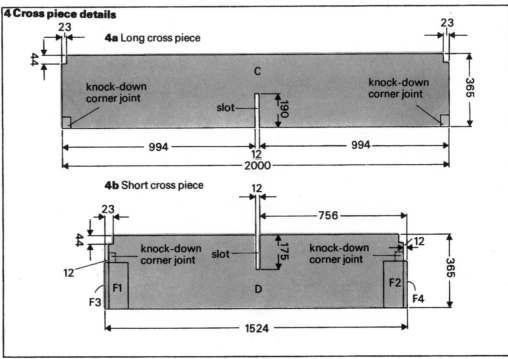

4a Long cross piece

23

44

C

knock-down corner joint

slot

190

knock-down corner joint

23

365

994

12

994

2000

4b Short cross piece

12

23

756

44

knock-down corner joint

slot

knock-down corner joint

12

12

175

365

12

F1

D

F2

F4

F3

1524

5 Drilling plan for base boards

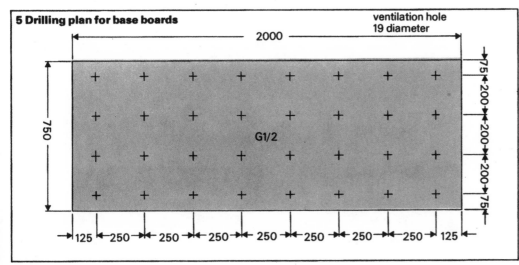

ventilation hole 19 diameter

2000

75-200-200-200-200-75

750

G1/2

125 250 250 250 250 250 250 125

6 Drawer front detail

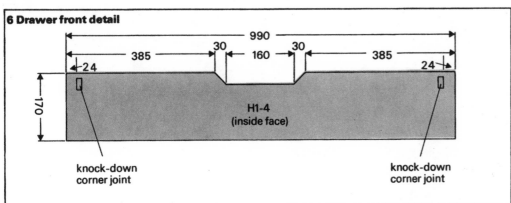

990

385

30

160

30

385

24

24

170

H1-4 (inside face)

knock-down corner joint

knock-down corner joint

the 16 castor mounts M and fix them to the underside of the drawer base in each corner, using 19mm long panel pins. Wipe off all excess adhesive. Hold the castors centrally against the bottom faces of the castor mounts and mark with a bradawl through the holes in the castors onto the mounts. Fix the castors firmly in position on the mounts with the 19mm long screws of the correct gauge for the castors.

stage 5

Fill all holes, cracks and abrasions with cellulose filler or matching plastic wood. Rub all surfaces smooth with medium fine, then fine, glasspaper and give a final rub over with flour glasspaper for a really smooth finish. You can take the main assembly of the bed completely apart just by unscrewing the knock-down corner joints and machine screws and separating the cross pieces C and D. We painted the bed to match the bedroom colour scheme. Apply a primer, undercoat and a top coat, allowing plenty of time for each coat to dry before applying the next. You could give the bed a natural finish and apply two coats of clear matt polyurethane lacquer. The base boards G need no finish.

nail punch. Wipe off all excess adhesive.
Screw the knock-down corner joints to the drawer fronts H, the drawer backs J and the drawer sides K according to the dimensions shown (see 6, 8 and 9). Apply adhesive

to the outside edges of the drawer battens R and fix the drawer sides firmly and squarely in position with the 32mm long panel pins so the bottom, front and back edges are flush (see 7). Fix the drawer fronts H and the

drawer backs J in position in the same way and secure the knock-down corner joints; check the drawer is square. Punch all pin heads below the surface and wipe off all excess adhesive.
Apply adhesive to one face of

7 Drawer assembly

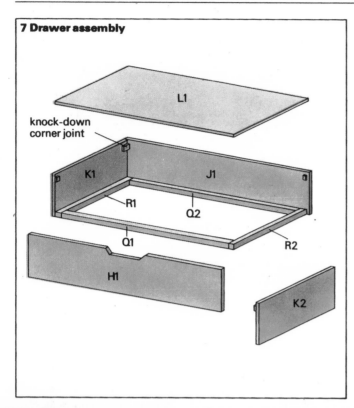

knock-down corner joint

L1

K1

J1

R1

Q2

Q1

R2

H1

K2

8 Drawer back detail

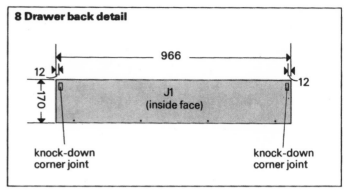

966

12

12

170

J1
(inside face)

knock-down corner joint

knock-down corner joint

9 Drawer side detail

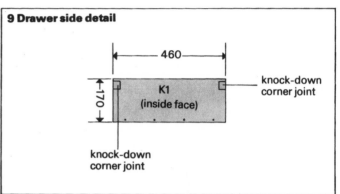

460

170

K1
(inside face)

knock-down corner joint

knock-down corner joint

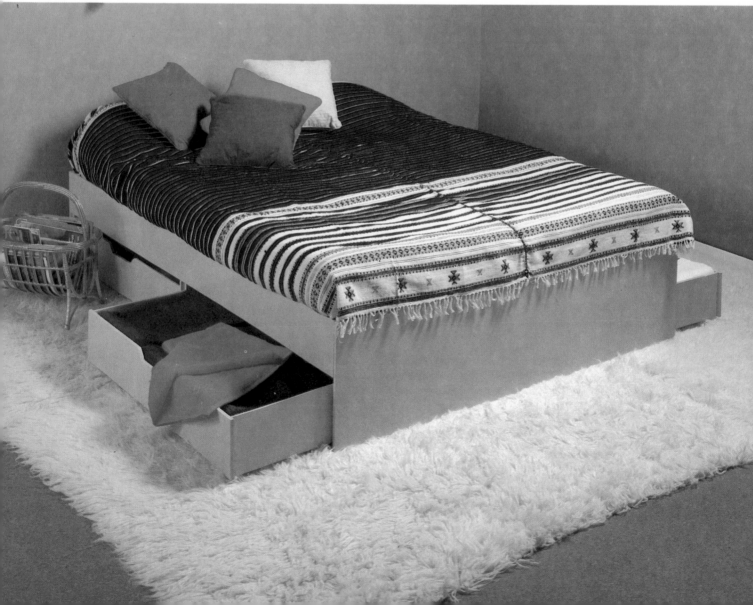

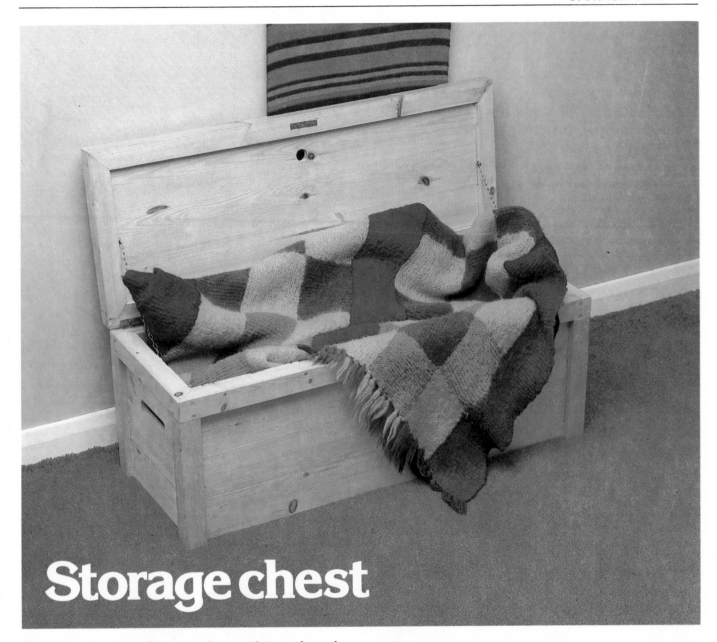

Storage chest

This pine storage chest can be used anywhere in the home and a lock has been fitted to deter children and protect valuables. Keep the finish plain to bring out the natural effect of the wood.

Tools and materials

timber (see cutting list)
measuring tape, pencil and try square
hacksaw, tenon saw, fine-tooth panel saw, pad saw
sharp trimming knife and metal straight-edge
medium fine, fine and flour glasspaper
electric drill, 9, 20 and 25mm bits, mitre box (or guide)
screwdriver, bradawl, hammer and nail punch
12 and 25mm chisels, two sash cramps
woodworking adhesive and clean cloth

For assembly

panel pins 19 and 32mm long, 5mm of 9mm diameter dowel
four steel furniture glides
500mm of brass chain
914mm of 25mm wide brass piano hinge and screws to fit
lock mechanism (if used)
matching plastic wood, Danish oil or polyurethane
    lacquer (for finish)

Cutting list for softwood & plywood.

Description	Key	Quantity	Dimensions
Long lid and frame battens	A	4	974 × 44 × 44mm
Short lid and frame battens	B	4	382 × 44 × 44mm
Frame uprights	C	4	294 × 44 × 44mm
Long planks	D	9	886 × 98 × 16mm
Short planks	E	6	294 × 98 × 16mm
Long base supports	F	2	870 × 22 × 22mm
Short base supports	G	2	322 × 22 × 22mm
Centre base support	H	1	278 × 32 × 22mm
Base panels (plywood)	J	2	457 × 322 × 6mm

stage 1

Measure and cut with a tenon saw all the softwood pieces according to the dimensions shown (**see cutting list**). Mark out the cutting lines on both sides of the plywood to the dimensions shown (**see cutting list**) and score along these lines with a sharp trimming knife held against a metal straight-edge. Cut the base panels to size with a fine-tooth panel saw and cut a 14mm square recess from the two corners on one short edge of both panels with a tenon saw. Smooth all surfaces of all cut pieces with medium fine, then fine, glasspaper.

Using a tenon saw and a mitre box (or guide), mitre both ends of all the long and short lid and frame battens A and B.

Mark out the handle slot in the top short planks E1 and E4 according to the dimensions shown (**see end elevation**), drill a 25mm diameter hole at both ends of each slot (placing a piece of scrap wood under the drilling area in each case) and remove the rest of the waste from between the drilled holes with a pad saw. Mark out and drill four 20mm diameter ventilation holes in what will be the top long plank D4 at the back of the finished chest (**see assembly diagram**), drilling them centrally in the plank 20mm and 300mm in from the ends. Mark the finger-pull hole in the long plank D3 according to the dimensions shown (**see plan**) and drill a 25mm diameter hole at this point, placing a piece of scrap wood under the drilling area. Bevel the edges of the hole with glasspaper.

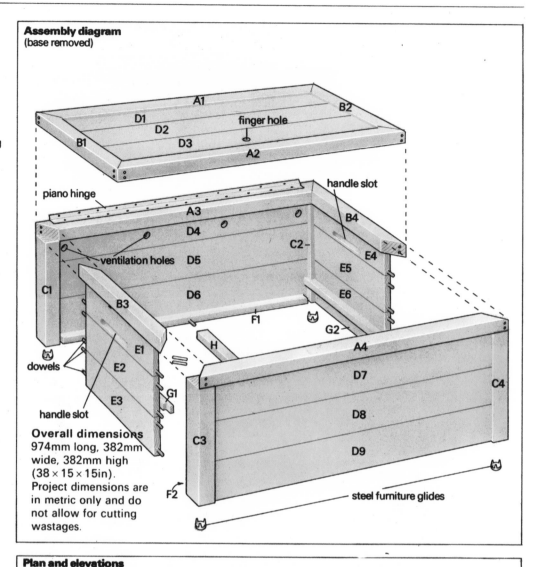

Assembly diagram
(base removed)

finger hole

piano hinge

handle slot

ventilation holes

handle slot

dowels

Overall dimensions
974mm long, 382mm wide, 382mm high (38 × 15 × 15in). Project dimensions are in metric only and do not allow for cutting wastages.

steel furniture glides

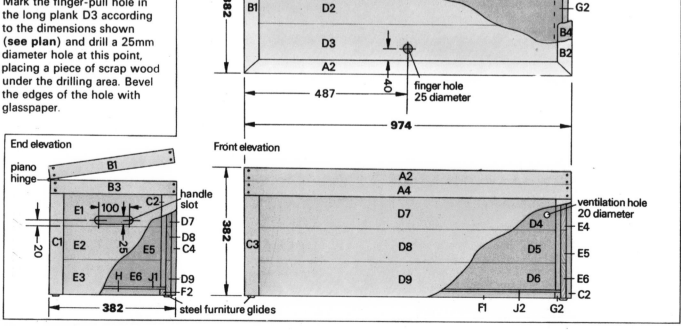

Plan and elevations
(dimensions in millimetres)

Plan

382

487

974

419

40

finger hole
25 diameter

End elevation

piano hinge

handle slot

100

25

20

382

steel furniture glides

Front elevation

382

ventilation hole
20 diameter

stage 2

Drill all the 9mm diameter dowel holes, 15mm deep, on the inside edges of the long and short lid battens A1 and A2 and B1 and B2 (see 1a and 1c) and drill the dowel holes on the bottom edge of the long and short frame battens A3 and A4 and B3 and B4 according to the dimensions shown (see 1b and 1d).

Mark out and drill the dowel holes on the inside edges of all four uprights C according to the dimensions shown (see 1e).

Mark out and drill the dowel holes in all four edges of the long and short planks D and E according to the dimensions shown (see 1f and 1g), drilling into only one long edge of what will be the bottom planks D6, D9, E3 and E6 on the finished chest (see assembly diagram).

stage 3

Cut the 9mm diameter dowel into twenty-eight 30mm lengths to assemble the lid. Pour some woodworking adhesive into the dowel holes in the long planks D1, D2 and D3 and apply some to the fixing edges; fix these planks firmly together with the cut dowels and fix the long and short battens A1 and A2 and B1 and B2 onto the protruding dowels (see 2). Tighten two sash cramps across the width of the lid until all the adhesive has set hard. Wipe off excess adhesive with a clean dampened cloth. While the adhesive is setting, drill two 9mm diameter dowel holes through each mitre joint between the battens A and B at the dimensions shown (see 2 inset). Cut eight 60mm lengths of the 9mm diameter dowel, apply adhesive to these dowels and push them into the holes in the mitre joints so both ends of each dowel protrude. Wipe off excess adhesive. When the adhesive has set hard, trim off the protruding dowel ends with a sharp chisel.

stage 4

Cut forty-eight 30mm lengths of the 9mm diameter

dowel to assemble the front and back of the chest. Pour some adhesive into the dowel holes in the long planks D and apply some to the fixing edges; fix D4, D5 and D6 together, then D7, D8 and D9, with the cut dowels (see 3). Apply adhesive to the ends of the long planks D and pour some inside the dowel holes; fix the uprights C and the long frame battens A firmly in position on the protruding dowels (see 3). Tighten two sash cramps across the width of the assembled back and front of the chest until the adhesive has set. Wipe off all excess adhesive.

Cut eighteen 30mm lengths of the 9mm diameter dowel to assemble each end of the

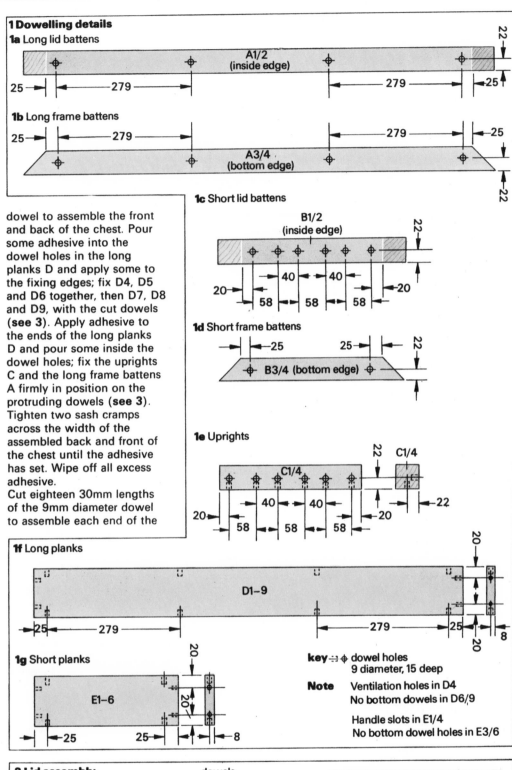

1 Dowelling details

1a Long lid battens

A1/2 (inside edge)

25 — 279 — 279 — 25

22 | 22

1b Long frame battens

25 — 279 — 279 — 25

A3/4 (bottom edge)

22 | 22

1c Short lid battens

B1/2 (inside edge)

20 — 40 — 40 — 20
58 — 58 — 58

22

1d Short frame battens

25 — 25

B3/4 (bottom edge)

22

1e Uprights

C1/4

22

C1/4

20 — 40 — 40 — 20
58 — 58 — 58

22

1f Long planks

D1–9

25 — 279 — 279 — 25 — 8

20 | 20

1g Short planks

E1–6

25 — 25 — 8

20 | 20

key ⊕ dowel holes 9 diameter, 15 deep

Note Ventilation holes in D4
No bottom dowels in D6/9

Handle slots in E1/4
No bottom dowel holes in E3/6

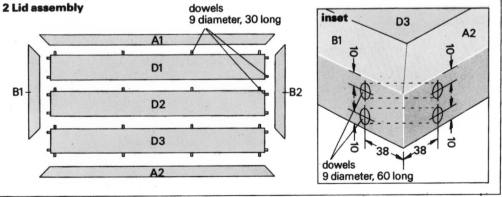

2 Lid assembly

dowels 9 diameter, 30 long

A1

D1

B1   D2   B2

D3

A2

inset

D3

B1   A2

10   10

10   38 — 38   10

dowels 9 diameter, 60 long

chest. Pour some adhesive into the dowel holes in the short planks E and apply some to the fixing edges; fix E1, E2 and E3 together, then E4, E5 and E6, with the cut dowels, making sure E1 and E4 are the right way round (**see 4**). Fix the short frame battens B in position on E1 and E4 and tighten two sash cramps round each end assembly until the adhesive has set. Wipe off excess adhesive.

stage 5

Mark out and drill the 9mm diameter dowel hole, 15mm deep, on both of the long base supports F at the dimensions shown (**see 5a**). Drill the 9mm diameter dowel hole, 15mm deep, in both ends of the centre base support H (**see 5b**) then mark out and cut with a tenon saw the rebate at both ends of both short base supports G according to the dimensions shown (**see 5c**). Mark the fixing position of the long base supports onto the long planks D6 and D9 at the dimensions shown (**see 3**), apply adhesive to the fixing edge of both base supports F and fix them firmly in position with the 32mm long panel pins; space these at about 100mm intervals and ensure the dowel hole on both supports is facing inwards.
Cut two 30mm lengths of the 9mm diameter dowel, pour some adhesive into the dowel hole in F1 and F2 and push the cut dowels inside.
Apply some adhesive to the ends of the short planks E and to the protruding dowels in the base supports F1 and F2; also apply adhesive to the mitred end of the long and short frame battens A and B and to both ends of the centre base support H. Fix the end assemblies to the front and back and the centre base support onto the protruding dowels in the long base supports F (**see assembly diagram**).
Tighten two sash cramps round each end of the chest, making sure all joints remain square. Wipe off excess adhesive.
When all the adhesive has set hard, apply adhesive to the

fixing edges of the short base supports G and fix them flush with the bottom edge of the short planks E3 and E6 with the 32mm long panel pins (**see assembly diagram**). Apply adhesive to the top edges of all the base supports, lower the base panels J into position and hammer 19mm long panel pins through the panels into the supports at about 100mm intervals. Punch all pin heads slightly below the surface of the plywood with a nail punch and wipe off excess adhesive.
Drill two 9mm diameter dowel holes through each mitre joint in the long and short frame battens A and B on the chest in the same way as for the lid. Cut eight 60mm lengths of the 9mm diameter dowel and glue these inside the holes as before, trimming off the protruding dowel ends when the adhesive has set.

stage 6

Fill all holes, cracks and abrasions with matching plastic wood and rub all surfaces smooth with fine, then flour, glasspaper.
For the finish, we applied two coats of Danish oil although you could use a polyurethane lacquer.
Hammer a steel furniture glide centrally into the bottom end of each upright C (**see assembly diagram**).
Cut the brass piano hinge to length with a hacksaw and cut a recess for the hinge in the long lid and frame battens A1 and A3 so the hinge will be 30mm in from each end of the lid. Fix the hinge inside the recess in the

lid with 25mm long brass screws of the correct gauge for the hinge you are using. Fix the lid in position on the chest by screwing the unattached leaf of the hinge to A3, making sure the lid will close accurately.
Cut two 250mm lengths of the brass chain and fix them

inside the chest and lid to support the lid when open. You can fit a lock to the chest so the contents will be out of the reach of children.

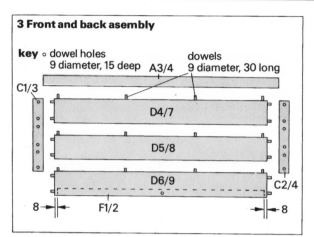

3 Front and back asembly

key ∘ dowel holes
9 diameter, 15 deep   A3/4   dowels
9 diameter, 30 long

C1/3

D4/7

D5/8

D6/9   C2/4

8   F1/2   8

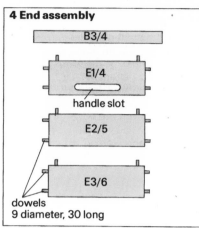

4 End assembly

B3/4

E1/4

handle slot

E2/5

E3/6

dowels
9 diameter, 30 long

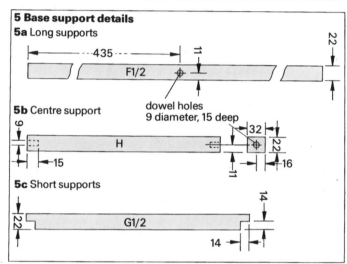

5 Base support details
5a Long supports

435   11   22

F1/2

dowel holes
9 diameter, 15 deep

5b Centre support

9   32

H   22

15   11   16

5c Short supports

22   14

G1/2

14

Sandboat

This fun idea for a sandpit in the shape of a boat, which involves simple techniques, will keep the children amused for hours.

stage 1

Measure and cut with a panel saw all the pieces of timber (except the four seat supports F) to the dimensions shown (**see cutting list and cutting plan**).

To cut the seat supports F, place the timber rail in a vice or mitre box and make the 45 degree angle cuts with a tenon saw at the dimensions shown (**see cutting plan**).

Tools and materials

timber (see cutting list)
measuring tape, pencil, try square
panel saw, tenon saw, vice, mitre box (or guide)
hand or electric drill, 2, 5 and 25mm bits
screwdriver, bradawl, countersink bit
hammer, nail punch, block plane, mallet (if used)
water-resistant woodworking adhesive, clean cloth
sharp knife or chisel, medium fine and fine glasspaper
No 10 rustproof countersunk screws 50 and 63mm long
oval nails 50mm long
1829mm of 25mm dowel (for mast)
exterior grade cellulose filler or plastic wood
clear gloss polyurethane lacquer (for mast)
primer, undercoat and gloss top coat paint (for finish)
50 and 100mm paint brushes

Overall dimensions
2439mm long, 1220mm wide, 225mm high (86 × 48 × 9in).
Project dimensions are in metric only and do not allow for
cutting wastages.

Assembly diagram

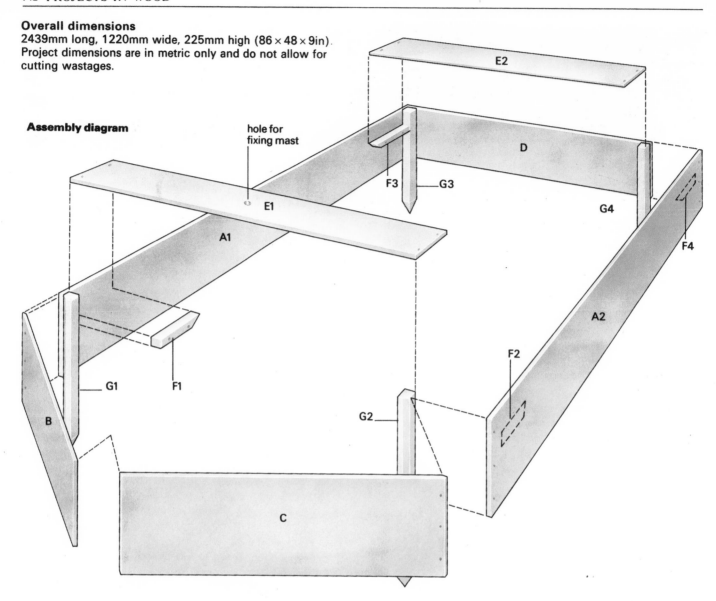

Make four cuts with a tenon
saw at the bottom of all four
uprights G to shape the
points for fixing the sandpit
firmly into the ground (**see
1a**). Mark the chamfer on the
square end of the uprights G1
and G2 to the dimensions
shown (**see 1b**) and remove
the waste with a block plane.

stage 2

Drill three 5mm diameter
clearance holes 44mm in
from one end of both sides
A, placing them 25mm in
from the edges of each plank
and one in the middle (**see
side elevation**).
Drill three 5mm clearance
holes 12mm in from the other
end of both sides A and
countersink all the holes to
take No 10 screws.
Drill three 5mm clearance
holes 22mm in from either

end of the back D, placing
these 30mm in from the
edges and one off centre
between them. Countersink
them to take No 10 screws.
Apply adhesive to both ends
of the back D and fix the
back ends of both sides A
(the clearance holes are
44mm in from the back ends)
squarely to the back D with
the 50mm long oval nails,
avoiding the clearance holes.
Hold the uprights G3 and G4
in position in the joints
between the back and the
two sides so the top edges
are flush and mark with a
bradawl through the
clearance holes in A and D
onto the uprights. Drill 2mm
pilot holes at these points
and glue and screw G3 and
G4 firmly in position with the
50mm long screws. Wipe off
excess adhesive with a clean
dampened cloth.

stage 3

Hold the uprights G1 and G2
against the other end of the
sides A so the back edge of
the chamfer on each upright
is flush with the end of each
side A. Mark with a bradawl
through the clearance holes
in the sides onto the uprights
and drill 2mm pilot holes at
these points. Glue and screw
both uprights in position
with 50mm screws and wipe
off all excess adhesive.
Drill three 5mm clearance
holes, 35mm in from
one end of both bow sections
B and C and countersink
them to take No 10 screws.
Mark the 45 degree mitre on
the drilled end of B and C
(**see plan inset**) and
carefully remove the waste
from each with a block
plane to form the mitre.
Glue and nail the square end

of the right bow section B
squarely to the square end of
the left bow section C with
the 50mm long oval nails
(**see plan**). Wipe off excess
adhesive.
Hold the assembled bow
section in the required
position against the uprights
G1 and G2 so the top edges
are flush (**see plan and side
elevation**), making sure the
mitred ends of B and C are
pressed hard against the
uprights G and the sides A.
The outside edges of the
mitred ends of B and C will
protrude, but don't trim this
off until you have assembled
the sandpit.
Mark with a bradawl through
the clearance holes in B and
C onto both uprights G and
drill 2mm pilot holes at these
points. Apply adhesive to the
chamfered edge of G1 and
G2 and fix the bow section

Cutting plan for softwood

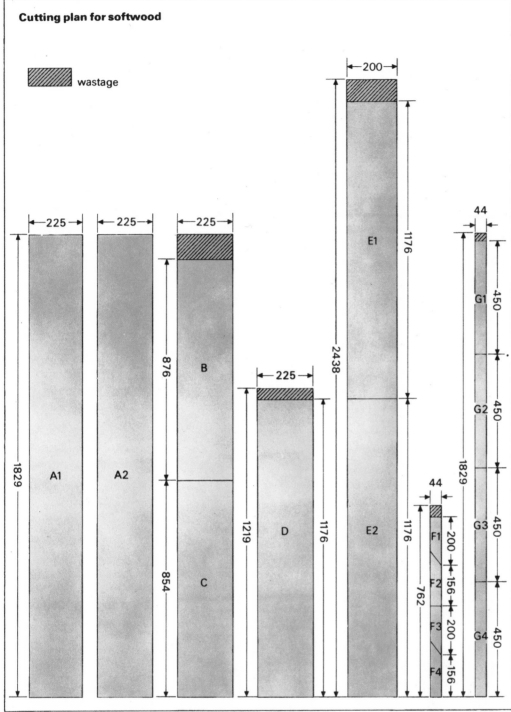

wastage

seat supports onto the sides A and drill 2mm pilot holes at these points. Apply adhesive to the fixing edges of the seat supports and glue and screw them firmly in position with the 63mm long screws. Wipe off excess adhesive.

Drill two 5mm clearance holes 22mm in from each end and 35mm in from each edge of both seats E and countersink them to take No 10 screws. Place the seats in the required position on the seat supports (**see plan**) and mark with a bradawl through the clearance holes in the seats onto the seat supports. Remove the seats and drill 2mm pilot holes at these points, apply adhesive to the top faces of the four seat supports and fix the seats firmly down with the 50mm long screws. Wipe off excess adhesive. Remove the waste wood at the two joins between the assembled bow section and the sides A with a block plane. Apply two coats of gloss polyurethane lacquer to the 1829mm length of 25mm dowel to make the mast weatherproof.

Drill a 25mm diameter hole in the centre of the front seat E1, make a point at one end of the 25mm dowel with a knife or chisel and insert this dowel through the hole in the seat. When the sandpit is in position, drive the mast at least 150mm into the ground.

stage 4

Fill all holes, cracks and abrasions with exterior grade cellulose filler or plastic wood and rub all surfaces smooth with medium fine, then fine, glasspaper.

Apply a coat of primer, an undercoat and at least three top coats of gloss paint for a durable, weatherproof finish. Allow each coat to dry before applying the next. Place the sandpit in a level part of your garden and hammer each upright G a little at a time into the ground, using a mallet or hammer and a block of wood, until the bottom edges of the sides A are at ground level. Fill the boat with about ¼cu m (or ¼cu yd) of silver sand. Don't use builder's sand since this will stain clothes.

Cutting list for softwood

Description	Key	Quantity	Dimensions
Sides	A	2	1829 × 225 × 22mm
Right bow section	B	1	876 × 225 × 22mm
Left bow section	C	1	854 × 225 × 22mm
Back	D	1	1176 × 225 × 22mm
Seats	E	2	1176 × 200 × 22mm
Seat supports	F	4	200 × 44 × 44mm
Uprights	G	4	450 × 44 × 44mm

in position with 50mm screws. Wipe off all excess adhesive. Drill a 5mm clearance hole 50mm in from each end of the four seat supports F and countersink them to take No 10 screws. Hold the seat supports in the required position against the sides A 80mm down from the top edges of the sides A and with the square ends of the seat supports touching the uprights G (**see side elevation and plan**).

Mark with a bradawl through the clearance holes in the

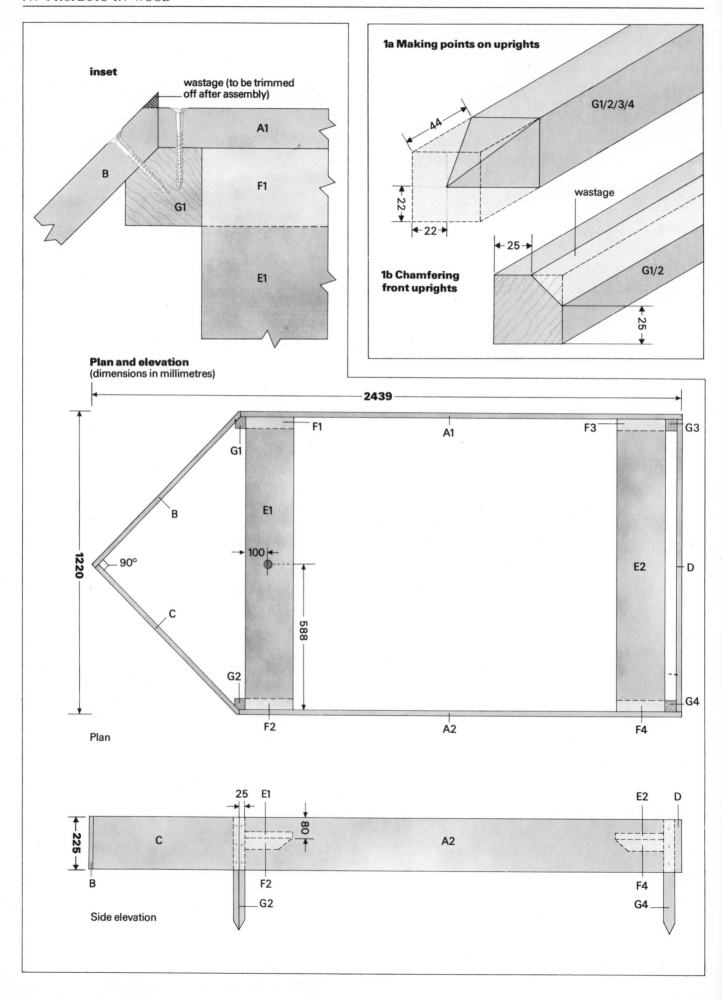

inset

wastage (to be trimmed off after assembly)

A1

B

F1

G1

E1

1a Making points on uprights

G1/2/3/4

44

22

22

wastage

25

G1/2

25

1b Chamfering front uprights

Plan and elevation
(dimensions in millimetres)

2439

F1 A1 F3 G3

G1

B

E1

90°

100

C

588

1220

G2

F2 A2 F4 G4

Plan

25 E1 E2 D

80

C A2

225

B F2 F4

G2 G4

Side elevation

Flap-down
ironing board

You can buy an ironing board quite cheaply in the shops but where do you put it? Store it in a cupboard and you have to struggle with broom sticks and mops every time you want to use it. Our ironing board looks very attractive on the wall or on a cupboard door and flaps down easily whenever you want it. With a simple change in the length of the legs shown on the cutting list you can make the board a suitable height for sitting or standing to work. First decide on the desired work position and make up the legs to suit.

Tools and materials

timber (see cutting list)
measuring tape, pencil, try square, spirit level
panel saw, tenon saw, coping saw, pair of compasses
screwdriver, bradawl, countersink bit, masonry bit
hammer and nail punch, 38mm chisel, marking gauge
hand or electric drill, 2, 3, 4, 5 and 6mm bits
medium fine and fine glasspaper
woodworking adhesive
thixotropic impact adhesive

For assembly

panel pins 19, 32 and 38mm long
No 8 countersunk screws 32mm long
No 12 countersunk screws 38mm long and wall plugs
No 6 raised head screws 18 and 32mm long
two 300mm long brass joint stays, two 25mm wide back flap hinges and 300mm of 32mm piano hinge, with 18mm long countersunk screws and 12mm long chipboard screws to fit
one roller blind kit and 1.4m of 43cm wide fabric
1m of 40cm wide calico (for ironing board cover)
1m of 400 × 6mm polyether foam
290 × 180 × 6mm 'safe' asbestos (for iron-rest)

For finish

cellulose filler or plastic wood
wood stain or dye and lint-free rag; or primer, undercoat and top coat and 50mm paint brush (if used)

Overall dimensions (when folded)

1220mm, 490mm wide, 108mm front to back (48 × 19 × 4in). Project dimensions are in metric only and do not allow for cutting wastages.

Cutting list for chipboard & softwood

Description	Key	Quantity	Dimensions
Work surface (chipboard)	A	1	1120 × 300 × 18mm
Legs	B	2	800* × 35 × 22mm
Foot	C	1	250 × 35 × 22mm
Fronts	D	2	1220 × 44 × 16mm
Sides	E	2	1220 × 92 × 16mm
Cross battens	F	3	490 × 44 × 22mm
Top	G	1	458 × 73 × 16mm
Latch	H	1	125 × 32 × 9mm
Latch block	J	1	66 × 44 × 22mm

* Reduce this measurement to 700 if you prefer sitting down to iron.

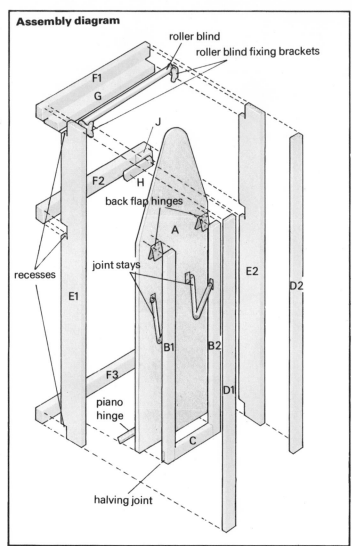

Assembly diagram

roller blind
roller blind fixing brackets
F1
G
J
F2
H
back flap hinges
A
joint stays
recesses
E1
E2
D2
B1
B2
F3
D1
piano hinge
C
halving joint

stage 1

Measure and cut all the pieces of timber to size according to the dimensions shown (**see cutting list**). The chipboard work surface A should be cut with a panel saw and the softwood parts with a tenon saw. Rub all surfaces smooth with medium fine, then fine, glasspaper. Mark out the shaping lines on the work surface A to the dimensions shown (**see 1**), draw a 70mm radius circle with a pair of compasses and cut off the waste with a panel and coping saw, making the straight cuts with the panel saw and cutting the curve with the coping saw.

stage 2

To make the leg frame (**see 2**) mark out the halving joint at one end of both legs B and both ends of the foot C. Apply adhesive to all these joints and bring them together, securing them with the 19mm long panel pins. Wipe off all excess adhesive with a clean dampened cloth and make sure all joint edges are flush by rubbing over with medium fine, then fine, glasspaper.

Fix one leaf of each back flap hinge centrally to the top inside face of the two legs B with the 18mm long countersunk screws so the knuckle of the hinge is clear of the end of the leg and fix the other half of the hinges to the underside of the work surface A at the dimensions shown (**see side section**) with the 12mm long chipboard screws. There should be a 25mm gap between the frame and the sides of the work surface A. Open the leg frame out at right-angles to the work surface, using a try square for accuracy, and screw the joint stays to the inside edges of the legs and to the underside of the top so the stay is fully

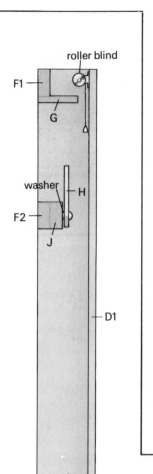

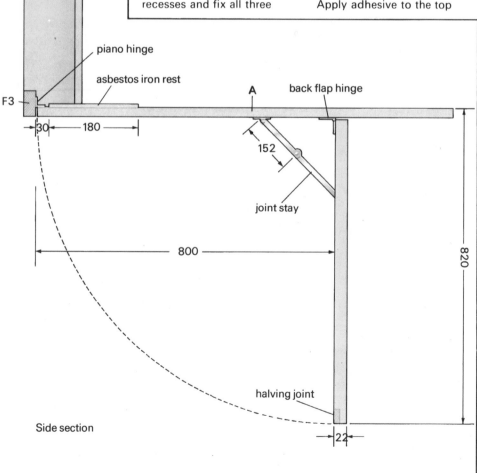

roller blind

F1

G

washer

H

F2

J

D1

piano hinge

asbestos iron rest

F3

A   back flap hinge

30   180

152

joint stay

800

820

halving joint

22

Side section

extended and locked in position when the legs are at right-angles.

Mark out the recesses in the two sides E at the dimensions shown (**see side elevation**) making sure they are exactly 22mm deep. It is best to use a marking gauge for accuracy. For each recess make two cuts with a tenon saw to the depth line and chop out the waste from between the cut lines with a 38mm chisel. Drill a 5mm diameter clearance hole 8mm in from each end of all three cross battens F and countersink these to take No 8 screws. Place the two sides E, front edge down, on a flat surface and position the cross battens in the recesses so the clearance holes line up with the middle of the recess in every case. Mark with a bradawl through the clearance holes onto the sides E, remove the cross battens and drill 2mm pilot holes at these points.

Apply adhesive to the inside of the bottom and middle recesses and fix all three

cross battens firmly in position with the 32mm countersunk screws. Don't apply adhesive to the top slot or batten as it will have to be removed again. Wipe off all excess adhesive.

Apply adhesive to the front edge of both sides E and fix the fronts D in position with the 32mm long panel pins so the top and bottom and side edges are flush. Wipe off excess adhesive.

stage 3

Remove the top cross batten F1 and screw the roller blind brackets (with the screws provided) to the top inside edge of the two sides D (**see 3**), making sure to place the slotted one on the left as you look at the ironing board from the back. Both brackets must be flush with the top edge of the sides. Cut the roller and fabric to size and make up the roller blind so it is 435mm wide, not including the pins on the end of the roller.

Apply adhesive to the top

recesses in the back edges of the two sides D and screw the top cross batten F1 back in place. Apply adhesive to the bottom edge of F1 and fix the top G in position with the 32mm panel pins so the back edges are flush. Wipe off all excess adhesive and drill two 6mm diameter clearance holes in F1 and F3 at the dimensions shown (**see front elevation**), countersinking them to take No 12 screws to take the fixing screws when screwing the board to the wall or door

stage 4

Cut the foam with a pair of scissors so it is 20mm wider than the work surface A. It is set 210mm back from the hinged end to allow the iron-rest to sit directly on the chipboard. Coat the top surface and all edges (except the back edge) of A with thixotropic impact adhesive and coat one side of the foam; leave all glued surfaces until touch-dry. Press the foam firmly in position taking care to fold it down and glue it to the edges of the chipboard as well.

Cut a 96.5 × 40cm piece of calico and fix this over the foam by tacking it (with the decorative tacks) to the underside of the work surface, spacing the tacks at 200mm intervals. The raw edge of the calico should be turned over for a neat finish.

Chamfer the edges and round off the corners of the asbestos iron-rest with medium fine glasspaper; drill a 4mm diameter clearance hole 20mm in from each corner and countersink them to take No 6 screws.

Warning When working with asbestos always wear a protective mask so you do not inhale the poisonous dust.

Place the iron-rest in the required position on the work surface A at the dimensions shown (**see 4a**) and mark with a bradawl onto the chipboard. Drill 2mm pilot holes at these points and fix the iron-rest firmly down with the 18mm raised head screws. Screw the piano hinge to the top of the work surface A so it is flush with the end and sides (**see 4a and 4b**) and

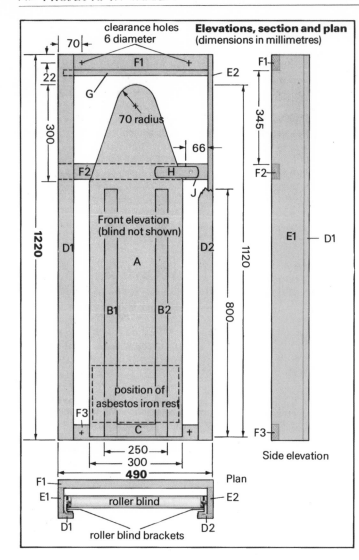

clearance holes
6 diameter

Elevations, section and plan
(dimensions in millimetres)

70

F1

22

G

70 radius

300

66

F2   H

J

Front elevation
(blind not shown)

B1   B2

1220

D1   D2

A

position of
asbestos iron rest

F3

250

300

490

C

F1

E1   roller blind   E2

D1   roller blind brackets   D2

F1

E2

345

F2

1120

E1 — D1

800

F3

Side elevation

Plan

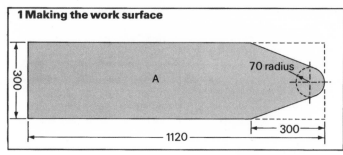

1 Making the work surface

300

A

70 radius

1120   300

nail through the previously
drilled 6mm diameter
clearance holes in the cross
battens F1 and F3. Drill holes
of the correct diameter and
depth for the wall plugs you
are using (if fixing to the wall)
or drill 3mm diameter pilot
holes (if fixing to a wooden
door) and screw the board
firmly in position, fitting the
assembled roller blind to the
brackets on the top inside
edge of each side D.

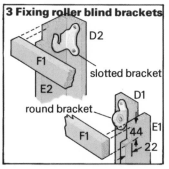

3 Fixing roller blind brackets

D2

F1

slotted bracket

E2

round bracket

D1

F1   E1

44

22

2 Leg frame assembly

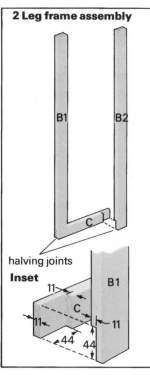

B1   B2

C

halving joints

Inset   B1

11

C

11   11

44   44

4a Fixing asbestos iron rests

piano hinge   asbestos

5

290

calico
covering foam   A

5

180

30   + clearance holes
4 diameter

Inset (section)   foam
calico   6 thick

A

decorative tacks

4b Fixing piano hinge

asbestos

countersunk
screw

A

piano hinge

F3   16

20

30

18

5 Fixing latch

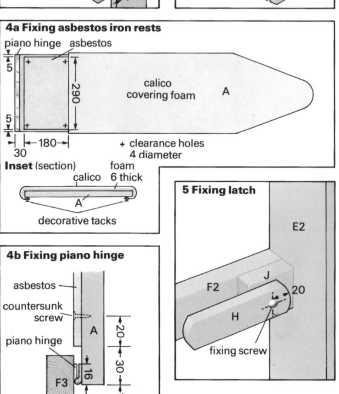

E2

F2   J   20

H

fixing screw

screw the other half of the
hinge to the bottom cross
batten F3 at the dimensions
shown (**see 4b**) with the
work surface A lowered.
Glue and pin the latch block
J to one end of the middle
cross batten F2 with 38mm
panel pins. Using a small
round object as a template,
mark the curve at each end of
the latch H and cut off the
waste with a coping saw.
Smooth the cut curves with
medium fine, then fine,
glasspaper.
Drill a 5mm diameter clearance
hole centrally 20mm in from
one end of H and countersink
it to take a No 8 screw. Hold
H in the required position
against the front edge of the
latch block J (**see 5**) and
mark with a bradawl through
the clearance hole in H onto
J. Drill a 2mm pilot hole at
this point and screw the latch
onto the block with the No 8
raised head screw 32mm
long, placing a washer
between the two as a spacer.

stage 5

Fill all holes, cracks and
abrasions (other than the
clearance holes for the wall
and latch fixing screws)
with cellulose filler or plastic
wood and rub all surfaces
smooth with medium fine,
then fine, glasspaper.
Apply a stain to all timber
surfaces (except the underside
of the work surface A) with a
lint-free rag. Apply another
coat if you want to darken
the stain.
If you decide to paint the
ironing board to match or
contrast with your colour
scheme, apply a coat of
primer, undercoat and top
coat, allowing each to dry.
To hang the board, place it in
the desired position on a wall
or a cupboard door with the
work surface A lowered and
the joint stays locked fully
extended. Check with a spirit
level to ensure the work
surface is level in all
directions and mark with a

Book rack

Use up some of those pieces of scrap timber you have lying round the workshop to make this attractive book rack—we used parana pine.

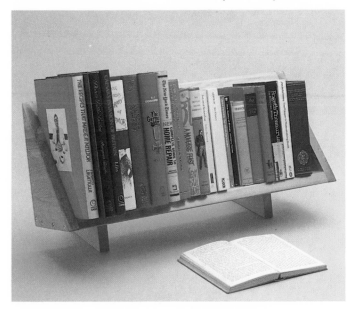

Cutting list for softwood

Description	Key	Quantity	Dimensions
Sides (to shape)	A	2	225 × 175 × 22mm
Back pieces	B	2	610 × 98 × 22mm
Base	C	1	610 × 149 × 22mm
Feet (to shape)	D	2	136 × 132 × 22mm

Assembly diagram
(dimensions in millimetres)

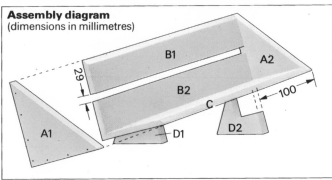

Side elevation

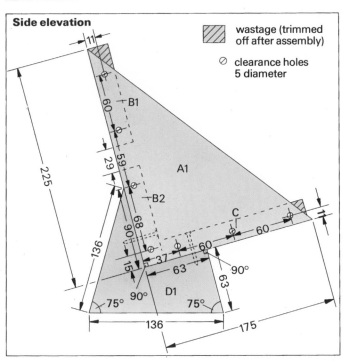

wastage (trimmed off after assembly)

⊘ clearance holes 5 diameter

stage 1

Measure and cut the back pieces B and the base C with a fine-tooth panel saw to the dimensions shown (**see cutting list**).
Mark the cutting lines on the sides A and cut with a fine-tooth panel saw to the dimensions shown (**see side elevation**). If you have a 22mm piece of softwood 225 × 175mm, you can obtain both sides from this by cutting it diagonally in half. Using a protractor and a tenon saw mark out and cut the two feet D to the shape shown (**see side elevation**). Smooth all cut edges with medium fine, then fine, glasspaper.
Drill the seven 5mm diameter clearance holes in both sides A at the dimensions shown (**see side elevation**) and countersink them to take No 8 screws.
Hold the bottom back piece B2 in the required position against one of the sides A and mark with a bradawl through the clearance holes in A onto B.
Drill 2mm pilot holes at these points, apply adhesive to this edge of B and fix it firmly in position onto A with No 8 countersunk screws 38mm long.
Glue and screw the top back piece B1 onto A1 (**see side elevation**), then fix the side A2 onto this assembly.
Hold the base C in the required position inside this assembly (**see side elevation and assembly diagram**) and mark with a bradawl through the clearance holes in the two sides A onto it. Drill 2mm pilot holes at these points, apply adhesive to both ends and to the back edge of the base and glue and screw it firmly in position with No 8 countersunk screws 38mm

long. Pin through the bottom back piece B2 into the base C (using 38mm long panel pins), placing the pins at 50mm intervals and punching all pin heads below the surface with a nail punch. Wipe off all excess adhesive. Using a panel saw, remove the bulk of the waste from the top edge of the top back piece B1 and from the front edge of the base C. Then use a block plane to remove the remaining waste from these edges and from the bottom front corner of both sides A (**see side elevation**).

stage 2

Hold one of the feet D in the required position 100mm in from one end of the rack and mark onto the back piece B2 and the base C where to drill clearance holes for the fixing screws; only two screws are needed to fix each foot; drill one 5mm clearance hole in B2 10mm up from the top face of C and another in C 30mm in from the front face of B2 (**see side elevation**).
Countersink these holes to take No 8 screws, hold the foot back in position and mark with a bradawl through the clearance holes in B2 and C onto the fixing edges of the foot. Drill 2mm pilot holes at these points, apply adhesive to the fixing edges of the foot and fix it firmly in position with No 8 countersunk screws 38mm long. Wipe off excess adhesive. Fix the second foot in the same way.
Fill all holes, cracks and abrasions with matching plastic wood or stopping and rub all surfaces smooth with medium fine, then fine, glasspaper; give a final rub over with flour glasspaper. Apply two coats of teak oil to highlight the grain.

All-purpose storage unit

This compact unit is ideal for use in any room in the home. Children can store their treasures in it or you can house a hi-fi system, records and cassettes. The laminate top makes it suitable as a coffee table and it is fitted with castors so you can wheel it anywhere you want.

Overall dimensions
851mm long, 577mm wide, 465mm high (34 × 23 × 18in). Project dimensions are in metric only and do not allow for cutting wastages. Overall height excludes castors.

Cutting list for Timesaver panels & chipboard

Description	Key	Quantity	Dimensions
Base	A	1	807 × 533 × 15mm
Main uprights	B	2	533 × 369 × 15mm
Small upright	C	1	369 × 125 × 15mm
Dividers	D	3	381 × 369 × 15mm
Shelves	E	2	381 × 110 × 15mm
Drawer fronts	F	2	407 × 140 × 15mm
Long plinths	G	2	763 × 63 × 15mm
Short plinths	H	2	459 × 63 × 15mm
Top (chipboard)	J	1	851 × 577 × 18mm

Tools and materials

Timesaver panels and chipboard (see cutting list) measuring tape, pencil, try square, metal straight-edge panel, tenon and hacksaws, block plane, fine flat file trimming knife, screwdriver, bradawl, countersink bit hand or electric drill, 2, 5 and 8mm bits, domestic iron woodworking adhesive and clean cloth, impact adhesive

For assembly
200mm of 8mm diameter dowel for six dowels 30mm long
16 joint blocks, eight white shelf supports
2m of plastic drawer runner profile
3m of 100mm profile of Formica Timesaver drawer system
four 100mm corner posts and four 100mm front plates
two pieces of 361 × 346 × 3mm hardboard (for drawer bases)
1m of 9mm square softwood fillet (for drawer base supports)
No 6 round head screws 12mm long
No 6 countersunk chipboard screws 19mm long
No 8 Pozidriv countersunk chipboard screws 38mm long
one pack of white plastic Pozi tops
four 90mm high plate-mounted castors, two drawer knobs
900 × 625mm decorative laminate (for top and edges)
5m of 15mm iron-on edging strip

Assembly diagram

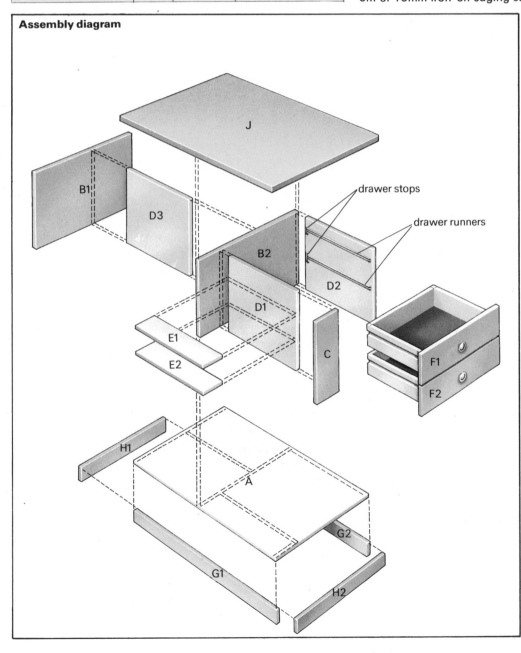

stage 1

Mark lightly with a pencil all the cutting lines on the Timesaver panels according to the dimensions shown (**see cutting list and cutting plan**). Label each part with the appropriate letter. Scribe along the cutting lines with a sharp knife held against a metal straight-edge to avoid damaging the melamine surface when sawing the panels to size. Cut all the Timesaver panels and the chipboard top J with a panel saw and smooth all cut edges with a block plane.

stage 2

Cut three 30mm lengths of the 8mm diameter dowel with a tenon saw and fix the small upright C to the divider D1 with these dowels, placing them 38mm in from each end and one in the centre. Wipe off excess adhesive with a clean dampened cloth.
Cut three more 30mm lengths of dowel and join B1 to D3 at the dimensions shown (**see plan**) in the same way. Fix laminate strips to the edges of the chipboard top J with impact adhesive and trim all edges flush with a block plane and fine flat file. Fix the decorative laminate sheet to the chipboard top in the same way. Cut four 350mm lengths of plastic drawer runner profile

Cutting plan for Timesaver panels

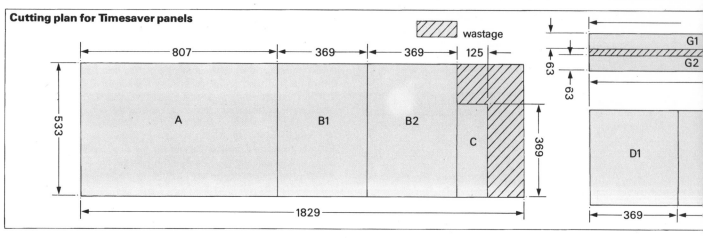

wastage

807 369 369 125

A B1 B2 C

533

369

1829

G1
G2

63
63

D1

369

Elevations and plan
(dimensions in millimetres)

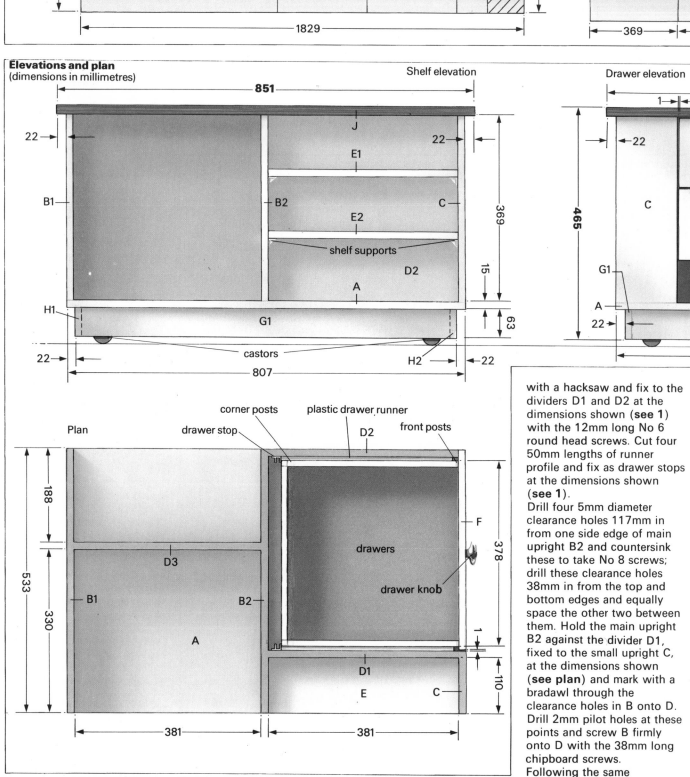

Shelf elevation

Drawer elevation

851

22

J

22

22

B1

E1

B2

C

C

369

E2

shelf supports

D2

465

A

G1

15

H1

A

G1

63

22

22

castors

H2

22

807

Plan

corner posts

drawer stop

plastic drawer runner

D2

front posts

188

533

330

D3

B1

B2

drawers

drawer knob

381

381

A

D1

E

C

F

378

1

110

with a hacksaw and fix to the dividers D1 and D2 at the dimensions shown (**see 1**) with the 12mm long No 6 round head screws. Cut four 50mm lengths of runner profile and fix as drawer stops at the dimensions shown (**see 1**).

Drill four 5mm diameter clearance holes 117mm in from one side edge of main upright B2 and countersink these to take No 8 screws; drill these clearance holes 38mm in from the top and bottom edges and equally space the other two between them. Hold the main upright B2 against the divider D1, fixed to the small upright C, at the dimensions shown (**see plan**) and mark with a bradawl through the clearance holes in B onto D. Drill 2mm pilot holes at these points and screw B firmly onto D with the 38mm long chipboard screws.
Following the same

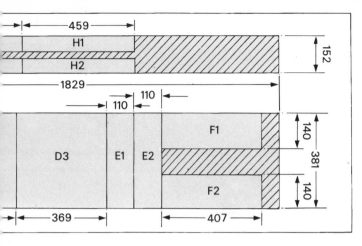

27mm in from the left edge with the 19mm long No 6 countersunk screws.
Fix the drawer fronts F onto each three-sided drawer assembly at the dimensions shown (**see 3**); make a pilot hole centrally on the front face of each drawer front and screw on the drawer knobs.
Fix a castor to the underside of the base A in each corner, far enough in from the plinths to allow the castors to swivel without obstruction. Push the plastic Pozi tops in any screw heads that will

show and, using a 'warm' iron over brown paper, press on the self-adhesive edging strip to all exposed chipboard edges.
Wipe off all pencil marks with soapy water and position the two shelves E on the previously fixed shelf supports.

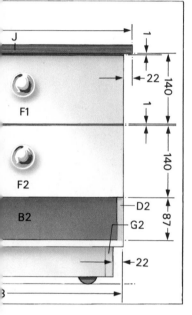

techniques, fix the divider D2 to the main upright B2, and D3 (already fixed to B1) to B2 at the dimensions shown (**see plan**) making sure all joints are square.

stage 3

Place the top J, with the laminated surface underneath, on a flat surface and position the basic assembly on top of it so there is a 22mm overhang all round. Fix the assembly to J with six joint blocks, placing these at the positions shown (**see plan**).
Place the base A on top of the assembly and mark on both sides of it the fixing positions of the two main uprights B, the small upright C and the three dividers D. Make sure all joints in the basic assembly remain square. Drill 5mm diameter clearance holes at 100mm intervals along the lines you have just marked and countersink them

to take No 8 screws. Place the base A back on top of the basic assembly and mark with a bradawl through the clearance holes onto the middle of the various panel edges. Remove A, drill 2mm pilot holes at these points and fix A firmly back in place with the 38mm long No 8 chipboard screws.

stage 4

Fix the two short plinths H between the long plinths G with a joint block placed centrally in each corner, making sure all joints are square and all edges flush (**see 2**).
Place this plinth assembly on top of the underside of the base A and fix it down using six joint blocks in the positions shown (**see 2**). There should be a 22mm gap between the outside edges of the plinths and the edges of the base.
Drill holes of the correct diameter and depth for the shelf supports you are using in the main upright B2 and the small upright C at the desired heights (**see shelf elevation**). Push the shelf supports in position.
Construct two three-sided Timesaver drawers, cutting the drawer profile into four 340mm lengths and two 349mm lengths.
Warning These sizes may vary due to errors in construction so check carefully before cutting your drawer profiles to size.
With a tenon saw cut the 9mm softwood fillet into two 340mm lengths and fix these to the inside face of each drawer front F at the dimensions shown (**see 3**),

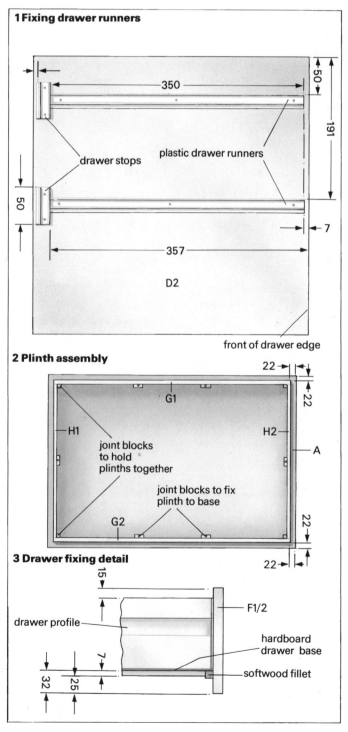

1 Fixing drawer runners

drawer stops
plastic drawer runners
D2
front of drawer edge

2 Plinth assembly

G1
H1   H2
joint blocks to hold plinths together
joint blocks to fix plinth to base
G2
A

3 Drawer fixing detail

drawer profile
F1/2
hardboard drawer base
softwood fillet

Appendix:

Woodworking tools and how to use them

There is a huge range of tools suitable for woodworking – both hand and power – and you should be familiar with them and how to use them. You obviously won't need to buy them all; plan carefully what you really want to start with and build up your collection gradually. Power tools can cut out a lot of time and effort and will be a great asset if you can afford them. You must have sufficient equipment for holding the work, otherwise you will find it very difficult to do the job properly. Always buy the best you can afford – whatever the tool – and make sure you look after it; this way it will perform well and last you.

Braces and hand drills

Braces and hand drills are a valuable addition to any tool kit. Although slower than power drills, they are more easily controlled and enable you to work in tight corners and where there is no electricity to run a power drill. They are particularly suitable for intricate work.

Swing brace

Often called a carpenter's or bit brace, this is particularly good for quick drilling of accurate holes in wood. The swing brace is measured by the diameter of the circle formed by the grip and sizes are 200–350mm (8–14in), the most popular for general work being 250mm (10in). You can get a fixed brace or one with a ratchet action. The ratchet type is more useful since you can drill a hole by working the grip backwards and forwards through 90 degrees rather than through 360 – a real advantage when working in confined spaces. The ratchet can be locked in a clockwise or anti-clockwise direction or so it moves through 360 degrees, like the fixed brace. The type of jaws fitted to the brace is important since the jaws determine what sort of bits can be used: Universal jaws will take both tapered and straight shanked bits, while Alligator jaws will take only bits which have a tapered shank.

There are small braces available for specialist jobs. These include the electrician's brace, which has a diameter, or sweep, of only 150mm (5⅞in), and the joist brace, which has a short drilling shaft with Universal jaws and is fitted with a long side arm which turns the shaft.

Using the swing brace When drilling through wood, ensure a clean hole and prevent the face of the timber breaking away by marking the position of the hole with a bradawl or nail punch. Place the point of the bit in this mark and turn the brace gently to drive the bit into the wood. When it starts to appear on the other side, withdraw the bit by turning the brace handle in the opposite direction. Complete the drilling by turning the wood round and placing the bit in the hole you made from the other side. If you cannot drill from both sides or if the timber is too thin, clamp a piece of scrap wood behind the point where you want the hole and drill right through into this.

If you are drilling to a fixed depth, fit the bit with a depth stop; either buy a special rubber collar or wrap round a piece of adhesive tape. Drilling holes squarely with a swing brace may prove difficult at first, so sight the bit against a try square to ensure accuracy.

Hand drill or wheel brace

This can be used with wood or masonry twist drills to make holes of up to 8mm (5⁄16in) diameter in a variety of materials. Single pinion hand drills are available, but better quality types have two pinions: the second pinion balances the gear wheels so the cogs meet perfectly. You can get hand drills where the gears are enclosed to protect them from dust and shavings.

An additional side handle is supplied with most models. This is detachable and should be used when more pressure and control are needed. With the side handle removed, you can work in tight corners which may be inaccessible with a power drill.

Using the wheel brace Turn the handle at a constant speed, but not too fast. Small twist drills tend

to clog quickly so withdraw the bit frequently to clear the waste. To withdraw the drill, keep turning the handle in the same direction and pull the drill away from the work. For normal work grip the main handle in your fist; when more pressure is needed, press the main handle into your body and grip the side handle to keep the brace straight as you use the turning handle.

Hand drills need very little maintenance apart from keeping the gears free of dust and occasionally giving the drill a light oiling. After a great deal of use the jaws may become worn and fail to grip the bit securely; but replacements are easily fitted. Twist the chuck as if opening the jaws and remove it from the brace. Hold the body of the chuck in a vice, unscrew the back cap, remove the chuck from the vice and take out the jaws. Squeeze the new jaws together and push them into the chuck, refit the back cap and screw the cap back onto the brace.

Breast drill

Used for heavy drilling jobs, the breast drill has two speeds, the slower one being used for tough materials such as masonry and steel. A breast pad is fitted at the top of the drill shaft so you can put your full weight behind the drill; the pad is adjustable for either horizontal or vertical drilling. A detachable side handle is also a standard feature.

The chuck of the breast drill will take any bit up to 12mm (½in) with parallel-sided shanks. It will also take bits up to 25mm (1in) with turned down shanks. Like the hand drill, various types are available, including one with completely enclosed working parts.

Push drill

A pump action drill which you use with only one hand. It is ideal for light work, such as making pilot holes (especially for hinges where you can hold the hinge in place with one hand and use the drill with the other), and for drilling small holes in thin plywood and mouldings. Interchangeable drill points are available from 1.6 to 4.4mm (1⁄16 – 11⁄64in).

Circular saws

As with any power tool, a circular saw must be handled with care and respect. Properly treated, it is a valuable addition to any handyman's workshop – taking the hard work out of sawing – and the wide range of blades available will enable you to tackle virtually any cutting job necessary. If you do not want to buy the purpose-built unit, an attachment to your electric drill can do the same job.

If you have a lot of accurate saw cutting to do, you may find the purpose-built unit, rather than an attachment to your electric drill, is worth buying. The attachment does provide a faster and more accurate cut than a conventional hand saw; and used with the correct blade you can cut all types of timber, as well as ferrous metals, aluminium, lead, asbestos and ceramic tiles, laminated chipboard and other laminates. But the attachment runs at lower speeds than the purpose-built unit and is therefore less efficient.

Alligator jaws

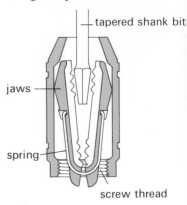

Universal jaws

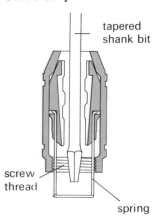

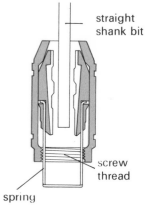

Above The two types of jaws fitted to a swing brace. Universal jaws take both tapered and straight shanked bits; alligator jaws take only tapered shanked bits

Right A range of circular saw blades used for (**top to bottom**) aluminium, stone, laminates, corrugated and flat sheet metal, man-made boards, ripping, flooring, general purpose, smoothing woodcuts and cross-cutting

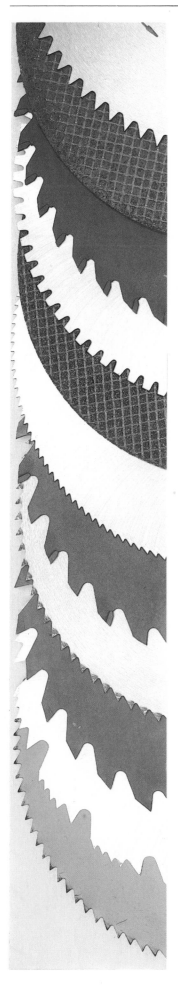

The saw blade is most efficient when used at high speeds: and the larger the blade diameter, the more power needed for maximum efficiency. Blades are commonly available in diameters of 125–229mm (5–9in). Larger blades are available for bigger saw units. When buying extra blades make sure they will fit your unit because just as blade sizes vary, so do methods of fitting them. And before you buy an attachment you should check with the manufacturer or supplier whether your power drill is suitable to take the attachment you want. The power of the average drill offers a maximum speed of around 2400rpm, while an integral unit gives a speed of 3000rpm.

Saw blades

A general purpose blade – normally supplied with the attachment or integral unit – is a combination of a rip and cross-cut blade, suitable for cutting across and along the grain. Usually a 24 point blade, it can also be used for light boards. Several blades and cutting discs are available for use with either type of saw, and some specialist blades.

Cross-cut blade Used for cutting timber to length.

Rip blade For sawing timber along its length and parallel to the grain.

Planer blade Hollow ground to give a smooth finish to a saw cut.

Tungsten carbide blade The hardened steel teeth cut more quickly, therefore making it suitable for cutting materials with a high resin content, such as plastic laminate and chipboard, which generally blunt normal steel teeth.

Metal cutting blade Has fine teeth and will cut most soft metals.

Flooring blade Suitable for cutting floorboards. It will also cut through nails.

Metal cutting wheel Used for cutting metals and plastics.

Masonry cutting disc This will cut brick, ceramic tiles, slate, marble, soft stone and non-ferrous metals.

Laminate blade Available in a tungsten carbide-tipped version. Because plastic is a difficult material to cut we recommend you sandwich it between two pieces of scrap wood and saw through all three layers to achieve a clean cut and prevent damaging the decorative surface.

Reinforced abrasive blade This will cut marble.

Friction blade For high-speed cutting of corrugated and flat steel sheets.

Warning Before fitting a blade make sure the saw is not connected to the power supply. You must always treat the electric saw with respect and care: it is one of the most useful tools in the home, but it can be one of the most dangerous if not handled properly. Never leave it on a bench where children may have access; when you have finished using it, always lock it away.

Fitting the blade

It is vitally important you fit the blade correctly. The direction of the blade is usually marked on the outer side by the manufacturer so there can be no mistake in fitting it. Check your blades regularly to make sure they are sharp: working with a blunt blade will cause it to overheat and be damaged; it will also spoil your work.

Changing the blade

This is a simple operation if you follow a set procedure. Hold the blade in a fixed position by inserting a screwdriver or special key into a hole drilled through the saw blade (making sure the power is switched off). Loosen the blade retaining bolt with a spanner, remove the old blade, and fit the replacement blade, retightening the retaining bolt. On most models the blade guard will have to be pulled back to do this.

Depth of cut This is adjusted by releasing a locking nut and raising the sole plate so the required depth of blade protrudes through the sole plate opening and relocking the nut to the hold position.

Using the saw

With a circular power saw the cut is usually made by one run of the saw blade, when the blade should be set slightly deeper than the thickness of the material being cut. When sawing thick timber or hard materials, however, you should cut in two stages. On the first run, set the blade depth to about half the thickness of the material you are cutting and follow up with a second run, setting the depth of cut to complete the sawing. This will prevent unnecessary stress and wear on the blade.

Rip fence guide This passes through a slot in the sole plate and is locked into position when the 'T' section of the fence is set at the required distance from the blade. Because it is adjustable it enables an accurate parallel cut to be made to a true straight edge of a piece of timber. This is particularly useful when ripping along a length of timber where a uniform width of cut is required. It can also be used across the grain if sufficiently close to the end. Remove the fence guide when using the saw to cross-cut timber beyond the reach of the fence.

When ripping through a long length of timber, the cut might be inclined to close behind the saw blade, causing it to overheat. You can prevent this by inserting a thick wedge of timber at the start of the cut before proceeding past the halfway mark on the timber being cut.

Large boards can be cut through the centre along an accurate line by clamping or pinning straight edge timber to the surface. This will act as a guide to the edge of the sole plate and the blade can be set at an accurate distance from the edge of the guide timber.

Warning Make sure the board is well supported along all edges and that sufficient clearance is provided under the cutting line.

Angle sawing This can be done by a simple adjustment to the sole plate, allowing the saw to cut accurately at a constant angle of 5–45 degrees. A protractor scale is a standard fitting to most units and attachments so the required angle can be set against the scale for accuracy. Once the angle has been set and locked, the blade can be set for the depth of cut as previously described. The teeth should project through the base of the material as for vertical cutting.

Groove cutting Set the blade to the required depth and make a series of runs within the chosen width of the groove by fractionally adjusting the fence guide. Leave a thick sliver of timber standing between each run to ensure an accurate line to the groove; these can be cleaned out later with a sharp chisel. Any attempt to clean the groove by joining the saw cuts is likely to result in the fence slipping from the line, leaving a ragged groove.

Grooves can be undercut in dovetail fashion by using an angled saw as already described.

Taking precautions

Always wear protective spectacles when using a saw. Flying sawdust can be irritating and dangerous to the eyes.

The cutting action of the teeth on a circular saw blade is in an upward direction, so always lay material with a decorative finish with the decorative surface face down – especially when cutting decorative laminates and veneer facings – or you will rip up the decorative surface.

Clamps and grips

Holding work securely is all important for safety and to do a good job. Here we describe the range of vices, clamps and grips available and some clamps you can make yourself – as well as how to use them.

Woodworking vices

Clamps and cramps are indispensable woodworking aids in certain circumstances, while your range of devices can be improved by several simple improvised pieces of home-made equipment. However, there is no real substitute for that most versatile clamping device, the traditional woodworking vice. Used properly, with plywood facings inside the jaws to protect the work from damage, a woodworking vice will prove to be the most useful piece of clamping equipment you can buy. Some vices are permanently mounted below the bench top, while various other models clamp on and can be removed as necessary. The jaws should have the largest possible surface area to minimize damage to the work, while at the same time giving a strong grip; they should also open wide enough to accommodate large cross-sections of timber. For best results, use a vice where the jaws have been drilled to allow replaceable protective plywood facings to be fixed easily in place. It is also useful to work with a vice which has a quick-release mechanism so you can open and close the jaws in seconds.

Some aluminium body vices have L-shaped jaws, which hold the work horizontally or vertically, and an offset clamp, which allows the vice to be fixed to the front and side of a bench and which can also be used as a G-clamp. A more versatile device is an all-purpose portable workbench. This has as its top a vice, which can be as wide as 740mm (or 29in) with a 100mm (or 4in) wide jaw opening, although there are smaller models available. On the largest model, swivelling vice pegs which press into the top of the bench allow items up to about 250mm (or 10in) wide to be gripped, while extender arms will accept sheets of wood up to about 1800 × 900mm (or 6 × 3ft) and picture, door and window frames. The vice jaws can be operated either in parallel or with a taper action.

Bench holdfast

This is used to hold wood down firmly on a bench top during work. The notched step of the cramp is passed through a hole in the bench top and levered over sideways by an arm. The arm exerts considerable pressure on the workpiece as the adjusting screw, which bears down on the top of the stem, is tightened. A holdfast can hold long timbers or large panels either on, or over, the edges of a bench.

It is important you protect the surface of the workpiece by placing a piece of scrap wood under the pressure point.

When fitting a holdfast, make sure the bench top is thick enough to take the iron collar, which comes with the tool, without bending. If necessary, reinforce the area where the collar will be fitted by gluing and screwing a 25mm (or 1in) thick hardwood block under the bench. Also make sure the collar is fixed away from under-bench drawers and cupboards. It is usually fitted at the end of the bench opposite the vice and you should keep it on the centre line of the bench top, about 450mm (or 18in) in from the end. The collar is countersunk in the bench top and screwed in place so it is level with the surface. There are two sizes commonly used: one with a maximum opening of 175mm (or $6\frac{7}{8}$in) and the other with a maximum opening of 194mm (or $7\frac{5}{8}$in). Extra collars are available to enable a holdfast to be used in several positions. When not in use the holdfast can be removed from the workbench and stored out of the way.

Bench hook

Although not strictly a clamping or gripping tool, the bench hook is useful for holding small pieces of timber while they are cut across the grain with a tenon saw. It is made of hardwood with a batten on the underside which rests against the top edge of the bench, and another on the top surface, where the wood rests and where you grip it by hand when cutting. You can make a bench hook from 18mm (or $\frac{3}{4}$in) thick hardwood. A useful platform size is 250 × 230mm (or 10 × 9in).

Home-made clamps

Purpose made clamps can be quite expensive, especially the larger size ones which you probably will not use very often. To save unnecessary expense, and with a minimum of time and effort, you can make highly effective clamps yourself.

Spanish windlass This can be used in many situations where clamping is required. It is a loop of cord or strong string which is placed around the framework to be held together; you twist a lever, such as a screwdriver or scrap of wood, round in it to increase the pressure. To prevent the string from damaging the wood you should protect the edges with scraps of timber or man-made boards. For large frames, use two loops across the frame or place the loop right round the frame to pull the corners together. The latter arrangement is particularly suitable when you are gluing mitred edges together; in this case it is important you also have four notched corner blocks to guide the string and act as buffers.

Workbench vice To clamp frames small enough to rest on your workbench, you can use an ordinary workbench vice. Screw a length of timber to the bench to act as a temporary stop and rest one side of the framework against this with the other side close to the vice. Fix a piece of stout timber to the face of the vice with the top edge above the level of the bench top. When you tighten the vice against the length of fixed timber the frame is securely clamped.

Folding wedges Two wedges placed face-to-face make a versatile clamping device. You can cut the wedges from any type of scrap timber; but it is better to make them from hardwood if you are going to use them frequently, since this type of wood is more durable than softwood.

Place the framework or timber to be clamped on

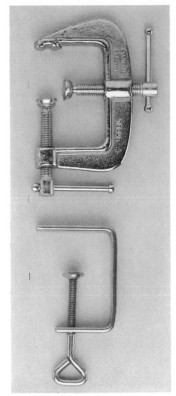

Top Edging clamp used to hold edging strips and lippings to a straight or curved workpiece
Above Fretwork clamp

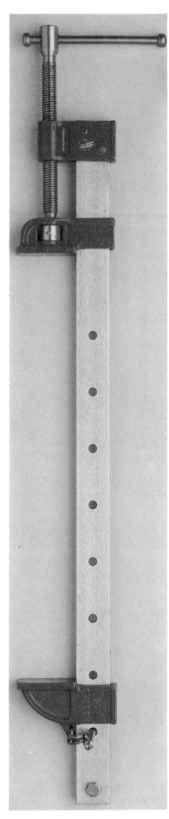

Sash bar cramp used for holding large frames or panels while they are being glued

a flat surface. Rest one side of the work against a timber stop and fix another stop close to the opposite side of the frame, leaving room for the folding wedges. Place the wedges together and use a wood mallet to tap their ends inwards to increase pressure on the workpiece. Alternatively, you can use stout screws as the stops and drive the wedges between the screws and the workpiece.

Timber frame When the workpiece to be clamped cannot be held flat on a bench, you can make a timber frame to fit around the work. Place folding wedges between the temporary frame and the workpiece to clamp the joints tightly.

Besides woodworking vices and bench holdfasts there are other clamping (or cramping) tools you can buy. Some of these are expensive, but they do enable you to carry out a whole range of jobs which are often beyond the scope of the simpler devices.

G-clamps

You will find these tools nearly as useful as the woodworking vice. They can be used to clamp together two items which are being glued or they can be used to hold timber down on a bench while it is worked.

G-clamps are available in many sizes, the most common being about 50–300mm (or 2–12in). The size indicates the width of the jaw opening. Special long reach or deep-throat clamps with extra deep openings are also available in sizes from about 50mm (or 2in) to 100mm (or 4in). The screw jaw is fitted with a swivel shoe which adapts to uneven surfaces. The strongest clamps have ribbed frames of malleable iron or steel with steel screws, while those for lighter work, such as fretwork clamps, have spring-tempered all-steel frames.

When using a G-clamp place scraps of wood between it and the timber being worked to protect the timber from marking. If the timber is being glued, put greaseproof paper between the work and the protective scraps to prevent them sticking together. You should never overtighten a G-clamp since this will dent the work and may bend the frame of the clamp.

Edging clamp A special version of the G-clamp, this is used to hold edging strips and lippings to a straight or curved workpiece. The width of the jaw opening is usually about 60mm (or $2\frac{3}{8}$in) and the throat depth up to 32mm (or $1\frac{1}{4}$in). Attach the clamp to the workpiece and tighten the secondary screw onto the edging.

Quick-acting cramps

There are many models of quick-acting cramps manufactured, but most work on the principle of a sliding cramp arm which can be moved and locked in any position on a steel bar. A particularly useful type is multi-directional, with two or more arms which can face either way on the steel bar to handle the most complicated cramping jobs. It can be used to cramp pieces of timber together – and to force them apart – and is supplied on a standard 305mm (or 12in) bar, though bars up to 1220mm (or 48in) are available. Maximum throat depth for this type of cramp is 92mm (or $3\frac{5}{8}$in).

Sash cramps

These relatively expensive cramps are used for holding large frames or panels while they are glued. Most have a rectangular cross-section steel bar on which the shoes slide. You place one shoe in

position according to the width of the work and fix it with a pin through the bar and then adjust the tension by screwing up the other shoe.

Depending on the thickness of the bar, the capacity of a sash cramp can be about 457–1676mm (or 18in–5ft 6in). Lengthening bars can increase the capacity of some sizes by a further 1220mm (or 4ft). Alternatively, you can make two sash cramps into one large one by removing the pegged shoes and linking the two cramps with nuts and bolts passed through the adjusting holes so the screw heads are at either end.

Rectangular section sash bar cramps tend to bend in use and to combat this, use three cramps on the workpiece – one on one side and two on the other. Alternatively you can use a stronger, more expensive T-bar sash cramp. The heavy weight of sash cramps, particularly in the larger sizes, can pull a frame out of true; to overcome this, make sure the framework is well supported. Similarly, the weight of the cramps can make a frame seem flat when they are in place, but when they are removed the frame may revert to its original shape.

Cramp heads

These are much cheaper than all-metal sash cramps, since you buy only the cramp heads themselves and use them in conjunction with a length of 25mm (or 1in) thick hardwood, which is of sufficient width to take the strain of cramping without bending. You need to drill holes for the locking pins at approximately 100mm (or 4in) intervals along the length of the beam.

Web-clamps

As a cheap means of holding large frames and panels for gluing, you can use a web-clamp – basically a more sophisticated version of the Spanish windlass. Pass a length of nylon webbing tape around the work and tighten it by passing the free end through a steel clamp, which has a ratchet handle and a mechanism to tighten the tape. You can use web-clamps on almost any shape of framework with an all-round measurement up to slightly less than the length of the webbing supplied, which is usually about 3.5m (or 12ft).

Frame clamps

These are another alternative to the Spanish windlass, but this time used for holding light work such as a picture frame. The frame clamp has four right-angle jaws of polypropylene plastic, which protect the corners of the frame, and 3.5m (or 12ft) of terylene cord, which you pass through a plastic cleat to draw the corner pieces together.

Corner cramp

This is another cramp for holding a framework at the corners. Also known as a mitre cramp, it is particularly useful for holding mitre joints at a right-angle while they are pinned and glued. The cramp point is designed so only a minimal mark is made on the moulding. The cramps can also hold awkward shapes and they usually have a capacity of 50–108mm (or 2–$4\frac{1}{4}$in).

You can make corner cramps yourself by cutting springs from an old upholstered spring chair or bed into the shape of a C.

Mitre joint cramps

Cramps of this type are particularly suitable for holding picture frame joints under light pressure.

They are made of spring steel and you apply them to the corners of the frame by expanding and relaxing them with special mounting pliers.

This type of cramp incorporates a saw guide at 45 and 90 degree angles so you can use the cramp to make accurate corner joints. They are available in six sizes with the smallest taking mouldings of 10–15mm (or $\frac{3}{8}$–$\frac{5}{8}$in) wide and the largest taking mouldings of 65–90mm (or $2\frac{1}{2}$–$3\frac{1}{2}$in) wide.

Drill bits

Drilling accurately into wood will be made easy if you use the right equipment. A whole range of bits is available for use with swing braces, hand drills (sometimes known as wheel braces) and electric drills, although swing brace and drill bits are often not interchangeable because of the type of fitting. Each bit is specially shaped to do a specific job, so it is important to check which one you need for the work in hand. Bits are available in a range of sizes, with width measurements in both metric and Imperial.

Auger bits
Used specifically for drilling into wood, the most common auger bits have a clearly defined spiral so the waste is cleared rapidly from the hole when drilling. Auger bits with tapered ends must be used exclusively with a swing brace fitted with Alligator type jaws. Straight shank bits can be used with a swing brace fitted with Universal jaws. Two types of auger bit are used with the brace, the Jennings and solid centre pattern bits.
Jennings pattern The most common type, this is particularly suitable for drilling deep holes since the long spiral keeps the hole straight.
Solid centre pattern Although this is not as accurate as the Jennings pattern, it has a slightly faster drilling action.

Twist bits
Often referred to as twist drills, twist bits are the most common drilling tools used by the handyman with either a hand or electric drill. You can buy them individually or in sets; the usual sizes are 0.8–6mm ($\frac{1}{32}$–$\frac{1}{4}$in). Designed for drilling small holes, they do tend to clog quickly so when drilling deep holes (especially in hardwood) the bits should be withdrawn regularly to remove the waste.
Warning Take particular care when using the smallest sizes since these bits are thin and brittle. Always hold the drill square to the work and apply only light pressure when drilling.

Specialist bits
Depending on the type of work and material used, special purpose bits are available, some for use with a brace and some for use with a hand drill or an electric drill.
Expansive bit Suitable for drilling into softwood, it has an adjustable cutting head so you can drill different size holes into wood at least 13mm ($\frac{1}{2}$in) thick. However it is difficult to keep straight when drilling deep holes.
Forstner bit Ideal for accurate drilling of flat-bottomed holes. But you will have to apply a lot of pressure when using it.
Centre bit Its use should be restricted to drilling through plywood. Unlike the spiral twist auger bits, this type of head is inclined to wander off

course when drilling deep holes.
Countersink bit Different patterns are available for drilling with a brace or hand or electric drill. Its cutting edge funnels out the surface of wood to take the head of a countersunk screw. Once the cutting edge of this bit has worn down you will have to replace it.
Screwdriver bit For use with a brace or hand or electric drill. You must use a multi-speed electric drill since you have to work at very low speeds.
Dowel bit This bit, which drills flat-bottomed holes into wood, must be used with an electric drill at full speed. It tends to be difficult to control since it drills quickly without the accuracy of an auger bit.
Flatbit Popular for use with electric drills, it is suitable for drilling wider holes in wood. Take care, particularly when working with hardwood, because the bit tends to overheat and blacken along the cutting edge. This indicates the steel has lost its temper and the cutting edge is ruined. Keep the bit as cool as possible by using it only in short bursts. It is easy to sharpen and as long as the cutting face is kept sharp, there is little risk of this bit overheating quickly, therefore making it ideal for deep drilling into wood.
Screw sink bit Available in sets, this type is multipurpose since it drills a pilot hole of the correct diameter for the screw and countersinks for the head of the screw in one drilling operation.
Hole saw bit Useful when making large holes in thin gauge material such as plywood. Different diameter holes can be drilled by changing the ring saw around the centre pilot drill.
Spear point bit Used at slow speed for drilling glass. The point should be continually lubricated with turpentine or white spirit during drilling.
Yankee drilling point bit Special small drilling bit available for use with the push drill and Yankee pump action screwdriver. This is ideal for making small holes.

Heavy duty bits
These are designed for drilling into hard materials such as masonry, brick and concrete, because they have specially treated cutting edges.
Masonry drill This type of twist drill, used at slow speed, is suitable for drilling into masonry and brickwork. It has a tungsten carbide cutting edge which must be resharpened by the manufacturer.
Percussion drill Looks like the masonry drill and also has a tungsten carbide cutting edge. It is designed for use with a percussion or hammer drill for boring into concrete. Always use it at a slow speed. The cutting edge will have to be resharpened by the manufacturer.

Sharpening bits
You can resharpen slightly worn cutting edges on the Jennings and solid centre pattern bits and the expansive bit yourself, using a 100mm (4in) medium cut flat needle file. Work very carefully using the original angle of the steel as a guide until you have formed a keen edge on the bit. The Forstner bit will probably have to be returned to the manufacturer for resharpening. The screwdriver bit can be reground.

Twist bits must always be kept sharp, which used to be difficult because of the problem of maintaining a symmetrical cutting head by hand-filing. There is now an easy-to-use twist drill sharpener which will give most of the twist bits in the range a balanced cutting edge.

These specialist bits are (**from left**) a masonry drill and a percussion drill, both designed for work on hard materials, and a countersink bit (with a tapered shank) for countersinking holes already drilled

Files

Files come in many shapes (flat, tapered, round, half-round, square, three-square or triangular) and sizes, with various grades of teeth and cut. Shape and type of cut vary according to the work involved, the amount of material to be removed and the finish required. Usually, the bigger the job the larger the file you should use. Although the file is basically designed to be used for metalwork, you can do some fining down on wood or laminate edges with a file.

There are two basic styles of cutting edge on files: single-cut and double-cut (**see details at left**) and each has a different tooth formation for different filing effects.

Single-cut Here the teeth are arranged in one direction only, to give a smooth cut and to remove a fair amount of material with each stroke.

Double-cut With two sets of diagonal teeth crossing over to make the double cut.

There are three main degrees of coarseness (applying to both single and double-cut files) known as bastard, second-cut and smooth.

Bastard With a very coarse face, this type is used for removing material rapidly at the start of a job.

Second-cut Finer than bastard files and suited to in-between work.

Smooth Finer still, this cut is used for finishing off the surface.

There is no point in removing a lot of material with a fine file – all you will achieve is aching muscles and a worn-out tool.

Many files are made with a 'safe' edge – that is, one edge without teeth. If by accident you rub the file against the face adjacent to the one you are working on, you will not remove any material. Always use a file with a safe edge when working in restricted space or when you want to produce an accurate cut-out or right-angle.

Multi-purpose files

Several manufacturers have produced multi-purpose files for general use. These are dual-cut with very coarse teeth on one side and finer teeth on the other.

Specialist files

There are special files available for use on awkward corners or angles where conventional ones would be too big; you can also buy a range of small saw files which are designed for sharpening the teeth of specific saws.

Needle files Very thin, fine files which come in a variety of shapes. They are ideal for delicate work such as clockmaking.

Rifflers With curves or hooks at each end, or curved at one end and tapered and pointed the other, these come in many shapes. They can cope with intricate jobs and are mainly used by tool-makers and silversmiths.

Mill saw files Extremely useful for sharpening the teeth of a circular saw, these are single-cut with rounded edges that fit the gullet of the saw blade; you maintain the depth of the teeth as well as filing the top edge.

Cant saw files Triangular, single-cut for sharpening saws with long, slender teeth, such as pruning saws.

Round files These have a special spiral cut for filing the gullets of chain saws.

Rasp-cut files With individually formed teeth in

varying degrees of fineness (**see detail at left**), they can be used on most types of material, including wood, plastics and soft metals.

Using files

Clamp the work in a vice to leave both hands free. Make sure the vice is at such a height that, when you hold the file with its far end resting on the work, the file is horizontal and the file tip, your hand and arm are all in a straight line.

The jaws of a vice are usually serrated to grip firmly, but these edges will badly mark fine work. To overcome this problem, buy a pair of smooth face jaws (or grind off the existing ones) or use a pair of vice linings – shaped pieces of lead, plastic or other soft material which fit around the jaws to protect the work.

The stance you adopt for filing is important. Stand with your legs slightly apart, with the left foot forward and the right foot pointing sideways (if you are left-handed, reverse the position).

Accuracy depends on the correct grip: hold the handle of the file in your right hand, place the palm of your left hand over the end of the file and wrap your fingers underneath to grip it tightly (again reverse the position if left-handed). This will enable you to apply considerable pressure. For lighter work, particularly when sharpening small saws with a triangular file, change your hand grip to a finger-tip hold. Place the file on the work and push it across the surface, using firm strokes the full length of the blade and lifting the file on the backward stroke.

You will find the angle of the teeth allows you to vary the cutting action simply by changing the direction of the stroke. To ensure accuracy on long lengths, use the file in a sideways action, making sure the teeth are at right angles to the direction of the cut – if they go the other way you will score the surface.

Draw filing This gives a much finer finish than straight filing. You hold the file across your body, with one hand gripping each end. Stand at right angles to the work and draw the file across it, towards the body, giving a slicing action to the file teeth.

Care of files

The teeth of a file are accurately cut on the face of extremely hard steel and, as with most very hard materials, this is rather brittle. Always keep your files on a rack; if they are jumbled together in a drawer, their teeth will blunt and chip and they will never again cut with the same efficiency.

Certain soft materials, particularly aluminium, tend to clog the file teeth, reducing their efficiency. When filing such materials keep a wire brush handy and use it along the line of the teeth to keep them clean.

A better tool for cleaning the teeth is a file card. This is a piece of very thick, strong, woven material into which are embedded hundreds of tiny wire strands making, in effect, a very wide wire brush with fine bristles about 6mm ($\frac{1}{4}$in) long. You can either use the card in this flexible state or stick it to a piece of wood to make a flat, rigid structure.

One way to cut down, if not eliminate, the problem of clogging is to keep some French chalk handy and liberally dust this on the file when cutting soft metals. The chalk acts as a lubricant and prevents the metal from sticking to the file.

Warning Always fit your files with proper handles.

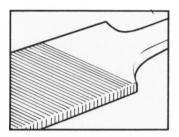

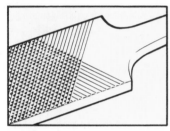

The two basic styles of cutting edges on files are the single-cut (**top**) and the double-cut with a safe edge (**centre**). The rasp-cut file (**bottom**) has individually formed teeth and can be used for most types of work

These may cost a few pence each, but they can prevent personal injury since a slight slip, a file catching on a sharp edge or a careless moment may result in a nasty hand wound.

Hammers

In many household tool kits there is just one hammer to tackle all the jobs, from driving in a small panel pin to hitting a chisel. When a comparatively modest outlay will bring you an excellent kit of hammers offering a lifetime's service it is a pity to stick with just one type for every job.

Hammers are sold according to the weight of the head and the extensive range available enables you to choose the right weight for your strength. Buy a good quality, well-balanced hammer with a forged steel head since the cheaper cast heads tend to shatter. The striking face should be domed with slightly chamfered edges so if you hit a nail at a slight angle it should still go in straight.

There are six main types of hammer: claw, Warrington cross pein, pin, club, ball pein and wood mallet – this last often associated just with banging in cricket stumps or tent pegs.

Claw hammer
Available in various weights from 455–680g (16–24oz), the claw hammer is used mainly for heavier woodwork (fence building or other constructional work). It is dual purpose; one side of the head is for banging, while the other side is shaped to a long curved claw tapering to a fine 'V' for removing nails and pins. You will not then need a pair of pincers to withdraw badly knocked-in nails. Claw hammers come with steel or wood shafts; the steel shaft is stronger, but its rubber or leather handle grip becomes slippery if your hands sweat. If this happens, wipe the rubber with a wet rag to to remove any grease.
To extract nails Hook the claw of the hammer round the nail and work the handle in a lever action. Keep the handle as upright as possible and remove the nail with a series of pulls. If extracting a long nail, slip a block of wood under the hammer head once you have partly withdrawn the nail. This will increase the leverage and help the nail come out more easily; it will also protect the surface of the work from bruising.

Warrington cross pein hammer
A good all-round woodworking hammer available in weights from 170–455g (6–16oz). It has a flat wedge shape (the pein) on one side of the head for starting small nails and panel pins. A good quality type will have a handle made of ash which is a tough, flexible wood capable of withstanding continual jarring.

Pin hammer
The lightest of the Warrington hammers, available in 100 or 115g (3½ or 4oz) weights, this is used on fine pins which would bend under the weight of heavier hammers. It is ideal for woodworking involving panel pins, such as picture framing.

Club hammer
Mainly used with a bolster chisel to cut bricks and paving stones and for masonry jobs and light demolition work. Club hammers are sold in 1135, 1360 and 1815g (2½, 3 and 4lb) weights, the heaviest

being ideal for structural building work. Hold the club hammer about halfway up the handle for maximum efficiency with the minimum of effort.

Ball pein hammer
This type of hammer has a hardened steel face which is not easily damaged and is therefore ideal for metalwork and for driving in masonry nails. One side of the head, formed in the shape of a round knob, is specially designed for hitting rivets or for beating metal. It is available in a range of weights from 155–1135g (4oz–2½lb).

Mallet
Usually made of beech, the mallet is used with wood handle chisels or gouges which would be damaged by a steel hammer. The handle slots into the head and is unlikely to work loose since the head tends to tighten onto the handle with use. Mallets are sold according to the size of the striking face of the head, which is usually between 100–150mm (4–6in).

Using a hammer
Hold the handle near the end, not in the middle (except with a club hammer), so you use the full weight of the hammer. Always keep your eye on the nail head and tap it gently until the nail grips. Then strike it with increasing firmness, keeping the handle at right-angles to the nail.

Always keep the striking face of the hammer clean by rubbing it occasionally with emery paper – grease on the face can cause the hammer to slip, resulting in damage to the work surface or possibly injuring your fingers.

Handsaws for timber

A saw blade consists of a series of teeth bent out on alternate sides of the blade. This formation is called the set and enables the sawdust and chips of wood to be carried away in the gullets between the teeth to prevent clogging. It also makes the saw cut (or kerf) slightly wider than the blade so the blade slips through without jamming and can be turned fractionally if it goes off the cutting line.

Saws are sold according to point number, which is always one more than the number of teeth per 25mm (1in). The more teeth there are the slower and finer the cut; a 14 point saw has 13 teeth per 25mm and cuts slower but more finely than one with ten teeth per 25mm.

Most handsaws are available with hardpoint teeth for extra wear. These will take a long time to blunt but cannot be sharpened: they have to be guillotined off and new teeth cut into the remaining blade, preferably by the manufacturer. You can then sharpen these new teeth as necessary.

Made of steel, some blades have a non-stick coating (such as Teflon) which helps prevent jamming and rusting. Handles are usually plastic or wood, the latter being not as strong as plastic but more comfortable to use over long periods.

Hang up the saw after use. Keep a blade guard over the teeth to protect the cutting edge and always oil an uncoated blade after use, remembering to wipe it clean before beginning fresh work. If an uncoated blade starts to rust, clean it with steel wool dipped in rust remover or white spirit. Wipe with an oil-soaked cloth after treatment. Remember never to use abrasives on Teflon-coated blades.

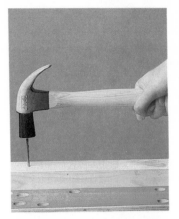

When using a hammer, always hold it near the end of the handle to ensure you use the full weight on the nail (**top**). When extracting nails with a claw hammer (**centre**), hook the claw round the nail and use the handle like a lever. When you need extra leverage for extracting long nails, put a block of wood under the hammer head (**bottom**)

When ripping timber (cutting with the grain), saw at an angle of approximately 60 degrees

Panel saw

The best type of all-round handsaw for cutting large timber to size. For general work we recommend an 8 point saw with a 550mm (22in) blade. The panel saw has cross-cut teeth for cutting across the grain: the tooth angle is the same on both sides of the point and the saw cuts equally well on the push and pull strokes. It will also cut with the grain (rip-sawing), but this is hard work on boards more than 25mm (1in) thick.

Rip saw

Designed specifically for cutting timber fast with the grain, this type is worth buying only if you have a lot of board-ripping to do. It is generally 4 or 5 point and the teeth resemble a series of chisels: one side is angled much more steeply than the other and the saw cuts only on the down stroke, when the chisel edges are driven into the wood.

To use a panel or rip saw Grip the handle with your index finger pointing along the blade. Support the timber in a vice (a bench vice if you have one) or on trestles or chairs, and use your knee and free hand to steady the wood. Start the cut by firmly drawing back the blade, holding it square to the wood at a shallow angle. Use your free thumb to guide the initial cut towards you; never push the saw forward with your thumb close to the cutting line as the saw may jump and hit the thumb. Keep your shoulder behind the line of the saw.

Always saw on the waste side of the cutting line; if you saw on the line the wood would be undersize when filed or planed smooth. Scribble arrows on the waste side of the line to remind you on which side to saw.

Saw steadily and rhythmically, using the full length of the blade and applying light pressure only on the downward stroke. Keep the blade at about 45 degrees to the wood when cross-cutting and at about 60 degrees when rip-cutting. Always let the saw do the work. When you near the end of the cut, support the waste end to prevent it tearing away from the main piece. When cutting across the grain, always have the waste end overhanging the trestle or the saw will jam. If the saw jams, remove it and lubricate the blade by rubbing it with a candle.

Tenon saw

For cutting joints and all fine and accurate work, both with and across the grain. The blade is rectangular and has a spine (or back) which gives you more control when cutting small pieces of wood. For all-round use we recommend a 15 point saw with a 250 or 300mm (10 or 12in) blade. Hold the tenon saw as you would the panel saw, with your index finger pointing along the blade to steady it. Always use the full length of the blade.

Small veneer-type tenon saw

Similar to the tenon saw, but without the spine, this enables you to make a fine cut at a deeper angle in sheet material such as thin plywood or veneer.

Specialist saws

Although the saws mentioned above will cope with basic woodworking jobs, you will need specialist saws for more intricate work.

Bow saw

Consisting of a narrow blade stretched in a wood frame, this type is used for cutting curves in timber more than 12mm (½in) thick.

Coping saw

A smaller version of the bow saw, to use on thinner wood, this has an adjustable blade fixed in a steel frame.

Both of these saws can cut only as far into the timber as the distance between the blade and the saw frame. To cut a hole in the middle of a piece of wood you must first drill a pilot hole through which to thread the saw blade. You can then fix the blade to the frame and begin sawing. Take care not to force the blade as it will wander from the cutting line and may break.

Pad (or keyhole) saw

This saw overcomes the problems of frame size presented by the bow and coping saws since it has a narrow blade clamped to a handle at one end only. It is invaluable for cutting holes in the middle of large panels. Again you will have to drill a pilot hole to insert the blade before you can begin sawing.

Jig saws

You can use the power jig saw, available either as a purpose-built unit or as an attachment to an electric drill, to cut a wide range of materials accurately. Interchangeable blades make it suitable for use on softwood and hardwood, man-made boards such as chipboard, plywood or blockboard, steel and other ferrous metals and non-ferrous ones such as copper and aluminium. It is ideal for complicated cutting jobs, but can also be used for straightforward sawing work.

The jig saw attachment works best with a two-speed or multi-speed drill. If you only have a single-speed drill, it is better to buy an integral jig saw unit. Some units have a two-speed control switch incorporated into the trigger switch; use the high speed for wood and laminated boards and the low speed for work with plastics and thin sheet metal. The same applies to jig saw attachments.

Cutting blades

At high speed the jig saw blade travels up and down at over 3200 strokes per minute, which places it under considerable stress; so you must check the blade is sharp and in good working order. Discard worn blades since they are too hard to be re-sharpened. The units and attachments are usually supplied with one general-purpose cutting blade, although a variety of blades is available. Coarse blades increase the speed of cutting through material, while finer blades cut less quickly but greatly reduce the risk of splintering.

Fitting blades Make sure the jig saw is disconnected from the mains before fitting a blade or making any other adjustment. The blade is secured in the chuck either by two screws locked by an L-shaped (Allen) key or by a slotted screw which you tighten with a screwdriver. You should insert the blade with the teeth facing forward, centre it in the chuck and tighten the screws against the blade, taking care not to overtighten them.

Using the saw

Check the unit or power drill is switched off before connecting it to the mains. For the best results, clamp the work to a bench or table. Mark the line to be cut on the surface of the material and guide the saw along the cutting line; a blower behind the blade directs air through a plastic tube to sweep dust from the line so it is not obscured. Always grip the jig saw firmly and see the lead is kept well away from the blade. To obtain maximum efficiency press down on the sole of the saw but never force the blade forward. Make sure any large overhangs of cutting material are well supported or the blade may be gripped by the work as the saw nears the end of the cut. Always let the motor stop before removing a blade from an unfinished cut.

Decorative surfaces The cutting action is on the upward stroke and you should always work with the non-decorative face of the material on the top so any tearing that might occur does not spoil the work. When there are two decorative surfaces place the main one face down. To prevent splintering put adhesive tape over the cutting line or score along it with a sharp knife before sawing.

Preventing fusion Friction heat may cause materials such as vinyl plastic sheet to melt and fuse solidly behind the blade. To prevent this, place adhesive-backed paper over the cutting line and saw through it using a general-purpose blade. Don't remove the protective paper until the cutting is completed or you will scratch the surface.

Padding To prevent chipping when cutting sheet laminates, tightly clamp a thin sheet of hardboard or plywood above and below the laminate at the cutting line. Clamp ferrous sheet and non-ferrous metals onto a backing of softwood or plywood to stop vibration and tearing.

Lubricants For metal and plastics spread a thin film of lubricant along the cutting line before sawing. It is important to use the right lubricant – cutting oil for steel, water or turpentine for aluminium and water for plastics. You can cut most other materials dry.

Warning Always wear protective spectacles when operating the jig saw. If the tool accidentally slips from the work area, don't attempt to catch it as the blade could easily tear your hand – it is wiser to sacrifice the blade. Never place the jig saw on the bench until the blade has stopped, then lay the tool on its side. Make sure it is placed on an uncluttered area when not in use and, when work is finished, store it away safely out of reach of children and animals. To keep it in smooth running order, lightly oil the lubricating points regularly.

Types of cut

The jig saw power tool is most effective when cutting intricate shapes and curves. Run it in from a starting point at the edge of the material and it will follow curved lines without effort. On some models you can tilt the shoe of the jig saw which enables you to cut angles up to 45 degrees.

Pocket cutting You can use this tool to cut a shape out of the middle of a piece of material, known as pocket cutting. The blade can be inserted in the middle of a panel without first having to drill a hole (though for thick material it is advisable to drill a pilot hole in the waste and saw out from this). First measure and clearly mark the surface to be cut, then tilt the saw forward so the rounded tips of the shoe rest on the work surface, but with the blade well clear of it. Switch on the power and move the saw in the tilted-up position until the blade is exactly over the point where you want to start cutting. Lower the rear of the shoe towards the work surface, keeping a firm pivoting pressure on

the shoe tips with the blade exactly on the line. Never try to move the saw forward until the blade has cut through the material and the shoe comes to rest flat on the surface.

Although a rounded section may be cut in one operation, several cuts are needed for rectangular shapes. Use the saw along the full length of one side of the square or oblong to be cut and, with the motor still running, bring it back, curving it smoothly away from the first cut to work on the second side. Leave the waste piece in the corner to be cut out later. Repeat for the two remaining sides until most of the waste falls away, then reverse your working direction to complete the unfinished cuts and remove the corner pieces.

To cut a keyhole or other small opening, pass the saw backwards and forwards to take small pieces out of the material.

Straight cutting For accurate straight-line cutting, use the adjustable fence which locks into position with a small screw. If you are cutting widths wider than the adjustable fence, nail or clamp a straight batten at a suitable distance from the cutting line so the shoe of the jig saw runs along the batten to form the precise cutting line.

Nails and nailing

Nails provide the quickest and easiest method of fixing or joining together pieces of wood. Nailed joints will be considerably strengthened by also applying woodworking adhesive. A wide range of nails is available, so make sure you use the right type and size of nail for the job you have to do.

Types of nails

Nails and tacks are available in small quantity packs, but it is usually cheaper to buy them by weight. The number in any given weight will obviously depend on the size of the nail.

Round wire nails These large round head nails are mostly used for rough carpentry where appearance is not important but strength is essential. They are inclined to split a piece of wood. Sizes from 20–150mm ($\frac{3}{4}$–6in).

Oval wire nails Most suitable for joinery work where appearance is important since they can easily be punched below the surface. They are less likely to split the wood if driven in with the longer sides parallel to the grain. Sizes from 12–150mm ($\frac{1}{2}$–6in).

Round or lost head nails Stronger than oval wire nails, they can easily be punched below the surface of the wood. Sizes from 12–150mm ($\frac{1}{2}$–6in).

Cut clasp nails Rectangular in section, they are difficult to remove and provide a very strong fixing in wood and pre-drilled masonry. Sizes from 25–150mm (1–6in).

Cut floor brads Also rectangular, they have an L-shaped head and are nearly always used for nailing floorboards to joists. Sizes from 12–150mm ($\frac{1}{2}$–6in).

Panel pins Round lightweight nails used for delicate cabinet work and for fixing small mouldings into place. They can easily be punched below the surface. Sizes from 12–50mm ($\frac{1}{2}$–2in).

Veneer pins Very small type of panel pin.

Hardboard nails These have a diamond-shaped head which is virtually hidden when hammered into hardboard. Sizes from 9–38mm ($\frac{3}{8}$–1$\frac{1}{2}$in).

Clout nails Most are galvanized for use outside. Particularly suitable for nailing down roof felt as

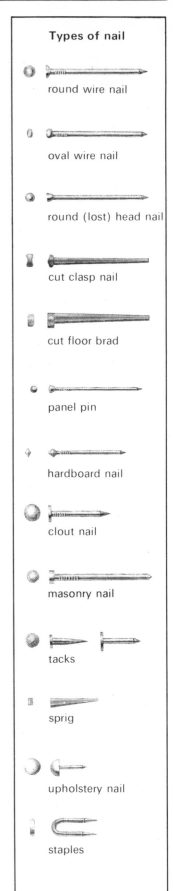

Types of nail

round wire nail

oval wire nail

round (lost) head nail

cut clasp nail

cut floor brad

panel pin

hardboard nail

clout nail

masonry nail

tacks

sprig

upholstery nail

staples

Use a nail punch to sink nails below the surface of the work and fill the hole for a neat finish

the large round head on these nails holds the felt firmly in position without tearing it. Sizes from 12–50mm ($\frac{1}{2}$–2in).

Masonry nails Toughened round nails which can be hammered into brick, breeze block and most types of masonry. Different gauges are available and lengths are from 19–100mm ($\frac{3}{4}$–4in).

Tacks Used for nailing carpets to floorboards or stretching fabric onto wood. They have very sharp points and large round flat heads. Sizes from 19–32mm ($\frac{3}{4}$–1$\frac{1}{4}$in).

Sprigs Similar to tacks but without heads. They are used mainly to hold glass in window frames before applying putty which covers them up. Sizes from 12–19mm ($\frac{1}{2}$–$\frac{3}{4}$in).

Upholstery nails Available in chrome, brass and other metallic finishes, they are used as a secondary fixing with tacks. The dome head gives a decorative finish when nailing chair coverings into place. Various head sizes are available.

Staples U-shaped round wire nails with two points to hold lengths of wire in position. Some staples have an insulated lining for fixing flex and electric cable.

Nailing methods

When joining two pieces of wood, the length of the nails used should be just under twice the thickness of the thinner piece of wood. Where possible nail through the thinner piece into the thicker piece in any joint and drive the nail in at a slight angle, where you can, to increase the strength of the joint. Always nail on a firm surface; if nailing unsupported wood, hold a heavy block behind it.

Preventing wood splits Nails easily cause both hardwoods and softwoods to split, especially near the end of a length. To avoid splits in hardwoods, for each nail drill a pilot hole slightly smaller in diameter than the nail. This also applies to chipboard and plywood.

Softwoods offer little resistance to nails but are still liable to split. Don't drive in nails close together in the same line of grain and always try to use oval nails with the longer sides parallel to the grain. It is also worth slightly blunting the point of the nail before hammering it into the wood and, if possible, cutting lengths of wood oversize so nails do not have to be driven in close to the end; you can trim the wood after fixing.

Clench nailing When joining two pieces of wood together the strongest bond will be made by clench nailing, preferably using round wire nails. Space the nails up to 12mm ($\frac{1}{2}$in) apart and drive them through the wood from either side, leaving at least 25mm (1in) showing through the other side. Bend over the projecting end of each nail with a hammer and drive right into the wood.

Angle nailing Any nail driven at an angle into the wood will give a stronger grip than if driven in at right-angles to the surface. You will achieve the strongest joint by driving one nail at a 45 degree angle to the wood and a second nail at the same angle from the opposite direction.

Using small nails and pins You may have difficulty in starting off panel and veneer pins, especially if you have large fingers. To prevent bruising your fingers, use the flat pein side of the head of a cross pein or pin hammer to strike the pin. Once it is secured, use the round striking face to drive it home. You can also hold the pin with thin long-reach pliers or push it through a thin piece of card and hold it with this until the pin grips enough to

need no further support. Remove the piece of card before driving the pin home.

Hidden or secret nailing With certain decorative woodworking jobs, lift up a sliver of wood with a sharp chisel and nail through underneath this, punching the nail below the surface. Use small oval or lost head nails. Glue the sliver of wood back into position with woodworking adhesive and rub over the area with fine glasspaper; the marks will barely be visible.

There is another method of secret nailing, useful when laying tongue and groove floorboards (and securing tongue and groove joints). Hammer the nail into the tongue at a 45 degree angle so it goes through the board (not through the other side of the tongue) and into the fixing surface. The nail will be concealed by the groove in the next board.

The easiest and quickest method of hiding a nail is to punch it below the surface and fill the hole with cellulose filler or plastic wood.

Nail punch A steel, pencil-like implement about 100mm (4in) long which enables you to sink pin and nail heads below the surface without damage whereas a hammer head would bruise the work on the last few blows. The punch should be of the same diameter as the head of the nail.

Using a nail punch Hammer the nail until it lies just proud of the surface. Place the tapered end of the punch on the nail head and strike it with a hammer until the head sinks below the surface. Fill the hole to give a smooth finish.

Warning Iron nails will rust easily if covered with a water-based filler and emulsion paint, causing brown patches to spread across the painted surface. Either use galvanized nails or make sure any iron nails are thoroughly treated with a rust-resistant metal primer before continuing decoration.

Gluing and pinning Apply a thick layer of woodworking adhesive to both faces to be joined. Select the appropriate nails or pins for the job and nail the two pieces of wood together while the adhesive is still wet. Wipe off any excess adhesive with a clean dampened cloth and leave to dry for up to 12 hours. Gluing and pinning gives a strong joint even when the fixing faces of two pieces of wood are quite small.

Planes, chisels and gouges

Precision instruments such as planes are necessary if you want to be quite satisfied the end product results in a job well done. Chisels and gouges also help to give an expert touch to many woodworking tasks in the home.

When working with wood, it pays to use high quality tools for the best results. As with all your tools, when buying planes, chisels and gouges get the best you can afford and look after them.

Planes

The basic job of a plane is to smooth wood to exact dimensions. For this purpose three types – smoothing, jack and jointer planes – are available. Planes are also used for shaping wood: the block plane is

When planing wood, it is important that the blade is set parallel to the bottom of the plane. You can check this by holding the plane upside down and squarely up to the light

for smoothing and shaping small work and there are various special planes for particular joints and shapes.

The blades of new planes have to be sharpened before use and regularly resharpened. If you do not want to go to the trouble of resharpening blades, you can buy a plane which takes throw-away replaceable blades. Other trimming tools are available, but are only suitable for jobs requiring less precision.

Most planes are now made of metal. Wood ones are very difficult to obtain and are rarely used by the home handyman.

Smoothing plane This comes in lengths of 200–250mm (8–10in) and is best used for smoothing small lengths of wood as it can create bumps and hollows on long lengths if not handled carefully.

Jack plane In 355 or 380mm (14 or 15in) lengths, this plane is long enough for most surfaces and less heavy than the jointer one.

Jointer plane Available in 560 and 610mm (22 and 24in) lengths, this plane is used for smoothing long pieces of wood. But it is heavy to use and quite expensive to buy.

Block plane A small plane which comes in lengths from 140–200mm (5½–8in), it can be used with one or two hands. The blade is set at a low angle with the bevel uppermost, making it ideal for cutting end grain. It is also used for shaping small work and is a convenient tool to use on chipboard and laminated plastic. However, the resin in these man-made materials quickly blunts the blade, which then needs frequent resharpening. Some planes have an adjustable mouth for coarse or fine work.

Special purpose planes The following planes are for specialized shaping jobs: a rebate plane cuts steps or grooves; an open-throat router makes grooves of uniform depth; a shoulder plane has a blade that cuts to the full width of the plane body so it can plane right into an angle. There is also a combination plane which can be fitted with various cutters.

Plane-type tools Aids to planing, such as the Stanley Surform and Aven Trimmatool, cannot be used with the same precision as conventional planes but are useful for levelling and shaping a variety of materials. They can also be used on painted wood and wood containing nails, which would normally ruin a conventional plane.

Using a plane

Before using a plane, make sure the blade is razor sharp and correctly adjusted to the required depth of cut. It takes experience to know just how far the blade should project for the desired cut, so it is worth practising planing on a piece of waste timber to find out how much the blade will remove when set in different positions. Turn the knurled knob to adjust the depth of the cut, then move the lever to straighten the blade along its width. Check the blade is parallel with the bottom of the plane; if the blade is not level, it will not cut evenly.

To level a long piece of timber, use a long plane since a small one will follow the undulations of the surface rather than straddle them. Always plane with the grain of the wood to get a really smooth finish. You will soon know if you are planing against the grain as you will tear the surface. This will be particularly noticeable on hardwood.

The right action Support the wood in a vice so you have both hands free to use the plane. Grip the knob at the front of the plane with one hand and place the other on the handle. At the beginning of

each stroke press down on the front knob and gradually transfer the pressure so it is on the back of the plane when you finish the stroke. This action will keep the plane level with the surface of the timber and will prevent the ends being rounded off. You will find it easier if you put all your weight on your front foot (the left one if you are right-handed) at the beginning of the stroke and gradually transfer it to the back foot as you shift pressure on the plane.

When planing the edge of timber, concentrate on keeping the plane square to the timber. Check regularly with a try square after a few strokes.

When trimming end grain, check regularly with a try square that you are trimming square, or use a shooting board. Always work from each edge towards the centre. It is also important to keep the blade razor sharp and adjusted to only a very slight projection. If possible, use a block plane with an adjustable mouth and keep it tightly closed.

Warning When planing, check regularly to see the wood shavings are not trapped under the blade. If they are, release the blade and clear away the shavings. When you reassemble the plane, check the blade adjustment before continuing work.

Chisels

These tools are for cutting out and paring pieces of timber. For some jobs you will have to tap the handle; if it is made of wood, you must use a mallet to prevent the wood splitting. A high-impact plastic handle is stronger and has the advantage that it will not be damaged if you tap it with a hammer when a mallet is not available. New chisels need to be sharpened before use.

There is a range of chisels to tackle different jobs, but the standard bevel edge type is suitable for most DIY work. Chisels are available in blade widths from 6–38mm (¼–1½in).

Bevel edge chisel The most versatile type since the blade has bevelled edges which enable it to cut into tight corners where a firmer chisel, which has square edges, would jam. The most useful widths are 6, 12, 19 and 25mm (¼, ½, ¾ and 1in).

Firmer chisel Here the blade is rectangular in cross-section and stronger than that of a bevel edge. It is suitable for tougher jobs where less precision is required, such as in frame joinery.

Paring chisel This has a longer blade, either bevel edge or firmer type, useful for making larger joints, or cutting housings for wide shelves.

Mortise chisel The blade has square sides and is virtually square in cross-section. Its strength makes it ideal for cutting mortises (deep rectangular holes used in forming joints). As a mortise chisel is almost always used with a mallet, it is essential the handle is made of high-impact plastic or of wood reinforced at the top with a metal band.

Using a chisel

Make sure your chisel is razor sharp and handle it carefully so you do not damage the blade. Never support the timber with your hand in front of the blade as you could cut yourself if the chisel slips. Clamp the timber firmly so you have both hands free to manoeuvre the chisel or to work with a chisel and mallet.

Always use a chisel with or across the grain of wood. If you cut against the grain you may split the wood or run off the cutting line. Paring across the

A jack plane, which you will find long enough for most jobs and lighter than a jointer plane

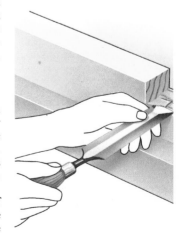

When cutting across the grain with a paring chisel, hand pressure is sufficient; there is no need to use a mallet

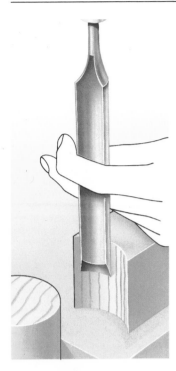

Use a scribing gouge for curved work, such as trimming the curve on the end of a rail to fit round a chair leg

grain can be done using hand pressure only. Keep one hand firmly on the handle to exert pressure and use the other hand to guide the blade.

When using a mallet, grip the chisel handle firmly and make sure the flat side of the blade is placed well inside the marked cutting area; the blade will move towards the cutting line when hit. A hammer may be used instead of a mallet if the chisel has a plastic handle, but always strike the handle with the flat side of the hammer.

Gouges

A special kind of chisel, the gouge has a curved blade and comes in two types. The firmer gouge has a bevel edge on the back of the blade, the scribing gouge a bevel edge on the front. Sizes relate to the width of the blade, not its arc, and range from 6–25mm ($\frac{1}{4}$–1in).

Using a gouge

This is handled in the same way as a chisel but each type of blade has its own particular use. A firmer gouge is used to cut shallow depressions, such as finger grips on doors, and curved grooves. To do this, work alternately from each end of the cut towards the middle until the required depth is reached. A scribing gouge is used to trim curves to match a rounded surface, such as shaping a rail to join a round leg of a chair.

Power drill

The electric drill is no longer an expensive luxury, but an essential part of your DIY tool kit. Apart from just drilling holes, it is the basic power unit for a wide range of attachments – from saws to polishers – which can be bought separately as required. And power tools also enable you to tackle jobs you might not have the strength to do by hand.

Choice of drill

One drill tends to look much the same as another, but there is quite a difference in price, performance and versatility between models. It will be worth your while to shop around to compare the considerable discounts that some shops offer.

Nearly all drills are mains-operated, although rechargeable battery-powered ones are available. Battery-only types are useful if you are working a long way from a power outlet or if you simply want a lightweight tool. Otherwise, choose one that operates off the mains.

Make sure the drill you buy offers a full range of attachments to fit it and check on the after-sales service before deciding on the best one for your needs.

The power of the drill is rated in watts, generally between 350 and 500 – the higher the wattage, the more powerful the drill. Higher-wattage drills are the most expensive, but they are also the strongest.

Chuck capacity Drills offer a range of chuck capacities. This capacity refers to the maximum size drill bit shank that can be fitted and the maximum size hole that can be drilled in steel. Special drill bits enable you to make holes twice as large in wood and up to one and a half times larger in masonry.

Usually the larger the hole to be drilled and the harder the material, the slower the drill speed you need. If you are likely to want to drill a variety of

materials, using various attachments, you should buy a variable-speed drill.

Variable-speed drill If the drill is fitted with an electronic switch, its speed can be varied between nil and maximum revs according to the pressure on the trigger switch. When the speed is reduced electrically, torque is also reduced unless the drill is fitted with an electronic feedback controller. There are other variations which you should ask your supplier to explain before you buy a drill.

Most drilling and other work with attachments, such as sanding and sawing, will be done at the top speed of around 2,000–2,400rpm. Drilling brickwork, concrete and holes of more than 6mm ($\frac{1}{4}$in) diameter in steel calls for a lower speed of around 900rpm. The very low speeds you can get with a variable-speed drill are also useful for making an accurate start to drilling (where otherwise the bit might bounce off the surface) and for drilling hard materials such as glass and ceramic tiles which might break or crack easily.

Two-speed drill Normally has a gearbox that mechanically reduces the working speed and simultaneously increases the torque or turning force.

Single-speed drill Operates at about 2,800rpm. You can use it to make holes in masonry, but the drill bit must be removed frequently from the hole to clear the waste dust and allow the tip to cool. You can get a plug-in electronic speed controller to fit in the supply cable, but it is better to buy a variable-speed drill to start with if you intend doing work that requires a slower speed.

Warning If you apply excessive pressure to the drill or try to make it work under strain, perhaps by using a blunt drill bit, the motor windings may overheat and burn out. To avoid this, remove the drill from the work at regular intervals and let it run freely to allow the fan to cool the windings. This is very important when using an electronic control drill at low speed because the fan only works efficiently at maximum speed. Some drills have an automatic overload cut-out to protect the windings from overheating.

Hammer (impact) action Generally a built-in feature that can be selected when drilling tough materials like concrete, stone or hard bricks. Hammer action is created by a ratchet-like rotary mechanism that delivers up to 40,000 percussions a minute as the chuck revolves. A specially strengthened masonry drill bit, called a percussion drill bit, should be used for this type of work.

Drill safety

Used sensibly, the electric drill is a very safe tool; but because it works fast, never take your mind off what you are doing.

● Keep children and pets away from the working area and always unplug the drill before making adjustments or changing the drill bit.

● Always use the chuck key to tighten the bit in the chuck and never try to tighten it by holding the chuck while the drill is still running or you could be seriously injured.

● Make sure the flex is well clear of the work area, don't wear a tie or scarf and if your hair is long tie it back; this will prevent anything getting tangled up in the drill, possibly throwing it out of control or again causing injury.

● Wear protective spectacles to guard your eyes against flying particles.

● Always check the extension lead is in good condition and suitable for the drill being used.

● Never use drills in the rain or under damp conditions.

● Make sure your drill is properly earthed (unless it is double-insulated and supplied with a two core flex) and the plug is fitted with a 13 amp fuse.

Power saw benches

A fixed bench saw is the ultimate refinement in any home workshop, but power saws of this type are expensive and require considerable space. The alternative is to use a saw bench or saw table attachment, which can be fitted with either a separate portable power saw unit or an electric drill with a saw attachment. The great advantage of having a mounted saw is that both hands are left free for handling the material to be cut.

Power tool manufacturers make saw benches and attachments to suit their drills and saw units, so choose the one recommended for your particular drill or unit. The range includes floor-standing models, portable folding benches and saw tables which can be mounted on a bench. A rigidly mounted saw table is the first requirement for safe sawing, so allow for the table legs to be screwed down to the surface where you plan to work – particularly important with small tables.

Nearly all saw tables have facilities for fixing fences and guides such as those supplied with the Workmate saw table.

Workmate saw table
Because the Workmate bench is portable, sawing jobs can be tackled anywhere inside or out of doors. The saw table is quickly assembled onto it by means of a mounting bracket bolted under the jaws of the Workmate on the side with handles. As it does not interfere with other work done on the Workmate, the bracket can be left permanently in position.

The saw table is clipped onto the bracket and brought flush with the jaws by means of adjusting screws. Once this adjustment has been made, the saw is clipped into the underside of the table. Any saw unit or attachment from the Black & Decker range will fit.

Even when the saw is fixed in position, the table remains firmly in place. The jaws of the bench itself provide an extra working surface, which is useful when you are feeding widths of timber or boards across the saw blade. The assembly remains stable while the saw is running, even when a long piece of timber is being ripped through.

Saw table fences
Three useful fences are supplied with the saw table attachment: the integral rip fence, the supplementary rip fence and the mitre guide.
Integral rip fence Can be used as a guide when cutting through long pieces of timber.
Supplementary rip fence Fits into the Workmate jaws and allows a wider cut to be made, enabling planks to be cut across the grain.
Mitre guide Useful for accurate angle cutting or mitring. It fits into a slot on the saw table and is held by a wing nut. The angle is set as required and the guide is moved forward down the slot to feed the timber across the blade while maintaining the correct angle.

Once all the necessary adjustments have been made, the power saw can be connected to the main supply. A red plastic handle grip is supplied to lock the switch of the saw in the 'on' position.

Using a saw table
Always start the saw and get it running at maximum speed before feeding timber to the blade; switch off the power only when the cutting is complete. This will reduce stress and wear on the blade and prevent premature blunting of the teeth.

When feeding timber to the saw blade, use a V-shaped piece of wood to push the work forward and keep pressure on it during cutting. To feed large boards across the blade, remove fences to allow the boards to lie flat on the table.

Remove any nails from the timber before attempting to cut with a power saw and never feed green, freshly cut timber across a saw table: only a tree saw should be used if you are cutting wet timber.

An electric saw tends to disperse dust over a wide area, so always wear protective spectacles and, when working inside, try to confine the work to a well ventilated workshop or room which is shut off from the rest of the house.

Screws and screwing

Screws are available in a variety of sizes and finishes – including steel, stainless steel, brass, chromium plated, black japanned and sherard-ized – and screw heads are either slotted, or cross slot – called Supadriv or Pozidriv. (You may come across Phillips screws in some of the fittings around the home, although these are no longer made.) Screws are bought by quantity, unlike nails which are bought by weight.
Countersunk The most common screw used in woodwork. The flat head tapers towards the shank allowing it to be driven slightly below, or flush with, the work surface.
Round head To hold in place fittings which have not been drilled with countersunk holes. These decorative screws are used where they have to be left exposed.
Raised head These can only be countersunk to the rim, so the head still protrudes above the work surface. Mostly used with fittings which have been drilled with countersunk holes.
Dome head For mirror and fascia fixings. The head is flat and should be countersunk. It has a threaded hole in the middle of the slot into which a decorative cap can be fixed.
Clutch head The specially shaped head makes it impossible to remove the screw. Suitable for fitting locks and other burglar-proof devices.
Self-tapping For sheet metal fixings. They cut their own thread when driven into a small pilot hole and are available with round, raised or flat heads.
Coach For heavy duty fixings. The head is bolt-shaped so the screws have to be fixed into the work with a spanner.
Dowel A double-ended screw for dowelling together two pieces of timber. The screw has a thread at both ends and a shank in the middle. Drive half of the screw into one piece of timber using a pair of pliers on the shank and then twist the other piece of timber onto the screw.
Chipboard The large thread profile gives a stronger grip in chipboard than an ordinary screw and the thread continues right up to the head.
Screw hooks and eyes Most hooks and eyes can be

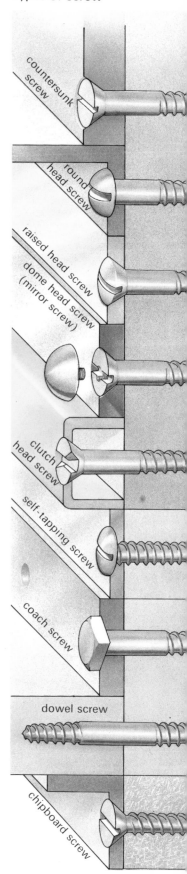

Types of screw

countersunk screw

round head screw

raised head screw

dome head screw (mirror screw)

clutch head screw

self-tapping screw

coach screw

dowel screw

chipboard screw

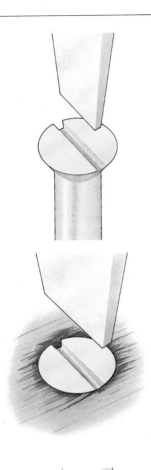

When using a screwdriver, make sure the tip of the blade fits perfectly inside the screw head (**top**). If the tip is too big, it will damage the timber on the last few turns of the screw (**centre**). If the tip is too small (**bottom**), it will damage the screw head and you will have difficulty removing the screw later

bought either plain or shouldered, in shapes and sizes to suit the job in hand.

Screw sizes

The size of a screw is measured in two dimensions – the overall length from head to point and the diameter of the shank (gauge). Most woodworking screws range from gauge Nos 4–14 and their length varies from 9–152mm ($\frac{3}{8}$–6in).

You must have all the necessary details available when buying screws – quantity, gauge, finish, type and length. For example you might ask for ten No 8 brass countersunk screws 38mm ($1\frac{1}{2}$in) long.

How to use screws

When joining two pieces of timber together, drill a clearance hole through the first piece so the shank of the screw can be passed through it. Drill a pilot hole (you can make some holes with a bradawl) in the second piece of timber; this hole should be slightly smaller in diameter than the threaded part of the screw. Pilot holes are especially important when using hardwoods to prevent splitting.

When using countersunk screws, countersink the clearance hole to take the head of the screw. This is done with a countersink bit which can easily be fitted into an electric or hand drill. There is a countersink bit with a handle which saves time as you do not have to insert it in the drill chuck. Use a bit with two cutting edges for softwoods and a multi-edged bit when countersinking into hardwoods.

Guide to clearance and pilot holes

Screw gauge	Clearance hole	Pilot for hardwood	Pilot for softwood
No 4	3mm ($\frac{1}{8}$in)	2mm ($\frac{5}{64}$in)	bradawl
No 6	4mm ($\frac{5}{32}$in)	2mm ($\frac{5}{64}$in)	bradawl
No 8	5mm ($\frac{3}{16}$in)	3mm ($\frac{1}{8}$in)	2mm ($\frac{5}{64}$in)
No 10	5mm ($\frac{3}{16}$in)	3mm ($\frac{1}{8}$in)	2mm ($\frac{5}{64}$in)
No 12	6mm ($\frac{1}{4}$in)	4mm ($\frac{5}{32}$in)	3mm ($\frac{1}{8}$in)
No 14	6mm ($\frac{1}{4}$in)	5mm ($\frac{3}{16}$in)	4mm ($\frac{5}{32}$in)

End grain Screws, like nails, do not provide a strong fixing when driven into the end grain of wood. The joint can be strengthened by inserting a dowel across the grain so screws driven through the end grain will penetrate the dowel.

Gluing and screwing This term is used when you need to strengthen a joint by gluing as well as screwing. Apply a coating of woodworking adhesive to one face of the timber pieces to be joined. Screw the two pieces together while the adhesive is still wet and wipe off with a clean dampened cloth any excess that squeezes out. Leave the adhesive to dry for 8–12 hours.

Washers, cups and sockets Washers are mostly used with round head screws to provide extra pressure at the fixing point. Screw cups are used when screwing into thin materials where countersinking would weaken the fixing. Sockets allow the screw to lie flush with the work surface and also give a decorative finish to the fixing.

Warning Steel screws will eventually rust if covered with a water-based filler or emulsion paint and cause brown patches to spread across the paint surface after application. To prevent this, use non-corroding screws or make certain any steel screws are primed with a rust-preventative metal primer before proceeding with any decoration, the effect of which could otherwise be spoiled.

Screwdrivers

It is crucial the tip of your screwdriver blade fits perfectly inside the screw head; you must therefore have a range of screwdrivers to use with the various screw sizes.

Matching screwdriver to screw

If your screwdriver is too small it will tear up the screw head and its own tip could also be damaged; if it is too large it will damage the surface of the work on the final few turns especially if the screw is to be countersunk. The most commonly used screw sizes range from Nos 4–14 and the following chart shows you what width of screw-driver to use for each gauge.

Screw gauge	Tip width
No 4	5mm ($\frac{3}{16}$in)
No 6	5mm ($\frac{3}{16}$in)
No 8	6mm ($\frac{1}{4}$in)
No 10	8mm ($\frac{5}{16}$in)
No 12	9mm ($\frac{3}{8}$in)
No 14	9mm ($\frac{3}{8}$in)

You will need a full range of screwdrivers for use with both slotted and Supadriv (which are now replacing Pozidriv) cross slot screws or a special Yankee type with interchangeable blades.

Yankee A useful screwdriver that houses a comprehensive range of interchangeable bits giving choice of blade sizes (including Pozidriv). It has the added advantage of a pump action mechanism to make certain types of work quicker.

Ratchet Has a device which prevents the screwdriver being turned in more than one direction at a time. Because of this, you do not have to release your grip on the handle when inserting or withdrawing a screw.

Pozidriver This type of screwdriver is available in various sizes and blade lengths and must be used with Supadriv or Pozidriv screws. Once again make sure you have the right size point for the screw being used. With this type the screwdriver tip holds the screw in place, whether in the vertical or near horizontal position, which is especially useful when inserting screws in awkward places.

Phillips Although similar to the Pozidriver this is designed for use with the old type Phillips screws which have a differently shaped slot in the head. Always use a Phillips screwdriver for Phillips screws and a Pozidriver for Supadriv or Pozidriv screws. If you use either type of screwdriver on the wrong screw you will damage the screw head and possibly the point of your screwdriver.

In tight corners If you are working in a really tight corner and you cannot manoeuvre a normal screwdriver, use a stubby one which has a very short blade. This type is available for both modern screw heads. There is also a specially shaped offset screwdriver for screwing round corners.

For electrical work Always use a screwdriver with a properly insulated handle. Some screwdriver blades are insulated with a plastic sleeve which is an extra safeguard should the blade accidentally touch the live terminal. Small mains test screwdrivers are ideal for use with most electric plug screws and incorporate a small warning light which illuminates the plastic handle when the blade tip touches a live terminal. If you drop the screwdriver make sure the light still works; if it does not, you could assume a

live terminal to be neutral – with disastrous results.
Old stubborn screws When screws have been left in position for a long time they sometimes prove almost impossible to remove. An impact driver, with a heavy body and interchangeable blades, makes this job a lot easier. When you hit the driver with a hammer the blade is turned in an anti-clockwise direction. By reversing the ratchet you can drive a screw tightly into position.

Squares and measures

When you are working with wood you will only achieve the perfect result if your measurements are accurate. And not only distances are crucial; angles and levels must be correct or your finished job will not only look untidy and unprofessional, but it may not fit together properly.

There are a variety of tools for checking your work is accurate and some you can improvise on or make up yourself.

Try square
This tool is essential if you are to saw a square end across a length of timber or if you want to check if a section of timber is square. It is available in three standard blade sizes – 152, 229 and 305mm (6, 9 and 12in). The tempered steel blade is locked firmly into the stock (handle) to form a perfect right-angle. Traditionally a wood stock was riveted to the blade, but now moulded plastic is used as an alternative.

A perfect try square will guarantee a 90 degree angle along both the inside and outside edges of the blade and you can easily check the accuracy of the right-angle. Lay the stock close against the straight edge of a piece of timber and mark a pencil line along the outer edge of the blade across the timber. Turn the try square over so the stock lies close to the timber but pointing the other way. If the blade is still parallel with the pencil line, your try square is accurate.

Combination square
This versatile tool, made from strong die-cast metal, provides both the inside and outside 90 degree angles of the try square and also a straight-edge/marking edge, depth gauge, adjustable mitre square, spirit level and scriber. You can buy a combination square that includes a protractor for 35–90 degree angles and a screw gauge for Nos 4–12 screws.

Sliding bevel
Available in various sizes, this tool adjusts to form any angle. The blade is easily held in position with a simple finger-tight lock.

Folding rule
Boxwood rule traditionally used by the carpenter. This folding type is available in 610 or 914mm (24 or 36in) lengths (when fully extended).

Steel tape
The retractable steel measuring tape is now the most popular for both the professional and the home handyman and is available in either metric or Imperial, or both. The range of lengths is 2–5m (6–16ft) and widths 6–19mm ($\frac{1}{4}$–$\frac{3}{4}$in). We recommend you buy one that has a sliding thumb lock and both metric and Imperial measurements on

the tape unless you are completely at ease working with the metric system.

Top sight This version, with a window at the top of the case, is particularly handy since you can read it easily when measuring into recesses. The most useful size, which is light in weight, is the 3m (10ft) long, 12mm ($\frac{1}{2}$in) wide tape.

For measuring tapes of 3m (10ft) long or more we recommend you buy the 19mm ($\frac{3}{4}$in) wide type, since this is more rigid when measuring over longer distances.

Long measure
The building measuring tape is essential for outside work when building, or setting out your garden. Available in lengths ranging from 10–30m (33–100ft), a useful working size is the 20m (66ft) one. It is made of either steel or cloth; although cloth tapes are quite satisfactory for long distances, avoid using this type for small carpentry jobs where precision is vital.

Rigid steel rule
Used for measuring metalwork, this rule is usually supplied in 305, 610 or 1000mm (12, 24 or 39in) lengths. It is also useful as a straight-edge or as a guide when using a laminate-cutter or cutting knife.

Lines and levels
When starting most structural projects and fitments, you must either form a true vertical or find a perfectly level surface. Specialist tools are available, although you will achieve a satisfactory result with some simple improvisation.

Plumb line
The accuracy of the vertical line is important, particularly when setting up shelf support rails and vertical sides of wardrobes and door frames and when hanging wall coverings. The force of gravity will ensure that any weight suspended from a string line will, if kept still, hang in a true vertical line – the plumb line. Although easy to make yourself with string and a balanced weight, a plumb bob is inexpensive and guarantees the correct shape weight necessary to reduce swing when suspended.

Once the string line is perfectly still, the exact vertical can be transferred in pencil onto the surface behind. An easy way to do this is to mark the position of the top and bottom of this line with crosses, remove the plumb line and join up the crosses using a pencil and straight-edge.

An alternative is a chalk line reel. The line is housed in a canister containing powdered chalk which coats the line each time it is extended. When the bob at the end of the line is stationary the line is held taut and plucked. A vertical chalk line is left on the wall which can easily be removed after use.

Spirit level
Level surfaces are crucial in a lot of DIY work and are usually checked with a spirit level. The longer the level, the more accurate it will be, since it covers a greater measuring length. If you have a small spirit level, use it placed on a longer straight piece of timber.

The spirit level has, set in the centre of its length, a capsule containing liquid and a bubble. Two lines are marked on the centre of the capsule the same distance apart as the length of the bubble. When

One way of checking your try square is accurate is to lay it across a length of timber with the stock butting against the straight edge of the wood. Pencil in a line across the wood. Turn the try square round so the stock points in the opposite direction and check that the blade still coincides with the marked line. If so, the try square is accurate

The plumb bob and line used to measure and mark true verticals

checking, the surface is level if the bubble sits exactly inside the two lines.

To check whether a spirit level is accurate, place it on a flat surface. The bubble should rest in exactly the same position when the level is reversed through 180 degrees; if it moves, take the level to your tool merchant for adjustment.

Home-made levels

A good spirit level can be quite expensive to buy. If your budget is limited, there are several ways you can improvise by making your own levels.

Using a try square You will get an accurate horizontal line by using a 90 degree angle set against a true vertical line. Mark your vertical line with a plumb line and weight (as already described) and set the outside edge of your try square blade flush against it. Mark a pencil line along the outer edge of the stock. Turn the try square over with the outside edge flush against the vertical line on the other side and again mark a pencil line along the stock. This will give you a true horizontal line.

Using a pointer or plumb line You can check whether a surface is level or not by hanging either a pointer or a plumb line on a specially marked T-shaped joint. Make the joint by screwing a long piece of hardwood midway along a shorter piece, checking with a try square that they meet at right-angles and the bottom edges of each piece are flush. Mark a line accurately down the centre of the upright and then drill two holes big enough to take small lengths of dowel, one near the top of the upright and one two-thirds the way down. Make a balanced pointer by chamfering one end of a thin piece of timber and drill a hole slightly bigger than the dowel in the centre of the other end. Insert the lower dowel to hang the pointer and the top dowel to hang the plumb line. You must saw a groove in the exposed end of the top dowel to insert the plumb line. Where the plumb bob hangs, cut out a square hole so the line rests near the upright. Mark out the square, drill holes in each corner and cut out with a coping saw. Lay the 'T' joint on the surface to be checked; the surface is level if the arrow or bob aligns with the marked vertical line on the upright.

Using transparent pipe Water, like all other liquids, always finds its own level. You can use it as an accurate measure by attaching a section of transparent pipe to each end of an ordinary hose-pipe (or use a full length of transparent pipe). Put the pipe in a U-shaped position and fill with water until it overflows, ensuring there is no air in the pipe. By raising or lowering either end of the pipe the water will move up or down. The water level at either end indicates true horizontal.

Sharpening planes, chisels and gouges

When you look at a plane, chisel or gouge blade, you will see two angles form the cutting edge. This edge is sharpened to a 30 degree angle and the long ground face slopes back more gradually at about a 25 degree angle.

Oilstone

The honed edge is kept razor sharp by rubbing on an oilstone; these are expensive and must be looked after carefully. They are usually 50mm (2in) wide

and 25mm (1in) thick; some are 150mm (6in) long, but a 200mm (8in) stone is better because it allows you to make a longer stroke.

Oilstones are available in coarse, medium and fine grades. There are also combination stones which are usually fine on one side and medium on the other. Coarse grade stones are required only when the edge of the plane or chisel blade is badly chipped and large amounts of metal have to be removed. The medium grade is used to get the blade ready for the final honing and the fine grade to give the final cutting edge.

Planes and chisels

Keep the oilstone in a box and put a few drops of light oil on it each time before use. Hold the blade at a 30 degree angle to the oilstone and, keeping the angle constant, work the blade backwards and forwards over the entire surface of the stone.

Keep rubbing until a feather-edge burr builds up on the flat side of the blade. With practice you will be able to do this freehand, holding the handle with one hand and maintaining pressure on the blade with the other. But at first you will find it much easier to keep the blade steady if you use a honing guide.

Turn the blade over and hold it flat on the oilstone until the burr wears thin and turns back to the bevelled side. Using less pressure each time, continue honing each side of the blade in turn (occasionally wiping the edge clean with a rag) until the burr wears off, leaving a razor-sharp edge.

It is most important for the oilstone to be absolutely flat otherwise the chisel or plane blade will not have a true, straight edge. From time to time lay the edge of a steel rule across the stone to check it is still flat. If it is seriously mis-shapen, buy a new stone. Slight irregularities can be removed by grinding the stone with water and carborundum (sold for gem engraving and polishing) on a piece of float glass. Always keep your stone clean.

Warning Use only float glass here as this is manufactured to ensure a true flat surface; sheet glass will have slight imperfections and the surface will not be sufficiently flat.

Gouges

The principle of sharpening a gouge is the same as that for a chisel or plane; a burr is built up on the cutting edge and worked until it drops off. But the method of rubbing is different and a slipstone is used in addition to an oilstone. A slipstone is smaller than an oilstone and is made in different shapes. The one used for sharpening gouges has its long edges rounded and is tapered to give two different radii. A cylindrical one may also be used. Keep it in its own box to protect it from dust and dirt.

Firmer gouge

Build up a burr on the inside edge by rubbing the angled side of the blade on an oilstone, holding the blade at 30 degrees to the stone. Use a sideways twisting action to ensure even contact with the stone along the length of the edge. When you have built up a burr on the inside, return it by rubbing a slipstone forward and back along the inside edge parallel to the blade. Repeat this two-step procedure until the burr drops off, leaving a razor-sharp edge.

Having suspended the plumb bob and line, you can then mark a true horizontal line by placing a try square up to the plumb line

When sharpening a chisel or plane blade, use a honing guide to ensure you maintain the 30 degree cutting angle. Move the guide up and down a lightly oiled oilstone

Scribing gouge

Sharpen a scribing gouge in the same way as a firmer gouge but reverse the sequence. First build up a burr on the inside edge by rubbing a slip-stone to and fro on the cutting edge, holding the stone at a 30 degree angle to the blade. When you have built up the burr, return it by rubbing the outside edge on the oilstone; hold the blade flat on the stone and twist it gently from side to side.

Grinding blades

If the blade of a chisel or plane is seriously chipped or badly worn, you can regrind it yourself on a grindstone wheel to restore a square edge and the 25 degree grinding angle. Regrinding a gouge is more difficult and we recommend you take it to your tool supplier.

Don't let the blade overheat; hold it only lightly against the grindstone, pointing against the direction of rotation of the wheel, and occasionally dip it in water. On no account must the cutting edge turn blue; if it does, this indicates the blade has lost its hardness.

After regrinding, restore the 30 degree cutting edge by honing the blade on an oilstone.

Metric conversion charts

Quick conversion factors – volume

1 cubic inch (cu in)	= 16.3871cu cm
1 cubic foot (cu ft)/ 1728cu in	= 28.3168cu dm/0.0283cu m
1 cubic yard (cu yd)/ 27cu ft	= 0.7646cu m
1 cubic centimetre (cu cm)/ 1000 cubic millimetres (cu mm)	= 0.0610cu in
1 cubic decimetre (cu dm)/ 1000cu cm	= 61.024cu in/0.0353cu ft
1 cubic metre (cu m)/ 1000cu dm	= 35.3146cu ft/1.308cu yd
1cu cm	= 1 millilitre (ml)
1cu dm	= 1 litre (lit) See **Capacity**

Quick conversion factors – capacity

1 fluid ounce (fl oz)	= 28.4ml
1 gill (gi)/5fl oz	= 142.1ml
1 pint (pt)/4gi	= 568.2ml/0.568 lit
1 quart (qt)/2pt	= 1.136 lit
1 gallon (gal)/4pt	= 4.546 lit
1 millilitre (ml)	= 0.035fl oz
1 litre (lit)	= 1.76pt/0.22gal
1ml	= 1 cubic centimetre (cu cm)
1 lit	= 1 cubic decimetre (cu dm) See **Volume**
1 US pint	= 5/6 Imperial pt/473.2ml/0.473 lit
1 US gallon	= 5/6 Imperial gal/3.785 lit

Quick conversion factors – length

Terms are set out in full in the left-hand column except where clarification is necessary.

1 inch (in)	= 25.4mm/2.54cm
1 foot (ft)/12in	= 304.8mm/30.48cm/0.3048m
1 yard (yd)/3ft	= 914.4mm/91.44cm/0.9144m
1 mile (mi)/1760yd	= 1609.344m/1.609km
1 millimetre (mm)	= 0.0394in
1 centimetre (cm)/10mm	= 0.394in
1 metre (m)/100cm	= 39.37in/3.281ft/1.094yd
1 kilometre (km)/1000m	= 1093.6yd/0.6214mi

Quick conversion factors – area

1 square inch (sq in)	= 645.16sq mm/ 6.4516sq cm
1 square foot (sq ft)/144sq in	= 929.03sq cm
1 square yard (sq yd)/9sq ft	= 8361.3sq cm/ 0.8361sq m
1 acre (ac)/4840sq yd	= 4046.9sq m/0.4047ha
1 square mile (sq mi)640ac	= 259ha
1 square centimetre (sq cm)/ 100 square millimetre (sq mm)	= 0.155sq in
1 square metre (sq m)/ 10,000sq cm	= 10.764sq ft/1.196sq yd
1 are (a)/100sq m	= 119.60sq yd/0.0247ac
1 hectare (ha)/100a	= 2.471ac/0.00386sq mi

Quick conversion factors – weight

1 ounce (oz)	= 28.35g
1 pound (lb)/16oz	= 453.59g/0.4536kg
1 stone/14lb	= 6.35kg
1 hundredweight (cwt)/ 8 stone/112lb	= 50.80kg
1 ton/20cwt	= 1016.05kg/1.016t
1 gram (g)	= 0.035oz
1 kilogram (kg)/1000g	= 35.274oz/2.2046lb/ 2lb 3.274oz
1 tonne (t)/1000kg	= 2204.6lb/0.9842 ton

Circumference, perimeter and surface area

Circles
diameter	= radius × 2
circumference	= diameter × 22/7
surface area	= radius × radius × 22/7

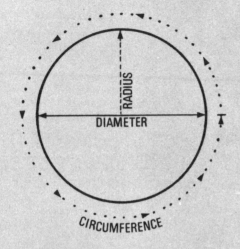

Triangles
height	= perpendicular distance from base to opposite corner
perimeter	= sum of length of three sides
surface area	= base × height ÷ 2

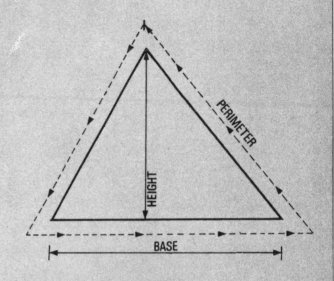

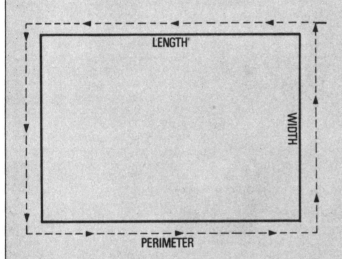

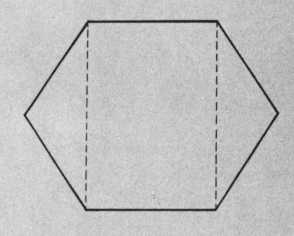

Rectangle/square
perimeter (rectangle)	= (length + width) × 2
perimeter (square)	= length of one side × 4
surface area	= length of one side × length of adjacent side

Planes (with more than four straight sides)
perimeter	= sum of all side lengths
surface area	= split up into triangles and rectangles, find all individual areas and add these figures to obtain total surface area

Temperature

To convert degrees Fahrenheit to degrees Celsius (Centigrade)
Subtract 32, multiply by 5, divide by 9.
e.g. $(212°F - 32) \times 5/9 = 180 \times 5/9 = 100°C$

To convert degrees Celsius to degrees Fahrenheit
Multiply by 9, divide by 5, add 32.
e.g. $(100°C \times 9/5 + 32 = 180 + 32 = 212°F$

Ice point $\quad 0°C = 32°F$

Boiling point of water $\quad 100°C = 212°F$
(under standard pressure)

Index

Numbers in italics refer to illustrations and tables